RAISING CHILDREN

WHO THINK

FOR THEMSELVES

Raising Children Who Think for Themselves

Elisa Medhus, M.D.

BEYOND WORDS Publishing INC

Beyond Words Publishing, Inc.
20827 N.W. Cornell Road, Suite 500
Hillsboro, Oregon 97124-9808
503-531-8700
1-800-284-9673

Editor: Laura Carlsmith
Proofreaders: Carol Franks and Michael Ashby
Managing editor: Julie Steigerwaldt
Design: Mary Beth Salmon
Composition: William H. Brunson Typography Services

Printed in the United States of America
Distributed to the book trade by Publishers Group West

Library of Congress Cataloging-in-Publication Data
Medhus, Elisa.
    Raising children who think for themselves / Elisa Medhus
        p. cm.
    Includes bibliographical references and index.
    ISBN 1-58270-047-8 (pbk.)
        1. Child rearing.   2. Self-reliance in children.   3. Self-esteem in
    children.   4. Parent and child.   I. Title.
HQ769 .M3873   2001
649'.1—dc21
                                                                    00-068076

The corporate mission of Beyond Words Publishing, Inc.:
Inspire to Integrity

Contents

DEDICATION   ix

ACKNOWLEDGMENTS   xi

THE BASICS

INTRODUCTION   3

What This Book Is About   3

The Five Essential Qualities of Self-Directed Children   6

Understanding Internal vs. External Direction   11

THE GAME PLAN
SEVEN STRATEGIES FOR RAISING SELF-DIRECTED CHILDREN

ONE • CREATING THE PROPER FAMILY ENVIRONMENT   19

Eliminating Elements That Foster External Direction   19

A Word about Sibling Influences   44

The Importance of a Family Identity   48

TWO • HELPING CHILDREN DEVELOP HEALTHY INTERNAL DIALOGUE   51

Eight Techniques to Encourage Introspection   51

Derailing Unhealthy Internal Dialogue   66

Helping Them Confront Their Unhealthy Internal Dialogue   66

Helping Them Rebound from the Effects of
  Facing the Truth   68
Helping Them Find Solutions through Honest, Healthy
  Internal Dialogue   69
Modeling Our Own Inner Honesty for Our Children   69

THREE • HELPING CHILDREN DEVELOP
NATURAL INTUITION   71
Modeling the Use of Our Own Intuitive Powers   72
Encouraging Them to Follow Their Own Hunches   72
Teaching Children How to Strengthen Their
  Intuitive Powers   72
Playing Intuition Games   74
Keeping an Intuition Journal   74
Teaching Children How to Receive Intuitive
  Signals More Clearly   74

FOUR • TEACHING CHILDREN EMPATHY   77
Teaching Children How "Benevolent Selfishness" Works   79
Helping Children Understand Others by Using
  the "Empathy Triad"   79
Helping Children Develop Empathy through Service   81
Helping Children Use Internal Dialogue to
  Develop Empathy   82
Helping Children Develop Empathy through Role Play   84
Using "I Messages" to Teach Children Empathy   85
Modeling Empathy   86
Teaching Children Empathy by Not Criticizing the
  Unfortunate   87

FIVE • DISCIPLINING TO PROMOTE INTERNAL
   DIRECTION   89
What It Means to Discipline in a Way That Promotes
   Internal Direction   89
The Twelve Basic Requirements of Self-Directed Discipline   91
Eight Discipline Techniques That Encourage Self-Direction 107

SIX • HELPING CHILDREN REBOUND FROM FAILURE   121
Discussing Our Own Mistakes with Our Children   123
Not Denying Opportunities to Excel As a Consequence
   for Misbehavior   123
Sharing Lessons We've Learned from Our Own Mistakes   124
Teaching the Value of Failed Attempts   124
Teaching Children to Strive for Personal Excellence,
   Not Perfection   125
Using Mistake Contests   126
Downplaying Past Failures   126
Teaching "Failure Tolerance" by Not Over-reacting
   to Mistakes   127
Encouraging Mistakes   128
Encouraging Independence   128
Teaching How to Separate Failures from Self-Worth   129
Accepting Suffering As a Good Thing   130

SEVEN • HELPING CHILDREN HANDLE
   REAL-WORLD INFLUENCES   133
Drugs and Alcohol   134
Violence among Children   137
Modern Technology   139

The Hurried Life 142

Consumerism vs. Simplicity 145

Sexuality 147

Body Image and the Perception of Beauty 151

The Winner-Loser Mentality and Competition 154

CONCLUSION 157

SPECIFIC CHILD-REARING CHALLENGES 159

LEVEL SYSTEM FOR TEENAGERS 275

RESOURCES 277

INDEX 283

Dedication

Truth resides in every human heart,
and one has to search for it there and
to be guided by the truth as one sees it.
But no one has the right to coerce
others to act according to his
own view of truth.
—Mahatma Gandhi

WITH MUCH FONDNESS I dedicate this book to my greatest teachers: my husband, Rune, and my five beautiful children: Kristina, Michelle, Erik, Lukas, and Annika. Filled with eternal optimism, I also dedicate this book to my fellow parents, who, shoulder to shoulder in the foxholes of life, are so willing to struggle and sacrifice for their children to defend the sacred priorities they hold dear. Their dedication, vision, and perseverance give humanity a gift of hope for the future that history has yet to behold.

Acknowledgments

Gratitude is the heart's memory.
—French proverb

THROUGH THIS LABOR OF LOVE, I have learned much from so many that have touched and enriched my life. In this wondrous process, I have crossed paths with teachers from many walks of life and from all levels of enlightenment, each with a gift that adds its own special flavor to this book's creation.

With profound respect, I give thanks to my mother and father, who never introduced the words "can't," "limitation," or "impossible" to my vocabulary.

I am also deeply grateful to my dear friend Sarah, who has taught me the goodness and comfort of a loyal friendship.

I would further like to acknowledge the many sages who, through their writings on parenting and spirituality, have inspired and ignited me.

My deepest love and appreciation go to my oldest sister Teri, who has always been my confidante, my mentor, and my dearest friend.

To my youngest sister Denise, whose spiritual growth gives me pause and loving respect and whose life has taught me so much about love and compassion, I give my undying affection and admiration.

To all of my friends and neighbors who so eagerly listened, supported, and advised me throughout my exploration of parenting.

To Tammy Richards, my PR agent, who, as my second voice, so professionally helps me spread this important message around the globe.

To Cindy Black, Laura Carlsmith, and all of the other wonderful folks at Beyond Words Publishing, whose enthusiasm for this message can be felt throughout these pages and whose expertise promises to mold me into the author I wish to become.

THE BASICS

Parents wonder why the stream is bitter,

when they themselves have spoiled the fountain.

—John Locke

Introduction

Mountains are removed by first
shoveling away the small stones.
—Anonymous

WHAT THIS BOOK IS ABOUT

How many of us liken parenthood to a perilous journey? As parents, we are constantly teaching our children to fend off outer evils like drugs, alcohol, gangs, violence, and suicide, as well as helping them sidestep inner pitfalls like cynicism, eating disorders, irresponsibility, and poor impulse control. These dilemmas can sometimes make our children's future appear downright bleak! In spite of all this, our job is to raise them to be successful, competent, self-confident, and independent.

As a physician, I have been fortunate to be privy to that part of human life to which others have no ready access. Patients could open a window to the world to me through their most intimate thoughts about their and their families' lives. What I witnessed over the years fascinated me. On the one hand, I had patients who seemed to have "everything," by society's standards anyway. But they were often unsatisfied, frustrated, and depressed, claiming their lives were empty shells. One man, in particular, had several cars, a big yacht,

Texas Hill Country property, and a 7,000-square-foot house in an exclusive neighborhood. He was able to dress his family in the finest designer clothes and send his children to the most elite schools. Despite these trappings, his life was a wreck. Two children were unemployed bums high on drugs more often than not, and a third had perished in a tragic accident. Marital emotional support for this poor soul was slim to none, because his relationship with his wife wavered from contentious to hollow. In a nutshell, here was a man who had succeeded in those ways that society had promised would bring him happiness. However, society did not live up to its end of the bargain. Here was a man whose unhappiness was the result of his basing his choices on the outside world's values instead of on what he felt and reasoned was best for him.

On the other hand was a patient with a lovely wife and six children who were living from hand to mouth in an old trailer home. He was a hardworking, low-wage machinist assistant for an oil tool company, and his hours revolved around the needs of his family, not around his need for image or escape. What a breath of life that family was when they waltzed in and out of my clinic with beaming smiles and sincere appreciation! Between each and every one of them, there were true love and admiration that were mightier than the external influences that could have torn them apart. They didn't care about Guess jeans or Sketchers boots. Attending public school was fine, as far as they were concerned, because both parents felt it was ultimately *their* responsibility to educate their children by involving themselves in the schools and supervising homework time closely. And, in their estimation, the mildewed wading pool behind their trailer could muster more laughs out of those kids than a fifty-six-foot motor yacht on Lake Travis. This was a man whose happiness came from making his own choices, by using his own reasoning powers to match his actions to his values and principles, instead of blindly adopting the choices thrust on him by an external world that had no conception of or concern for his individual values and principles.

Although I felt these observations were interesting, it wasn't until later that I caught on to their connection to all that is wrong in the world today. Every morning, I'd read horror stories in the newspaper and shake my head in disbelief, stories such as children killing their parents or siblings, gang members racking up kill quotas, and mothers chaining their children to posts in the cellars and allowing them to wallow in their own filth. These awful, despicable acts made me wonder how anyone could possibly depersonalize human life so easily ... the same lives I, as a physician, often fought so hard to save.

Then, one day, I read a story I couldn't dismiss. A young mother had killed her two-year-old son for some trivial annoyance, cut him into little pieces, fried him in a skillet, and served him to her dogs. Then and there, I felt I had to do something to help stop this madness, for the world that had given me so much and for the world in which my children would have to live their lives.

I decided to explore how others interpreted the state of the world today. I interviewed hundreds of teachers, parents, and children in Texas and California and even as far as Norway. Most of the children were interviewed during their lunch period or recess, with the permission of their parents and school principals. Others were interviewed by phone. Throughout these pages, you will see many references to these interviews.

This social reconnaissance mission inspired me to search for the most proximal cause of society's current predicament.

In my earlier research, I had found that humankind usually tackles social problems at the very tips of their branches rather than deep down at their roots, so that, at best, the disease is slowed but not cured. For instance, we pour money and other resources into anti-gang efforts, welfare reform, and drug and alcohol awareness programs. We declare war on drug traffickers and criminals. We do all this without ever asking ourselves one important question—*Why do we have these problems in the first place?*

My conclusion: the threats and challenges children face in society today stem from one source—*we are raising our children to be externally rather than internally directed.* In other words, we are teaching them to make choices in life to gain the approval and acceptance of others. In doing so, our children relinquish the one gift that elevates human beings above all other living creatures—the power to reason.

When children are self-directed, on the other hand, they use their power of reason like a sword to cut through the jungle of external influences: they use reason to examine all the possible consequences of the choices they consider, relying on it as an inner point of control. Self-directed children make a decision after giving it full consideration, because they believe that a choice is right for them, not because they believe others will think more highly of them. It is this reasoning, this internal dialogue that is the foundation of the self-directed child. We must endeavor to instill this self-direction in children— the earlier the better.

THE FIVE ESSENTIAL QUALITIES OF SELF-DIRECTED CHILDREN

Once children become skilled in their use of internal dialogue and can direct themselves from within, they develop two characteristics: a strong sense of self and a strong desire to be a vital and meaningful part of the group. From these two characteristics spring five qualities that define them as self-directed beings.

1. High self-esteem/self-confidence

Self-directed children feel good about themselves, because they've learned how to rationally assess themselves in a way that helps them grow rather than tears them down. Reason is truly an impartial and forgiving judge. It enables them to rebound from defeat, view failure as a learning opportunity, and tolerate their own weaknesses without letting those weaknesses undermine their sense of self-worth. Because such children don't react mindlessly to outside influences, they don't take things personally or defensively. To achieve this perspective, these children are invariably raised in an environment rich in unconditional love and approval.

2. Competence

Competent children have the ability to understand and manipulate their surroundings. Because self-directed children don't perceive failure as something that whittles away their sense of worth, they feel comfortable taking on new endeavors and exploring their own intellectual and physical limits. They are risk-takers. Although they will stumble on occasion, these children rack up an impressive list of accomplishments and skills over the years. They become keenly aware of their potential. All this success goes far in reinforcing their self-assuredness and, in turn, their self-esteem. Self-directed children are raised in an environment where they are encouraged to attempt new ventures and explore their abilities without fear of ridicule, criticism, or shame if they fail. They are not rescued from their mistakes.

3. Independence

Once self-directed children become competent, what follows is a sense of independence—the ability to rely on internally derived decisions. Their own reasoning helps them become independent thinkers and problem solvers. It also helps them resist external influences in making choices. It is the inability to resist external influences that is the defining attribute of an inept and dependent individual.

4. High moral character

Since self-directed children are free to make choices for the right reasons—reasons that have nothing to do with others' expectations or approval—their choices are more inclined to be ones that serve their own self-interest rather than the interest of others. And morally speaking, it's always in the best interest of the self-directed individual to do the right thing. For example, if Timmy finds an envelope with someone's lunch money in it on the playground, he will, if he's self-directed, use internal dialogue to conclude that keeping the money will make him feel bad about himself for causing problems for the rightful owner. In another example, suppose Kristina sees a group of "popular" girls picking on her best friend's questionable choice in fashions. Does she stand up for her friend and risk being ridiculed or shunned by the "in crowd"? Or does she slink away, hoping nobody notices? Worse yet, does she join in on the peer bashing? If she's self-directed, she will make the choice that honors her moral principles: she will choose to come to her friend's rescue. Her sense of reason tells her that not doing so would make her feel like a traitor. She also realizes that betraying her friend could possibly destroy their friendship—a consequence she's unlikely to find acceptable. Since she has such a strong sense of self and high self-esteem, she doesn't really need the approval of the popular girls to feel good about herself, anyway. So the decision is easy. Making rational choices that agree with moral principles and values accounts for the high level of self-control, self-discipline, and integrity in self-directed children.

5. Being an asset within the group

As the pack animal theory of human behavior postulates, we're all driven by an intense desire to belong and to have a meaningful place within a group, and we behave and think in ways that will satisfy that longing. Some children choose to belong by doing and believing whatever the group dictates. They choose to beg for the pack's acceptance by selecting conformity over contribution. Such children are externally directed—motivated by their need to gain the pack's approval. They choose to sacrifice their own identity and replace it with one fashioned by outside influences in hopes that it will be more acceptable to others. The payoff of raising children this way, and perhaps the biggest reason we do so, is they're much easier to manage if we're the ones whose wishes they're conforming to. It's so much easier to shape them into what we want them to be. Of course, this unfortunately holds true for other influences they're sure to encounter apart from ours—peers and the media, for example—and that's when Pandora's box of child-rearing nightmares is released.

Other children choose to belong by finding their own role or contribution within the pack—one that's meaningful to the child, and decided upon by him rather than by the group. They choose to earn rather than beg for the pack's acceptance. These children are self-directed. Since they don't need to look to the group to think for them and since they're not inclined to see their surroundings as threatening, they're able to carve out meaningful roles within that group. They don't have to blindly obey, conform, or withdraw. And because of their high level of competence, they can use any or all of their many skills to find a way to contribute and be an asset to their group. By helping the group, they feel a sense of belonging, which, in turn, strengthens their self-confidence, their sense of self, and their independence. See how this process reinforces itself?

With a strong sense of purpose and uniqueness, self-directed children can add to any group. They don't have to rely on an allegiance to just one to feel that they belong. Since they don't have to please the group to improve their own self-regard, they can objectively pick and choose their groups as well as those strengths and abilities they think would contribute most to the group's welfare. For instance, Sarah might use her organizational prowess to form a youth organization to help tutor learning disabled peers, yet she might use her well-honed skills in conflict resolution to keep the peace among her peers and siblings.

The downside is that self-directed children are often more difficult to manage, because, after all, they have their own minds and their own ways of handling life, and sometimes, their ways clash with ours. But in reality, our job is to guide, not manage them. And when you think about it for a moment, which path better serves evolution's intent, teleologically speaking? Would the Houston Astros fare as well if every player were a shortstop? No, of course not. A pack *has* to have leaders, mediators, sympathizers, hunters, gatherers, healers, inventors, teachers, and so on.

As parents, we can capitalize on this pack animal instinct by *guiding* them down the road to self-direction. After all, our children instinctively want to please us, the alpha wolves.

They want to feel that they belong and have something special to offer. Our job, with the help of this book, is to show them how to do so through their *own* inner identity rather than through outside influences—to *earn*, rather than *beg for*, the pack's acceptance, by contributing rather than conforming.

You may ask, "What will the payoff be for cultivating these qualities and creating self-directed children?" It is my contention that, if children have these five essential qualities, they have no reason to look to outside sources for approval. The less they rely on outside influences, the stronger these five qualities become and the less they need the external world to shape or reinforce their identity. It's a never-ending upward spiral toward self-actualization. In the end, they have what they need to get along happily in the world. Frankly, what more can we ask for?

UNDERSTANDING INTERNAL VS. EXTERNAL DIRECTION

Now let's learn a little more about what it means to be internally and externally directed. To understand fully, let's backtrack and examine how the concept of self develops in children from birth on. Throughout the following stages, you will see how a child's reasoning process matures until it reaches a pivotal point where he or she chooses, in varying degrees, either to abandon reasoning to external factors or to embrace reasoning to select what choices are truly appropriate to their sense of right and wrong. The former is the path of the externally directed and the latter, that of the self-directed.

Newborn stage

At birth, children have no real concept of self. How could they when they come into this world completely oblivious to their limits and possibilities? After all, self-concept doesn't develop in a vacuum. Children must have ideas and experiences that they can compare and contrast to those of others around them to get a concept of *who they are*. This is an essential step for them to be able to assess and define themselves. At this stage, our number one priority as their parent (besides taking care of their physical needs, of course) is to provide them with a strong sense of attachment. If we want them to accept our guidance on that bumpy road to self-discovery later on, our children need to feel that they are unconditionally loved and that we will always be there for them. Unconditional love is the key to helping children feel that whatever "self" they become will be accepted by us enthusiastically.

Infant/toddler stage

In this stage, children begin to interact with the rest of the world. They quickly realize that for every action, there's a reaction. From this fundamental law of nature, children begin to understand that there are consequences for what they do. When Johnny drops his black bean soup on the floor, it goes "kershplat" and Mommy scurries about yammering unintelligibly while she wipes his beautiful pièce de résistance off the floor. When Rachel sips from a cup for the first time, she notices the cheerleader section of the family hooraying, jumping up and down and generally acting like a bunch of raving lunatics. As you can see from these examples, our children's physical accomplishments and defeats shape their self-concept at this stage—all because of the outside reactions they provoke.

Preschooler to early elementary grades

In this stage, children are subjected, for the first time, to the judgments and evaluations of others. Not only are they exposed to more people (such as teachers, classmates, friends, and neighbors), but they also begin to realize that not everyone will love and approve of them unconditionally. Furthermore, children at this age are now old enough to rack up a number of skills that will then be scrutinized and perhaps criticized by others—how fast they tie their shoes, how well they read, whether they can kick a ball more than three feet, and whether they'll confess to watching Barney videos. This scrutiny, in the form of conditional approval, criticism, or praise, plays an important part in shaping a more abstract, externally directed concept of self.

Late elementary grades on

By the time they reach third grade, children are already relying heavily on comparisons to judge themselves and others. They are painfully aware that their moral character, social skills, personality, academic competence, physical appearance, athletic ability, and so forth are all being assessed by those around them. *This is often the critical crossroad in their lives where self-esteem is either built or broken*—where children choose between self-direction and external direction as their cognitive point of reference they will use to function in the outside world. We'll get to the factors that influence this choice later on.

Self-directed children operate from an internal point of control through which they filter and evaluate all external influences. This inner direction enables them to appraise themselves objectively—without any emotional attachment to the final judgment. They make choices because, given the possible consequences they have considered internally, they think these are the right choices for them to make. They *respond* to life, rather than *react* to it. These children are self-inspired— inspired by the products of their own reasoning.

Other children operate from an external point of control and can't filter outside influences through the process of reason. Their need for approval and acceptance clouds and shapes their choices. Eventually, this "reasoning by proxy" helps them create a social mask—the façade that becomes the made-to-order identity based on what they assume others want them to be. Sadly, the more they rely on their false identity, the less they trust their real one. So the process reinforces itself over time.

Another disadvantage of not using internal dialogue to make their choices or judgments is that externally directed children never learn to develop self-talk and self-monitoring skills. Without these skills, children don't self-regulate and, therefore, exhibit poor impulse control. Such children *react* to life. They are *externally directed*. In the pages ahead, we will look at the reasons why children take one path over the other. Most important, the book will provide proactive solutions for helping them change their path to the one that leads to self-direction.

As you read this book, you may find yourself gasping in horror or wringing your hands, because, like me, you've just spent the last ten years or so raising your children to be externally directed, and you thought you were doing a pretty darn good job! But before you panic, let me first applaud you for being one of those rare and commendable moms or dads who care enough about their children to tirelessly strive to become a better parent. Second, I can assure you that no matter how long you've been doing it the wrong way, once you become comfortable with the suggestions in this book, it won't take long for your children to become self-directed. In fact, don't be surprised if you wind up that way, too! I had been using *some* degree of externally directed parenting for fourteen years before I discovered and began practicing internally directed parenting techniques, and I soon saw dramatic changes in my children (and myself). You'll become more and more aware of externally versus internally directed behavior in your children, yourself, and other people. It is this awareness that makes this new parenting style self-reinforcing so that it becomes easier to implement over time.

Imagine, for a moment, a world of self-directed children! We'd have people who can appreciate their own unique strengths, translate them into meaningful roles, and contribute to the pack by fulfilling those roles, people who live according to their own thoughts rather than the thoughts of others. Compare this to an externally directed world where people frantically jockey for the best positions within the pack, stepping on others and their own moral principles along the way. Go one step further and imagine that it's within our power, as parents, to decide which of these paths humankind will travel! With a few tweaks of our parenting techniques, we can create a self-directed world. I'm not saying this process is going to be a walk in the park, by any means, because, after all, humanity has endured centuries of externally directed behavior advocated by individuals, leaders, and society as a whole. And since this indoctrination includes the way we were all raised, we've got a mighty cranky tiger by the tail. But, it can be tamed. Now, let's explore the tools that will help us take on this worthy challenge: the seven key strategies for raising self-directed children.

THE GAME PLAN

SEVEN STRATEGIES
FOR RAISING
SELF-DIRECTED CHILDREN

One

CREATING THE PROPER FAMILY ENVIRONMENT

> *The sun does not need help shining.*
> —*Anonymous*

OF THE SEVEN STRATEGIES, creating the proper family environment is perhaps the most fundamental. After all, if the family environment isn't conducive to raising self-directed children, we can apply the other six strategies until we're blue in the face, and it still isn't going to work any miracles! Might as well build the Golden Gate Bridge on a lily pad. So, let's start off on the right foot by first laying down a solid foundation. First, we must take a look at how we have all been inclined to shape the family milieu so that it fosters external over internal direction. Then we'll look at ways to correct these nasty little habits.

ELIMINATING ELEMENTS THAT FOSTER EXTERNAL DIRECTION

Three parenting behaviors promote external direction in our children: modeling externally directed behavior in our own lives, being conditional with our children, and not having faith in our children.

Modeling externally directed behavior in our own lives

The way we react to external influences is important because we design many of the blueprints for our children's sense of self by the behavior we model. How we act, feel, and think is crucial, because our children see us as a reflection of the outside world—as a glimpse into what they'll be like when they grow up. That's pretty scary stuff! And since most of us are externally directed to some degree, we want to be accepted by others too. If we're not careful, though, the behavior we model will reflect an overreliance on external influences.

Modeling external direction to have "the right image"

Our children are extremely adept at picking up the subtlest signs of our externally directed behavior. For example, when we struggle to get ahead—to look out for number one—our children notice. We work long and hard all day to make those credit card payments so that we can continue to have the things that make us look successful. We try to say the right thing, wear the right clothes, have the right "stuff," get the right job, have the right social status, rub elbows with the right people, all in an effort to pass society's popularity contest and win its approval. Our children see this in our actions, in our words, and in our feelings. Moreover, because our children are often extensions of our own egos, we often make them march to the same drum.

So how on earth can we stop these unhealthy reactions to the outside world so that we can jump free of this spinning hamster wheel? We might try to examine the motives behind everything we do and say as often as possible. Ask: are we making this choice because we think it's right for us, or is it just a means to win love and acceptance from the outside world? We might even want to try modeling this internal dialogue aloud for them. We can nurture their own self-talk by doing all the pondering, weighing, and considering parts of our decision-making out loud for them to witness and absorb internally.

Modeling external direction by placing conditions on the approval we receive

The conditions we allow others to place on the love and approval we *receive* is perhaps the biggest force fueling external direction in our own lives. For instance, we receive love conditionally when we beat ourselves up because of a screwup we caused at work. We feel we don't deserve love and approval, because we haven't met some fictitious set of conditions cooked up by ourselves, by other individuals, or by some group to which we seek a sense of belonging. When our children hear our self-depreciation, it sends them the message that we don't think we deserve love, because we're one of the outcasts or losers. What else can they possibly do but assume that those external influences are much more powerful than what lies within them?

To stop sending this subliminal message, we might try to avoid statements of self-depreciation. Instead of saying something like, *"I knew I should have sent the boss a more expensive birthday present. What an idiot I am! No wonder Cindy got the promotion instead of me!"* we might try saying something like, *"Gosh, I was really hoping to get that promotion. But at least I know I tried my best, and that makes it worth all the trouble. I bet something else good will come of it soon. I'll just keep doing the best I can."* This way, our children will notice that we are concentrating on what we did well and what benefits those efforts brought forth, not what others think. In other words, they will learn how to reflect on everything that is *within their power* instead of agonizing over the stronghold that external influences *beyond their control* have on them.

Modeling external direction through expectations of reciprocity and entitlement

Modeling our own expectation of reciprocity also teaches our children to focus externally when they make choices on how they should feel about other people and how they should behave towards them. For instance, we might cook meals for an elderly neighbor whose spouse is in the hospital and then come home and complain that "the old geezer didn't say thank-you once!" From this remark, our children learn that a good deed *must* be reciprocated. Furthermore, they start to believe that if their love and their tokens of kindness are not reciprocated, then we're unloved and unappreciated.

When we have expectations of reciprocity, we naturally develop an attitude of entitlement. One of the biggest threats to the economic stability in our country is that its citizens feel entitled to rights and privileges that aren't really justified. Many people complain about their rights to have free parking, job security, low-cost health insurance, etc. Although some of these demands are fair and should be defended, many aren't. When our children hear these complaints and demands over time, they eventually absorb this same expectation of entitlement, which once more teaches our children to react to factors in the outside world to shape their conception of how their lives should be. This attitude can come back to haunt you later. Believe me! Just remember this when your kids tell you that *you're* supposed to pay for the gas and insurance for *their* car!

This overblown sense of entitlement plays an unfortunate part in the formation of a corrupt and greedy society. We must make it clear to them that the only things to which we are entitled are our lives, our right to be productive, and anything that comes from either. For instance, we can ask Robert why he thinks he's entitled to receiving payment for watching his younger siblings while we attend a school meeting. When we help him walk through the reasoning process, he may soon realize that he mistook an obligation for an opportunity to profit.

So what does this have to do with external and internal direction? A great deal! These expectations send our children the message that they need people and things in the outside world to bolster their self-worth. To avoid instilling this attitude in them, we must try the best we can to give love or kindness to others, expecting nothing in return. Giving that love or kindness anonymously, if possible, goes a long way to fulfill this goal. We can show our children that we don't expect something for nothing and that we earn everything we have. This way, our children will grow up learning that hard work and good deeds are reward enough, and they begin to see that all they need for a healthy self-worth lies within them.

Modeling external direction by the mishandling of feelings

From time to time, all of us model the mishandling of our feelings in front of our children in several ways. First, we sometimes conceal sadness, disappointment, guilt, embarrassment, and anger. When Mom refuses to show her grief over Uncle Jack's death, her child interprets this as "feelings are very bad and should be buried." A second way we mishandle our feelings in front of our children is to misdirect them. When Dad comes home in a terrible mood because of some stressful events at work and then takes his anger out on his child, that child then gets the message that other people's feelings are his or her responsibility and perhaps even his or her fault. Finally, we mishandle our feelings when we cling to negative feelings like anger or grief for a long time without working them out. Sustaining negative feelings just teaches our children that really bad emotions have no solution. They're just something they need to put up with.

Modeling the misuse of feelings in front of our children fosters external direction in two ways. First, it helps them shape a more thick-skinned façade behind which to hide their true self. Second, it sends our children the message that external influences have so much power over us that our feelings, those vital avenues of communication with the world around us, must be muted, altered, retracted, or destroyed. Naturally, our children are going to assume that anything wielding this kind of power is a force to which they must submit. This all shifts their attention externally, leaving internal forms of communications stunted and ignored.

So we might try expressing our emotions in a healthy way, without suppressing them to avoid criticism or ridicule and without hanging on to them forever or using them as instruments of destruction against others. Think of emotions as a crate of fresh fish. It's okay to cook 'em up and eat them, because that's their purpose, after all. (I'm sure you'll find some fish that'll disagree with this statement.) But it's best not to keep those leftovers too long, because they'll start stinking soon enough! Use 'em and let 'em go. If they do start stinking, we mustn't wave them in poor Uncle Harry's face or try to lay the blame on him by saying they're his fish! Instead, we should take the responsibility for what we do with our own feelings (and fish).

Being conditional with our children

The second parenting faux pas is our behaving conditionally with our children. Nothing is more powerful in convincing them to look outward rather than inward for answers.

Conditional love is that love we ration out to our children only when they're behaving according to our wishes. We often show them our love just during their most love-able moments rather than those times when they need it most. Let's examine some of the ways we place contingencies on our love as well as approaches for breaking this harmful way of thinking.

Qualifying statements with conditions

We sometimes add endings to our remarks of affection like, "I really love you *when* you help me out like this," or "I love you, but you've really been a little snot lately." These "qualifiers" suggest that our love has strings attached, giving our children the message that they need to be as we want them to be to earn our love and acceptance. Once this sinks in, it's only a matter of time before they develop this kind of relationship with the rest of the world, too. So, to prove to them that our love has no conditions, we must try our best never to attach endings that suggest we'd love them more if ...

Showing them love when they're at their best

It seems as though we often show our children affection and praise only when they are nearly perfect. For instance, we reserve pats on the back for those times that they make the tennis team or get all A's on their report card. We hang only their best schoolwork on the refrigerator door, casting anything less than perfect in the garbage. In short, we usually sing the loudest praises only when our children achieve what *we* think is their best, sending them the message that they deserve love only when they meet *our* expectations of perfection!

To show that our love is truly unconditional, we need to show affection and appreciation regardless of the grades that they make, the opinions they hold, or the clothes they wear. We might try to proudly hang that B+ spelling test on the refrigerator door if Peter studied especially hard for it. We can give Alice a big hug, because she single-handedly cheered on her downtrodden teammates during a volleyball game they lost. We might tell Tommy how much we love him when he's being a cranky little fart after a long and difficult day at school.

Another way to demonstrate the unconditional nature of our love is by relying more on actions and less on words. This demonstration of love is a biggie with many rewards. Showing "I love you" in ways that entail effort or inconvenience is like shouting those three little words through a bullhorn. We might spend time coloring pictures in a coloring book alongside them. We can send love letters in their lunch sacks. Even a silent hug for no particular reason can send our children a powerful message about how much we love them.

It's easy to fall into the trap of focusing all our attention on what our children are becoming instead of appreciating who they already are. It's OK to let them know we appreciate the hard work it'll take them to satisfy their ambition to become a neurosurgeon, to get a good grade on their next physics test, or to run for class president, but not if we neglect telling them how remarkable they are right now. Bethany, age thirteen, says, "I know my mom likes me just the way I am, not just what she wants me to be. That makes me feel freer to be me."

Sometimes I enjoy sitting with my children, one on one, telling them how wonderful they are and how lucky I am to be their mom. I like to go through the whole list of why I think they're so special, what remarkable talents they have, what challenges they've met and conquered in the past, and so forth. Just keep one thought in the back of your mind—*to love them unconditionally, we must love our children for who they are, not for who we expect them to be.*

Not having faith in our children

Another common message that pervades many family environments is that we have little or no faith in our children to make the right choices. This lack of faith in them always encourages our children to place more trust in external signals than internal ones. Let's take a look at what we're up against and how we can tackle it.

Repression

From birth on, our children receive subtle signals that they're not quite good enough. They're led to believe that they're helpless and inferior and that parents and others in authority are there to fill in where they fall short. For example, when our children cry, we pick them up, rock them, and say, "Hush, baby, don't cry." Although we mean well, this message censures their need to express their feelings at a time in their lives when crying is the only means of expression at their disposal, unless you think dirty diapers qualify.

The repression our children experience goes on and on from there. Until age six or seven, our children actually remain surprisingly self-confident, despite prior failures and disapproval. There's nothing out of their reach and nothing they think they don't deserve. After all, it takes a lot to put out a forest fire!

Sometimes we see these qualities in our child as selfishness. This possibility scares some, because society considers selfishness a vice. We often worry that their being self-centered and expressive will make it difficult for our children to cooperate and coexist with the part of the world that is not *them*. We worry that this self-determination will make our children difficult to handle. I know I cringe every time one or all of my kids goes ballistic in public. God forbid that others think I "spoil" them or that I'm a miserable disciplinarian, because then the entire world will know what a terrible mom I am. So what do we do to calm our fears? Unfortunately, we usually teach our children that this self-expressiveness is wrong—even egoistic or foolhardy. For instance, when children reach out in innocent wonder to touch a candle's bright flame, we quickly slap their hand away instead of letting them figure out for themselves that the flame is hot and can burn them. It's important for children to learn how to apply their reasoning skills to their experiences as well as those of others.

I love the account of the African tribe that grants children this kind of free exploration. They calmly wash their clothes by the river, letting even the smallest children play at the water's edge without fear. They don't so much as bat an eye when their children play with machetes and other dangerous things that we won't even allow our kids to look at, much less brandish wildly in their hands! Interestingly enough, however, the mortality and morbidity rates for these children are low. Drowning and near-drowning incidents are almost unheard-of. Maybe it has something to do with our expectations. If we expect the world to be full of danger, it often is. If we expect that danger to harm our children, it often does. So our self-fulfilling prophecies often make our worst nightmares materialize.

So early on, our children's actions and thoughts are overridden to such a degree that the children become afraid to think for themselves. They must look to authority for guidance, parental or otherwise. This is when they stop looking inwardly for answers. Instead, they become highly skilled at reading the subtlest signs of acceptance and rejection to get whatever answers the outside world can give that will win them the most approval.

Parental control and domination

Over centuries, parents have been brainwashed into believing that the best way to raise children is to exert control by using size and experience to their advantage. The basic premise is that, if we choose to twist our children's arms into becoming the adults we want them to be rather than coach and guide them to making choices for themselves, we're setting them up to be like us: externally directed children.

We teach our children to stick to society's artificial standards of behavior and beliefs for two reasons. First, we want to protect them from ridicule, exclusion, and criticism. Everyone wants their children to fit in—to be happy and successful in the outside world. Second, some use their children to satisfy whatever they lack in their own lives. To these types, children are just trophies they can flaunt to the world. For these two reasons, parents unwittingly encourage their children to create a false self that satisfies the parents' needs as well as society's expectations but often leaves children confused, lost, and unhappy. Let's take a look at how we can correct those pesky little habits that have helped us bring all these problems to bear. There are three faces of parental domination we need to address.

- "How could you, you beast!"
- "Just leave the thinking to me" [also known as "Father (or mother) knows best"].
- "Let me show you who you need to be."

"How could you, you beast!"

This is probably the sneakiest type of domination, because children often don't see it as a form of control. It involves stealthy tactics like guilt, martyrdom, and shame. As you will see, these also convey a sense of conditional love and approval to children. Heidi, age fifteen, says, "My father pressures me to make good grades. If I make a B, he makes me feel so bad about myself. Once, in sixth grade, I made an 82 on a test, and he made me feel like I was really dumb." Here are some remarks I've overheard parents say that illustrate these ploys well:

"But, honey, if you really loved me, you'd try harder in school." (guilt)

"Oh, fine. I'll make your school lunch for tomorrow. I do everything around this house anyway, seeing as how I'm your personal slave."(martyrdom)

"What do you mean you failed your chemistry test? Your parents are both chemists, for God's sake! You're a disgrace to the family name!" (shame)

Although these examples are pretty hard-core, if we listen to some of the things we say to our children, we'll notice subtler forms of each of these.

"Can't you try to get up earlier in the morning? Every time you miss the bus I have to get up at the crack of dawn to take you. Then I'm beat the rest of the day." (guilt)

"You know I'll probably be fired for missing so much work, but it's OK. I don't want to be a rotten mom and miss all of your softball games, so it's a chance I'm willing to take, I guess." (martyrdom)

"You made a C on your spelling test? Wow, that's the lowest grade you've made so far! Did everyone else in the class do better than you?"(shame)

Even these subtler examples take their toll on our children's ability to become self-directed. One of the most common guilt- or shame-invoking remarks we make is "I'm so disappointed in you." It seems harmless enough. We all say it. But it programs our children to make choices based on what will please us rather than what they think is right. So, we really need to be aware of what's coming out of our mouths. We need to ask ourselves every time: "When I say this, am I being a coach or a dictator?"

"Just leave the thinking to me" {or "Father (or mother) knows best"}.

All parents are guilty of telling their children how to think and therefore how to behave and feel. Here are some comments from the children:

"My parents are always pointing out what's wrong with me."

"They're trying to run my life all the time. It drives me crazy. They should trust me more to handle things my own way. Hellooo, I think I can do most stuff myself without messing up like they think I will."

"God, sometimes I feel like I live under a microscope. I just go up to my room and close the door to get some peace."

*"I think my mom and dad don't think I have my own brain sometimes. Maybe they think I don't know how to use it yet. Anyway, sometimes it's **their** brains that need some work."*

"I wish my parents wouldn't butt into my life all the time."

Here are six tricks parents use to tell their children how to think, behave, and feel. Although we can't expect to stop these habits overnight, we might want to try our best to avoid them as much as we can.

- Criticism
- Judgments and evaluations
- Reprimand and illogical punishments
- Thought indoctrination
- Over-controlling
- Rescuing

1. Criticism

Criticism is the act of finding fault in someone. It's all right if its motives will help change things for the better, but if no good can come of it, eighty-six it. Nagging (criticism thinly disguised) is a close relative that almost every kid with a brain finds extremely annoying. Both are forms of evaluation that signal to children that they are on the wrong course toward shaping the acceptable self. Through criticism and nagging, we help our children to define themselves in terms of their flaws rather than their strengths. They therefore grow to believe that there are conditions placed on our love and approval of them.

Through "destructive" criticism, our children adopt beliefs about themselves from us and others in authority rather than through their own reasoning process. So we need to analyze any criticism to ensure it does more good than harm. There's so much we say that's better left unsaid.

2. Judgments and evaluations

Judgments and evaluations go far in discouraging self-direction in our children. Out of the same fear that our children won't satisfy social expectations, we often make negative assessments that convince our children that our beliefs and thoughts are superior. In other words, judgments and evaluations represent our own observations and conclusions being forced upon our children. Again, a ploy that smacks of conditional love. We all make such statements. See whether you recognize any of them.

> *"Life is going to be tougher for you since you're learning disabled."*

> *"That principal at your school doesn't know crap!"*

> *"Organic chemistry is a killer course."*

> *"You're just naturally clumsy. It's not your fault."*

Affirmations can even be a form of evaluation, too. Look at these examples:

> *"It's OK, I was totally obsessed with my hair in junior high, too."*

> *"Not to worry, when I was a kid, I had the same trouble with spelling."*

Any time we make statements like these, it sends our children the message that unless they're exactly like us, they're not OK, meaning they need to go back to the drawing board and rework the design of their false self. Whenever we make assessments about our children, we must be sure to get across to them that these are opinions, not edicts carved in stone. Again, making such distinctions takes being on our toes, listening to everything we say, and doing what we can to encourage them to think for themselves.

3. Reprimand and illogical punishment

A judgmental reprimand is also a weapon capable of transforming the most self-directed children into externally directed wimps. It's criticism taken one step further. Whereas criticism is a warning to our children that they've strayed off the course we've set for them, reprimand is the acknowledgment that they have arrived at the wrong destination. Reprimands often reflect our negative feelings, especially anger and disappointment. Take a look at how destructive these statements are:

"How dare you talk to me in that tone of voice, Mister!"

"You haven't even taken the trash out. I can't believe how lazy you are!"

Illogical punishment takes this negativity even further. It's reprimand coupled with parentally imposed illogical consequences. Examples include whipping children for not telling the truth, making them write "I will obey my parents" 100 times on a sheet of paper, and sending them to bed without supper for dallying over their homework. Such punishments only make our children focus their attention externally on how angry they are with us and accomplish little in correcting their bad behavior. Alternative discipline approaches, like logical, non-degrading consequences, will be discussed later in the book. For now, suffice it to say that illogical punishments dished out as authoritarian decrees are useless and just destroy our children's ability to guide themselves. Furthermore, children generally heed reprimand and punishment because they fear reprisal, not because it's the right thing to do. In this way, the "respect" they have for their parents is something that's demanded, not commanded.

4. Thought indoctrination

Thought indoctrination is extremely prevalent. Whereas all of the preceding indirectly transform the thought processes of our children, thought indoctrination does so more directly. Typical examples are remarks like

> *"You should be proud of yourself for making such a good grade on your report."*

> *"You should be ashamed! Your brother made the football team with no problem!"*

> *"You must feel so embarrassed about saying those nasty words in class."*

In this indoctrination, we directly tell our children what they must think. After a while, they stop using conscious thought to decide what to think or how to feel. Better ways of making the above statements include

> *"Wow, you really worked hard on that class presentation. No wonder you got an A. How does it make you feel?"*

> *"Oh, you didn't make the football team? Well I know you put out a lot of effort. How are you feeling? Are you going to try out next semester?"*

> *"How do you think your classmates felt when you said that in class. What are you going to do to make things right again?"*

As you can see, these examples all encourage children to use their reasoning skills to come up with their own assessment and solution, and this phrasing in no way forces them to accept an opinion or judgment that's not theirs.

5. Over-controlling

To ensure the creation of the consummate false self, we often use coercive techniques like directing, physical punishment, and threats and ultimatums.

In directing, we tell our children how to run their lives. It's the whole Gepetto and Pinocchio puppet thing. Some examples and their alternatives:

"Don't forget your backpack" instead of *"Is there anything you're forgetting before the bus comes?"*

"You need to wear your helmet if you're going outside to bike" instead of *"Biking without a helmet is unsafe."*

"Put your jacket on. It's freezing outside!" instead of *"It's supposed to get down into the twenties this afternoon."*

"Go ahead and get started on your homework right after your snack" instead of letting them figure that one out on their own. Hey, if they don't understand that they need to do their homework every night, they probably have bigger problems, like being able to do their homework in the first place!

"Be sure to call your friend Jerry and ask him to fax you that spelling list you forgot" instead of just letting them suffer the consequences come test time the next morning.

As you can see, although it's often easier to tell them what to do, it's much better either to give them the information that will help them use their own reasoning skills to figure things out or to let them suffer logical consequences for their bad choices.

Physical punishment is alarmingly prevalent, perhaps because of the stress inherent in living our lives at a frenetic pace and filling our schedules to the brim. Many parents feel that spankings are vital to raising an obedient child, while others, drowning in the pressures of the day, simply lose control and, in the heat of the moment, fail to see an alternative. Either approach has two unfortunate effects. First, it teaches our children that violence is an acceptable solution to many of their conflicts. Second, it tells children that they are inferior beings who need to be dominated and oppressed. This sends them the message that they are just a source of bother and not worth as much to the world as adults are. When we do goof up and hit or spank our children, we might try apologizing for our behavior immediately without attaching a disclaimer like, "I'm sorry I slapped you, *but* you were being so noisy, I couldn't help it."

It is easy to see the disastrous repercussions of physical punishment within our society today. The incidence of youth-related crimes like homicides, assaults, vandalism, and rapes has grown at a disturbing pace. Furthermore, the motivations behind violent crimes have become much more trivial in nature. Recent crimes like the eight-year-old child fatally shooting an elderly man in a wheelchair for fifteen cents illustrate this observation. Many may ask, "What was this child thinking?" That is exactly my point—he wasn't. He was unconsciously reacting instead of using his powers of reason to resolve a conflict or stop an impulse. He chose to be driven instead by the notion that violence is an appropriate and useful tool in problem solving and by the collective sentiment that he is entitled to something that he has not earned. He chose to adopt these beliefs and thoughts from others, because he relinquished the responsibility to create his own through conscious reasoning. In other words, he chose to act through external direction instead of self-direction.

Threats and ultimatums are powerful parental tools of control. Examples include

"If you don't get your butt down here right now, you're grounded for a month!"

"This is the last time I'm warning you. If your grades don't improve next term, the car goes. Skateboard to school, for all I care!"

"You say one more word like that to me, and I'll slap your teeth out."

Again, like physical punishment, these tactics just intimidate our children into doing as we wish. They react out of fear rather than reason. When we're guiding and disciplining our children, we need to be sure that we're leaving them room to think. To be self-directed, they'll have to come up with their own motives for behaving, thinking, and feeling a certain way. Self-direction takes a conscious effort, on their part, to add reasoning to their decision-making process.

6. *Rescuing*

In our society today, life seems stuck on fast forward. Caught up in this whirlwind pace, we often find it easier to live the lives of our children *for* them. Many times, I'd clean up my children's breakfast dishes, pick out their school clothes for the next morning, or do the telephone leg work to inquire about some cool-looking key chain one of them saw dangling from a friend's backpack. I often find myself wiping up milk they spilled and calling the school to see if calculators are allowed during the SAT. Mind you, these are activities my children could have easily done on their own. In fact, doing so would have accomplished much in furthering their assertiveness and their problem-solving and decision-making skills. But, it often seemed so much easier to do things for my children so that I could "get it over with" and not have to concern myself with the problem anymore. My fear was that if these tasks were left undone, it would unleash a barrage of nagging remarks on my part or the "poor little me" attitude on theirs. Either way, my externally directed strings were being pulled. I couldn't bear to be thought of as an inattentive, inept parent—by myself or by those around me.

Many parents even go so far as to choose friends, hobbies, sports, clothes, and other things for their children. Some are afraid to see them suffer from the consequences of a poor choice. Others cringe at the thought that their children's choices might make them look bad as parents. So they think for them, feel for them, and act for them. Denying children this practice in decision-making leads to terribly deficient problem-solving skills later, and the older children become, the higher the price tag their choices and consequences carry.

Here are some examples of the "rescue factor" and ways to keep from bailing our children out:

When our child says, *"Mom, I got a detention for being tardy, and it falls on the day of our most important football game! Help! Can't you talk to my teacher or something?"* I'd just say something like, *"Boy, that's rotten luck. But you're pretty sharp, so I'll bet you'll find a way to make things work, football game or no football game."*

When they make this plea for help, *"Dad, can you be a real pal and type up my report! I have the notes right here. I'd do it, but I have a date with Cindy tonight. Don't wanna disappoint her, ya know!"* I'd come back with, *"Gee, I'd like to help you, son, but I've seen you type. You're a speed demon. While you get started, would you like me to call Cindy to tell her you'll be running behind?"*

In summary, some parents come to their children's rescue, because they can't bear to see them suffer. Others do so because they don't want to look bad themselves. Still others do so because they don't want to be inconvenienced by their children's mistakes. Either way, it's commonplace in our society. And since it permits them to bypass the reasoning process, it further encourages them to hide behind a false self. These children grow to believe that there are no safe and reliable answers to be found from within, because they were never given a chance to look there in the first place.

"Let me show you who you need to be"

There are three externally directed parenting no-no's belonging to this type of domination: pressuring children to conform, comparing them with others, and using labeling and global assessments. Let's take a peek at each.

1. Pressure to conform

One fifteen-year-old interviewee says, "I know this girl whose mom tells her who to date, what to wear, and stuff like that. She's really afraid her daughter won't be liked and that'll make her look bad as a mom." We parents sure don't want to be oddballs, so why should we want our children to be? Not only that, non-conforming, highly individualistic children can sometimes be scary for us. We don't know what to make of effusive self-expression and creativity. Often, they don't conform to the artificial standards we hand down to them from society. Will they make others consider us bad parents who can't control their own children? Will our little nonconformists be handicapped when cast into the outside world? Will they disappoint and be disappointed?

But, as I see it, if children want to wear yellow socks, red shorts, and a purple shirt to school, it should make no difference to the parent—or to anyone else, for that matter. If they want to color the mane blue on their horse drawing, it should not only be allowed, but it should be encouraged. Sure, I've often cringed over some of the clothing combinations my children have worn as they happily dashed off to school. But, I suppose my hesitation was more colored by the dread of being considered a neglectful parent than by any doubts about my children's ability.

Here are some examples of the statements we make to pressure our children to conform:

"No one wears army boots with shorts! Are you crazy?"

"You can't go out like that; you'll be a laughingstock!"

"My God, you don't really listen to the Backstreet Boys, do you? Aren't they totally passé now?"

"You can't wear paisley with a plaid! They're two different prints! Go change into a solid-colored shirt."

We need to be acutely aware of any statements that could possibly compel our children to conform to the rest of society. We need to be okay about their being different, creative, and expressive in ways that are not common practice. Otherwise, we're just thinking and making choices for them. Squelching their individuality drives them to make all future decisions through external direction by using other outside influences to ensure conformity. Besides, you may actually have a real gem on your hands. Some of the most fascinating personalities who have contributed the most to humanity have been those with the most creative and eccentric quality about them. Take a look at Albert Einstein and Georgia O'Keeffe. Aren't these "oddballs" good enough role models?

2. Using comparisons

Some parents feel that comparisons are a useful tactic for pressuring children into being better than they are. Again, a ploy of conditional approval. These true-life confessions of interviewed parents paint a clear picture:

> *"Why can't you be like the other kids and try out for the soccer team?"*

> *"I heard Billy next door made straight A's on his last report card. The way I see it, if he can do it, so can you. So shape up, Mister!"*

There are no two ways about it. These comparisons just make children feel rotten about themselves. By comparing them to others, parents are just letting them know that they're not all we'd hoped for. Eventually, these children grow afraid to look within to evaluate themselves. They learn to rely on external measures such as the opinions of others to assess themselves personally. In other words, they become externally directed in the way they define themselves.

It is more helpful to compare our children to their past performance, rather than to other people. That way, they can figure out what changes, if any, they should make in themselves. When they learn to use themselves as measuring sticks, they become masters of self-evaluation—a pivotal attribute of the self-directed.

3. Labels and generalizations

There's nothing, short of flypaper, that sticks better than labels and generalizations. Both control strategies force our children into thinking of themselves in those terms upon which we've decided. It's unimportant whether these observations are accurate or not. And hey, we're bigger and supposedly wiser, so they fall for it every time! Here are some examples:

> *"Darling, you can't help it. You've always been a slow reader."*

> *"You're the brains of the family."*

> *"Hey 'El Destructo,' it seems like everything you touch breaks!"*

These remarks could become fodder for future excuses and justifications. One child admitted, "My parents sometimes call me lazy or fat, and I just use that as my little excuse to get out of doing stuff. It's like, hey, this is the way I am, what can I do about it? I was born that way." These children become confused about their own true identity. They need to figure out who they are on their own.

And then there are generalizations:

> *"You always lose everything! You'd lose your head if it weren't screwed on tight!"*

> *"You're always dawdling. Keep up!"*

> *"You never get anything right."*

Broad generalizations usually contain words like "never" or "always." These make our children give up all hope of shaking whatever assessment we have of them. It makes them think that these attributes are so sweeping that they pervade their every thought and action. In fact, it even deters them from going through the trouble of looking within to figure out who they really are. Self-directed children define themselves through self-evaluation alone. This sense of self is typically nonjudgmental and is derived from their past experiences and performances, their sense of purpose, their gifts and talents, their desires and interests, and their self-appointed unique way of contributing to the pack.

A WORD ABOUT SIBLING INFLUENCES

Your child's sibling can be his best friend or his worst enemy (depending on the time of day). Relationships between siblings can be the most intense and enduring relationships in your child's life. It's important to understand the dynamics of your children's relationships with one another because of the tremendous influences these relationships exert. This influence is triggered partly by their struggle to compete for parental love and approval. The more intense and gripping this struggle, the more externally directed our children will be where that sibling is concerned. They will grow to react to rather than respond to and learn from that sibling.

When our children vie for attention within the family, they learn to manipulate their siblings and us. To avoid this never-ending, child-sibling-parent power play, we can try to stay completely out of the conflicts our kids have with each other. No taking sides or intervening (unless there's a serious physical or emotional threat), because then, we're redefining ourselves as external influences. When we do this, they never learn to work things out for themselves through internal direction and sibling-to-sibling communication.

I believe the differences between siblings can be a wonderful source of wisdom and growth for our children, but only if children decide which of their sibling's characteristics, beliefs, and principles can help them grow on various levels. This conscious choice involves the internal dialogue that is typical of self-directed children. If we teach them how to develop this dialogue, by not allowing them to embroil us in their disagreements, by not comparing them to one another, and by not pitting one against the other, they will be less likely to mindlessly adopt the characteristics of their siblings just to make themselves more acceptable to us.

Here are some suggestions for helping to create a truce in the sibling wars so that our children will respond to the positive influences from their brothers and sisters rather than react to those negative ones in an externally directed way.

- We might want to avoid telling them we love each one equally, because then they don't feel that we have a unique and personal relationship with them. I tell my children that I love each of them in a special way.
- We must try not to compare one child against the other. Even subtle innuendoes can leave a lasting impression.
- We must try never to play favorites! Sometimes this is difficult, because, face it, all parents have one child they feel more connected with.
- Again, we should not interfere in sibling arguments unless broken bones or dismemberment are involved. It's actually rare for siblings to inflict serious physical harm on one another. This laissez-faire

approach means we must never collaborate with either side. When Johnny comes to complain about how mean Bobby was to pull his hair and kick his shins, it would be a mistake to agree with a statement like, "I know, Johnny. I hate when Bobby hurts you like that, but he's having a hard time at school lately, so maybe he's just cranky. I wouldn't get near him if I were you." It would be better to try something like, "I'm so sorry you got hurt, but I know you can find a way to handle your brother on your own. That's your job, not mine."

- We need to show our children how they can be positive role models for each other. For instance, we can ask the older siblings to read a bedtime story to the younger ones. Or we can get the younger ones to help the older siblings color a map for some school project if they happen to be more artistically inclined.

- We can teach our children how their disagreements with each other, as long as they don't draw blood, can help them explore and gel their own identity as well as their personal set of beliefs and opinions.

- We can avoid dismissing or opposing any negative feelings our children have for their siblings. They perceive such involvement as taking sides. It's better to stay neutral by just showing them that we understand how they feel. Here's an example:

  Rachel: *"Mom, Jimmy ripped the head off my favorite Barbie doll and tried to feed it to Rover!"*
  Mom: *"I'm sorry you and Jimmy aren't getting along. I know how upset that makes you feel."*

- It's good to encourage our children to work together so they can learn cooperative skills. *"Why don't you and Mary help me out by unloading the dishwasher?" "Robin, can you make sure Sarah stays quiet while I make a phone call?"*

- If one child is much older than the others, we can give him or her certain specific supervising roles. He or she can help make sure peace is kept among the wild and restless natives. He or she can also be encouraged to help teach the younger siblings. *"Tommy, you know your math facts by heart. Can you help Adam with his flash cards?"*

- When one of our children gets hurt, we can help evoke feelings of empathy in the others by enlisting their help. *"Sarah, your brother fell off his bike. Can you hold pressure on the wound so I can get a bandage?"* If our children feel needed by their siblings, it helps create a more nurturing relationship between them.

- We must try not to label our children. (*"Josh is our little scholar!"* or *"Joe is such a troublemaker!"*) Labels will only give the other sibling ammunition for the next sibling war.

- We can find many ways to encourage our children to regard each other as friends. When they go through the inevitable loss of a friendship, we can remind them how lucky they are to have their siblings as lifelong comrades. Even though they're bound to have spats, they will always love each other year after year, decade after decade.

- Having them sleep in the same bed can help the bond between them strengthen. By the time the sun goes down, so does their energy to bicker. Being stuck together in close quarters, they have to find some way to get along, or no one will get any sleep.

When those knockdown, drag-out fights do occur, always remember that we're the referee, not the judge and jury. This means we need to allow them to work things out for themselves, preferably outside our personal space. Some sibling arguments are helpful, actually. It's their way of testing the waters for the social boundaries for conflict resolution that they'll encounter in that wild and crazy world beyond the hedges of home. We just need to teach our children how to operate within those boundaries.

THE IMPORTANCE OF A FAMILY IDENTITY

Once we've eliminated those things in the family environment that foster external direction in children, building a family identity can go far in strengthening and maintaining the proper milieu for self-direction. The stronger the family identity, the more comfortable our children will be in their own skins—a crucial prerequisite for becoming self-directed. Children whose families have weak identities often seek guidance from external factors in order to achieve a sense of belonging that they haven't been able to gain within the confines of their homes.

Creating a family identity is an effective way to instill our children with a sense of permanence, belonging, and stability. Any way that we can convey this sense of identity is important. Family traditions and rituals, whether they accompany holidays or not, are something to which our children look forward. The families I interviewed say they create their family identity by going on yearly vacations to a specific destination, singing "Happy Birthday" in a special, wacky way, having little family sayings, serving special dishes at Thanksgiving, going out on "buddy days" with each child, having father-daughter dinners, mother-son outings, and so on. Watching family videos together and having photo albums that chronicle the years of family life handy can provide a strong sense of unity and a few belly laughs to boot. Many interviewed families feel that family dinners are crucial opportunities to strengthen this sense of identity. They see dinner as a wonderful time for children to freely express themselves as individuals as well as members of the family. However, it must be a completely safe environment free from evaluations, criticisms, or judgments that might hinder this freedom of expression. We should never denounce what they say and never feel compelled to offer a better idea every time.

A strong family identity makes the job of instilling values in our children easier. We might try saying things such as, "We don't tell lies in our family," or "The Vasquez family shows respect for their friends," "We use words in our family, not hitting." This voicing of values demonstrates what we hold dear as a family. For instance, to show my children the benefits of generosity, we enjoy going out on Christmas Eve to distribute blankets, socks, mittens, and jackets to the homeless. To show them the virtues of a strong work ethic as well as the importance of loyalty and responsibility, we volunteer as a family to staff the garage sales and other fundraisers for our schools. A family identity can even be used to advocate the tenets of self-direction. We might try saying things like, "In our family, we don't interfere with sibling arguments," or "In our family, we have faith in people to think for themselves," or "In our family, we listen to music/wear clothing/pick friends/do things, because we think it's the right choice for us."

Now that we know how to build and maintain a self-directed milieu within the family, our children may actually soak in some of the guidance we offer them in the six remaining strategies that follow.

Two

HELPING CHILDREN DEVELOP
HEALTHY INTERNAL DIALOGUE

As soon as you can say what you think,
and not what some other person has
thought for you, you are on the way to
being a remarkable man.
—*J. M. Barrie*

EIGHT TECHNIQUES TO ENCOURAGE INTROSPECTION

The most important tool of the self-directed is a keen ability
to use internal dialogue in making choices. With this tool,
they can process information from past and present experiences and add objective observations from the outside world.
They can then weigh pros and cons and predict possible consequences and outcomes for their potential choices. This ability to "converse with themselves" makes all the difference in
whether they respond to their external world or react mindlessly to it. It means they will make a choice because it's
right for them, not for others. Unless we nurture the development of their inner voices, they will pay more attention to
the voices of others. Look around you, or better yet, brace
yourself, and watch the news. You'll see that this reliance on
external direction has gotten us nowhere fast.

In the last chapter, I illustrated some of the ways we discourage internal dialogue in our children. Threats, ultimatums, prejudiced evaluations, criticisms, thought indoctrination, reprimands, directing, rescuing, endless chatter, pleading, bribing, negotiations, and so forth give our children little reason to come up with their choices for their own reasons. With these "in your face" parenting techniques, the choices they do make are for our reasons, not theirs. Now let's look at eight strategies that will encourage them to use introspection to make their own choices.

1. Questioning

One of the best ways to stimulate internal dialogue in children is through questioning. Throwing questions at children signals them that it's their turn to act. If the family environment encourages self-direction, children are likely to reflect upon various answers. Some guidance may be necessary, but only when they seem absolutely stuck. Of course, it doesn't count when we ask questions in an ugly way. We derail their internal dialogue when we shout out the question in an angry or frustrated tone. So we must try hard to keep our voices pleasant and respectful. Here's an example of the correct way to question:

> Mom: *"Billy, why are you sitting here all alone while the other kids are playing?"*
> Billy: *"Nobody wants to play with me!"*
> Mom: *"Did something happen?"*
> Billy: *"Well, yeah, Tommy called me names."*
> Mom: *"What did he call you?"*
> Billy: *"Cheater."*
> Mom: *"Why did he call you that?"*
> Billy: *"Because I peeked when I was counting for hide-and-seek."*

Mom: *"What do you think you could do to make things all right between you?"*

Billy: *"I dunno. Nothing I guess. He's a butt, anyway. I hate his guts!"*

Mom: *"But you were the best of friends yesterday. What's different today?"*

Billy: *"He made me feel like a lousy jerk!"*

Mom: *"Did you have anything to do with that?"*

Billy: *"Yeah, well, I guess I shouldn't have cheated."*

Mom: *"What do you think you should do?"*

Billy: *"I guess I can say I'm sorry."*

Mom: *"Sounds good. Give it a whirl, chief."*

How about another?

Dad: *"Rachel, you look angry. What's the matter?"*

Rachel: *"I hate my teacher. She gave me a detention for nothing."*

Dad: *"What were her reasons?"*

Rachel: *"No big deal, I just forgot to bring my math book to class, again."*

Dad: *"Why do you think the school has that rule?"*

Rachel: *"So the stupid kids in the class won't get stupider."*

Dad: *"Have you noticed any difference in your math grades this grading period?"*

Rachel: *"I guess they have slipped a little."*

Dad: *"So what do you think you should do?"*

Rachel: *"I guess I'll put a note on the inside of my locker so I won't forget next time."*

Dad: *"Hey, good idea! I think that might just work!"*

In both examples, you can see how the child was made to think. Compare this to the incorrect form of questioning:

> Mom: *"Billy, stop pouting and go play with the other kids."*
> Billy: *"But Tommy called me a cheater."*
> Mom: *"What! You cheated? Why did you go and do something stupid like that?"*
> Billy: *"'Cuz I don't want Tommy to win instead of me."*
> Mom: *"Do you really think you deserve to play with him now?"*
> Billy: *"I dunno."*
> Mom: *"Get your things, I'm taking you home right away."*

Here's another example of how not to question:

> Dad: *"Why the nasty scowl on your face, Missie?"*
> Rachel: *"You'd be mad too if you got a detention!"*
> Dad: *"What! How many detentions do you think you can get away with before they suspend you?"*
> Rachel: *"Who cares. I hate that school anyway."*
> Dad: *"And just how do you think you'll be able to make a living if you don't finish school?"*
> Rachel: *"Oh, just leave me alone!"*

What's the difference? The difference is a good day and a bad day. A good relationship or a bad relationship. A child that reflects inwardly on the choices she made or a child who reacts to her parent's remarks by focusing on what that parent did wrong. A self-directed child or an externally directed child.

2. Statement prompts

Simple statements can kick-start a child's internal dialogue mechanism, too. Some of my favorites are giving information, making observations, and using one- or two-word prompts.

Here's an example of **giving information**:

> Mom: *"David, it's not safe to run around the pool."*

David, thinking: *"Oh yeah. I remember that kid last year split his head right open. Gross, I don't want that to happen to me!"*

Compare that with

Mom: *"David, stop that running right now!"*
David, thinking: *"What a nag! I wish she'd stop treating me like a baby!"*

Here's an example of **making observations**:

Dad: *"I see you're not ready yet, and the invitation says the party starts at 9:00."*
Lizzie, thinking: *"Oh yeah! I forgot all about it. Gosh, I'm so glad he reminded me. What if he had forgotten too? Next time, I better write this kind of stuff down in my calendar!"*

Compare that with

Dad: *"Don't you realize what time it is? You're going to be late for the big party! If you're not dressed and ready in five minutes, you can find yourself another ride!"*
Lizzie, thinking: *"Geez, he really gets on my nerves when he's like that. Anyway, I can get ready in five minutes, no prob. I'm gonna call Jenny and ask for a ride. No way I'm sitting in the car with that monster!"*

Here's an example of **one- or two-word prompts**:

Mom: *"Eliza, the bus."*
Eliza, thinking: *"Oh my gosh, I'm late. I better eat breakfast on the bus, 'cuz I don't have time to eat at home now! Glad she reminded me. I have a spelling test this morning. I better wake up fifteen minutes earlier next time."*

Compare that with

> Mom: *"Eliza, I hear the bus around the corner, and I'm sick and tired of driving you to school when you miss it!"*
> Eliza, thinking: *"God I hate her! Like I need any more stress this morning. It's her fault, anyway. She should have waken me up when my alarm didn't go off."*

Again, these prompts all got the children thinking about their own problems and ways to solve them. Not using them just created an irrational reaction to an external influence, the parent.

3. Giving our children choices we can live with

Children become comfortable with their internal dialogue when we empower them with choices. For instance, let Sally decide where to sit in a restaurant, or ask Tommy to pick out the place setting for the Thanksgiving table. Of course, there's one small catch. We have to be happy with whatever that choice is! If we overrule it, our children will grow to think that their decisions stink! Over time, they'll rely less and less on internal direction and look to others to make choices for them.

4. Modeling internal dialogue

Our children can learn to develop their internal dialogue by watching us. Have you ever "thought out loud"? This is what this technique is all about. Let's jump right in to an example.

> You: *"Mr. Rask is so mad at me for not showing up to that meeting on time. I know how important it was to him. And there I was, finishing my crossword puzzle instead! I should have thought about how my being late would have made him*

feel. I think I'll go apologize to him right now. Maybe I can invite him to lunch, too. We can discuss whatever part of the meeting I missed, and maybe I can offer to help more with that project he was proposing."

Sure, they'll think you're a bit daffy at first, talking to an invisible audience, but it's a great way to teach values, problem solving, and the benefits of not engaging in self-deceit. It beats an offensive lecture. It might even get your children to reflect inwardly on these same issues.

5. Walk-throughs

Sometimes it helps to walk our children through their own internal dialogue by role-playing a scenario. Suppose Johnny is being terrorized by the class bully. You can offer to help like this:

> You: *"I know Chris has been giving you a hard time at school lately."*
> Johnny: *"Yeah, he pushes me a lot and says I look like a girl with my curly hair."*
> You: *"I know what, let's play a game. I'll be you, and you can be Chris. Maybe we can find a way to solve this problem together."*
> Johnny: *"OK. He usually says something like, 'Hey, Curly, where ya going, home to play with your dolls?'"*
> You as Johnny: *"I'm not gonna let people treat me that way. I know you could probably be a pretty good friend if you wouldn't pick on other kids."*
> Johnny as Chris: *"Says who, you little punk?"*
> You as Johnny: *"Says me. You throw a mean curve ball. I wish you could be part of our team, but we just don't need anyone who's rude."*

Johnny as Chris: *"Look, I'm sorry, pal. I didn't mean nothing by it. Shake and be friends?"*
You as Johnny: *"Okay, I'll give it a try. But remember, no more teasing."*

Of course, this conversation can go any one of a million directions, so role-play various outcomes, bad and good. By switching roles on occasion, your child can see the problem from different perspectives, which is crucial to the development of strong and healthy internal dialogue.

6. Pros and cons list

Helping children list pros and cons encourages them to develop the internal dialogue to solve problems and make difficult choices. They learn to weigh different variables in a decision and predict potential outcomes. Let's take a look at one scenario:

Tim: *"Mom, should I play soccer or baseball next year?"*
Mom: *"Hmm. That's a tough decision. Let's make a list of pros and cons."*
Tim: *"Huh?"*
Mom: *"You know, advantages and disadvantages for each choice."*
Tim: *"Oh yeah, I get it! Well I'm a lot better at baseball!"*
Mom: *"But then again, you might want to improve your soccer skills."*
Tim: *"Yeah, and Jimmy's going out for soccer. He's my best friend now."*
Mom: *"Your dad coaches for the baseball team. Is that a pro or a con?"*
Tim: *"Definitely a con. It makes me nervous when he hovers over me."*

Mom: *"Gotcha. When's practice for each one?"*
Tim: *"Soccer practice is right after school, so I get a break before homework, and I don't have to bum a ride."*
Mom: *"But you have to admit, the weather is nice and cool when you have practice after dinner."*
Tim: *"True. But I don't mind the heat. I think I'll go for the soccer team this year. Baseball will have to wait."*

This listing can be done orally or on paper. For those old enough to write well, a written list has special benefits in that it can be referred to over and over until the decision has been made or the problem solved.

7. Consequence list

A consequence list is simply a variation on the pros and cons list. Instead of listing advantages and disadvantages, children list only the consequences of each potential decision. For instance, if Sandra is agonizing over whether or not to apply for a school patrol position, together you might come up with this list of possible consequences:

I would have to get up thirty minutes earlier.
I would earn the respect of my friends and teachers.
I would be able to help smaller children cross the street.
I would have to miss after-school chess club for nine weeks.
I would get to wear that cool-looking badge.
I might be able to win a student council position next year.
I would learn how to be responsible and punctual.
I would be able to learn to organize my time.
I wouldn't be able to ride with Jenny on the bus every morning.
I would be able to practice my manners.

After discussing or reading the list, Sandra would find it easier to choose. And over time, she'd be able to transform this habit into automatic and lightening-fast internal dialogue, relying on herself, rather than others, to make choices.

8. Using praise and rewards that promote internal rather than external direction

The concept of praise and rewards is surrounded by a lot of controversy, because there are both beneficial and harmful forms of praise and rewards.

To preserve children's internal direction, we must ensure that they don't shape their behavior just to get praises and rewards. Such shaping means they are using an external influence to make those choices. One fifteen-year-old interviewee says it perfectly: "Sometimes I do certain things just to get a reward like a present or something. I don't even think of any other reason why I should do it." Our task is to determine which forms of praise and reward will encourage self-evaluation in our children. Let's start by examining the following praises and rewards and then explaining why each is either good or bad.

DO NOT praise children when they win stars, trophies, medals, or games or earn good grades. These are external factors. Saying something like, "Look how great you did! You got all A's on your report card!" places emphasis on their win/loss record (external direction) rather than on their hard work (internal direction.)

DO praise children for the actions that led them to earn those stars, trophies, medals, games, or good grades. Saying something like, "These A's represent lots of hard work and determination on your part. You must be proud," places the focus on the child's efforts so that he or she reflects upon them and learns to make the connection between effort and outcome.

DO NOT praise a child as a person: "You're such a good girl." This is an appraisal of self-worth. Such appraisals should never come from an external source, even a parent. It's up to our children alone to decide, internally, what kind of people they are.

DO praise their behavior, instead, by saying, "You are playing so nicely with your friends." This motivates children to reflect internally on something over which they have full control— their actions.

DO NOT give general or meaningless praise. Such praise smacks of subjectivity, because, frankly, they're just our opinions. And we certainly don't want our children to use the opinions of authority figures as the gold standard by which they shape their behavior and make their decisions in life. Examples of such empty praise include the following remarks:

"Wow, great job raking those leaves!"

"Hey, that's a terrific-looking picture you're drawing."

"What a beautiful map you've made!"

You can see how these forms of praise teach children that the only way they can distinguish right from wrong in what they say or do is by external approval or acceptance. Eventually, they develop a dependency upon the opinions of others. Even the statement "I am so proud of you" can give a child this same message, so I like to say "I bet you feel proud of yourself" instead.

Furthermore, when children receive general or meaning-less praise, their first reaction is often to think the opposite. Suppose a parent comments, "Billy, you are so organized!" I can almost guarantee that Billy's first thoughts will immediately go back to the times when he was sloppy and disorganized. If a parent says, "Jane, you're such a good girl," her first thought might be how badly she behaved the week before. She might even think, "No I'm not! I'm a rotten kid. Either you're just trying to be nice, or I've really got you horn-swoggled!" In short, this kind of praise often makes children reflect on past failures.

DO give children praise that is specific in nature. One way is to provide impartial observations, as in the following remarks:

> *"Wow, look how many leaves you raked up from the yard! Ten bags! That's a lot of work!"*

> *"I see you've already done all of your homework, and it's only six o'clock! You've checked over your math problems all by yourself!"*

> *"You sure used lots of nice colors on that geography map, and look how many things you thought to label—rivers, mountains, cities. Wow!"*

In addition, it helps to describe the benefits of their good choices:

> *"You finished all of your homework so fast, that you've allowed yourself two extra hours to play."*

Specific descriptions as a form of praise help children learn how to trust their own judgment, instead of relying on others' opinions and evaluations. As a result, children decide if their actions are truly worthy of their own approval. After all, to become self-directed, children must discover their greatness on their own.

DO give children praise that invokes introspection and inner praise like, "You must be proud of yourself." Again, this approach instructs children to assess themselves by reflecting on their actions. Consequently, they gain a sense of their own abilities and accomplishments, which, in turn, helps them further define their identity.

DO allow children to overhear your praise. While acting as though you don't know your child is listening, say something like, "Erik is good at figuring out how to put stuff together; let's ask him," or "Have you noticed how polite Michelle has been lately?" This type of praise is extremely powerful, because the child considers our evaluation sincere and completely free from ulterior motives. I believe overheard praise is one of the two most powerful parenting tools for raising self-directed children. The other one is sincerely asking for their help.

DO use silent forms of praise like nods, winks, the "thumbs up" sign, smiles, and pats on the back. When parents use gestures instead of words, the praise often packs a more powerful punch, because it appears more genuine and, therefore, more believable. It also motivates children to contemplate their praiseworthy actions.

DO NOT use excessive, indiscriminate praise. When subjected to this excessive praise year after year, our children don't learn to judge themselves realistically. They learn helplessness, because the abilities and talents they're told they have are often actually bogus or overinflated. When these children are thrown out into the real world, they become painfully aware that they're not as great in certain areas as they were led to believe. In fact, this false perception of greatness (a damaging external influence) may have actually hampered their motivation to better themselves in those areas.

This realization creates the opposite of that praise's intent—decreased self-esteem. I often see this artificial bolstering of self-esteem in elementary schools. So much emphasis is placed on external strengthening of kids' self-image and self-confidence. Praise, which is usually general in nature, is heaped on children in the form of stickers, teacher's comments, and so on. Filled with a sense of self-importance, they then enter middle school, where the true nature of their abilities is revealed. That's a rude awakening for any eleven year old.

DO NOT use praise that's overly gushy and insincere. Kids pick up on that insincerity, and it does nothing to encourage useful internal dialogue. One interviewee says, "I hate the way some grown-ups talk to younger kids, like they overdo the praise thing and treat the kid like a baby. It's like they treat them like they're stupid or something."

In conclusion, praise should always cause children to internally assess their behavior, instead of depending on others' evaluations. Children praised in a way that promotes internal direction rely on their reasoning skills to examine their choices, the consequences they experience, and the decisions they must make for the future. These are the qualities of a self-directed being—qualities we must all strive for, not only for our children, but for ourselves as well.

What about rewarding our children's good choices? I'm opposed to any kind of reward system that has the purpose of encouraging our children to do what we want them to do. Rewards are just external influences that distract our children from using internal dialogue to make their choices. For example, children should be willing to do their chores without pay, because it is reasonable to expect them to contribute to the family's daily tasks. After all, they're members of that family, too. Money for chores is just an external influence. On the other hand, I do believe that children should receive an age-appropriate allowance, but for a different reason. The family earns a certain amount of money over time, and being family members, our children should enjoy a part of that financial success. As far as schoolwork, rewarding children for good grades gives them the impression that the goal is in the grade rather than in the knowledge they can gain through their studies. Grades are an external influence. Children should do their best in school because learning is vital to their growth and welfare and because it's personally gratifying.

I also disagree with rewarding children for behaving well, but we'll go into this later on in the discipline chapter. They should, instead, receive negative consequences for their misbehavior and positive ones for their good behavior. It's fine, if you have the time and patience, to make up a behavior chart with certain goals for children to accomplish, but only for helping them monitor their own progress. And there should be no rewards for reaching a goal, except the satisfaction of behaving according to their own moral code. There are two acceptable types of rewards we can give our children. One is to offer words of encouragement when they're on the right track. For example, if Tommy carries out the trash without having to be reminded, we can say something like, "Whoa, you must be getting big! Do you realize I didn't have to remind you once to take out the trash? That sure helps me out!" Remarks like these stimulate them to evaluate their actions internally. The second is in the form of positive natural or logical consequences. For instance, if Brianna finishes her homework early, she can have extra time to play outside with her friends. Again, she's encouraged to reflect on her actions with internal dialogue like, "Wow! I *did* do my homework in record time, and now I get to play tons more! I'm going to try to do that *every* school day!" Other types of rewards are simply bribes, and bribes are external factors that make our children become unconscious, externally driven puppets.

DERAILING UNHEALTHY INTERNAL DIALOGUE

There's only one thing worse than relying on external influences to make decisions, and that's engaging in self-deceit, self-deprecation, and that evil triad: excuses, justifications, and rationalizations. And why do people engage in these self-defeating behaviors? Sometimes they find the truth too painful. Sometimes they're afraid of reprimand or shame. In any case, it's all about losing approval. If they reveal a part of themselves that they aren't exactly proud of, they think they won't be loved. If they discover something about themselves that they don't particularly like, they think they won't love themselves. If they don't love themselves, why should anyone else?

There are ways to keep our children on the healthier track of self-truth.

HELPING THEM CONFRONT THEIR UNHEALTHY INTERNAL DIALOGUE

Many times, we look the other way when our children give excuses or deceive themselves. We don't want to think of them as having flaws, we don't want to hurt their feelings, we don't want to be reminded of our own shortcomings, or we don't want to bother with the showdown that will result from calling their bluff. But it's always in their best interest to let them know we're on to them. Here are a couple of examples:

Danny: *"Ms. Wadsworth gave us way too much homework. She's so mean. I'm not going to do any of it!"* (self-deceit)

Mom: *"Mrs. Wilson says Hal has to study for a social studies test tomorrow. I know you guys are in the same class. And I know how much trouble you have with that subject. Is that what this is really all about?"*

Danny: *"Yeah, I guess. I was so embarrassed when I flunked the last test! Maybe you can let me stay home sick tomorrow just this once. Then I could have a little more time to study."*

Mom: *"Hey, I've already done the social studies bit. It's up to you to decide what to do. You know the consequences of studying and the consequences of not studying. You can figure it out yourself. I, for one, do not intend to lie for you. I just wanted you to know that you can't pull the wool over my eyes and I won't let you fool yourself either. How 'bout I help you go through the hardest parts?"*

Danny: *"Maybe if you quiz me with the questions at the end of each chapter!"*

One more example:

Debbie: *"I'm not going to be Jessica's friend any more. She's such a bore to be around."* (self-deceit)

Dad: *"You girls were practically attached at the hip last weekend. Tell me what really happened between you two."*

Debbie: *"I'm so mad at her. She told Jannika that I wasn't inviting her to my birthday party!"*

Dad: *"Is that true?"*

Debbie: *"Well, yes, but she didn't have to go and blab. Anyway, I can't be friends with her anymore, because she's not even in any of my classes."* (justification)

Dad: *"Sarah's not in your class, and she's been your friend for years. I just want you to know that it works best if you're honest with yourself and with me. That way, maybe we can figure out how to solve this together."*

Debbie: *"I guess you're right. I need to talk this out with Jessica tonight. Can you help me come up with some things to say?"*

So when we realize our children aren't being honest with themselves or others, the first step is to try to ferret them out of the hole they're digging for themselves and help them engage in healthier internal dialogue to solve their problem.

HELPING THEM REBOUND FROM THE EFFECTS OF FACING THE TRUTH

Once we've confronted deceit so that children face the truth, we need to help them get over whatever pain is involved:

"I know how difficult it was to talk about this problem. That took a lot of courage."

"Facing what you did wrong is tough. You must really be growing up."

"I'm glad you eventually came clean with me. I like feeling that I can trust what you have to say."

Even though it can be trying to deal with some of the problems they've been concealing, especially when those problems involve us, we need to work hard to make our children comfortable with the truth by not making comments that evoke feelings of guilt, shame, embarrassment, or anger. These comments include reprimands, insults, threats, ultimatums, and harsh or illogical punishments.

HELPING THEM FIND SOLUTIONS THROUGH HONEST, HEALTHY INTERNAL DIALOGUE

Once they've recovered from facing the truth, it's time to shift to finding a solution to the conflict. The eight strategies demonstrated in the first part of this chapter work well, because they change dishonest internal dialogue to dialogue that is more honest and open. If the problem is serious or complex or the child is old enough to have well-developed abstract thought processes, the walk-throughs, pros and cons list, and consequence list are probably your best options.

MODELING OUR OWN INNER HONESTY FOR OUR CHILDREN

If we want our children to engage in internal dialogue that's straightforward and truthful, that means we must do so too. If we slip, and make excuses or justification for a poor choice, we should expose this mistake out loud with our children as witnesses. It might even be a good idea to establish inner honesty as part of the family identity: "We're honest with ourselves in the Smith family," or "We don't believe in making excuses in our family."

Once our children are pros at having effective two-way communication with that little inner voice of theirs, the pull of external factors begins to atrophy. Over time, our children stand on their own and become stronger and stronger. They come to believe in themselves above all else.

Three

HELPING CHILDREN DEVELOP
NATURAL INTUITION

Intuition is proof that the soul is bigger
than we give it credit for.
—Anonymous

I LOVE THE WAY PSYCHOTHERAPIST Belleruth
Naparstek characterizes intuition:

> *Intuitive knowing brings through the normal sensory channels*
> *information that by all accounts we aren't supposed to be get-*
> *ting, because it's about someone or something other than us.*
> *It's as though our personal boundaries were extended over*
> *more territory than just our own skins, so we pick up data*
> *from the environment as if it were about us.*

Why is intuition so important to self-direction? Because it's
better to seek guidance from our own soul rather than from
external influences that can't possibly understand our personal
circumstances.

The intuition of children is particularly uncanny, but,
because they express their intuitive feelings without reservation,

we often chide them for their "overactive imaginations." But this special sense is a gift that helps children stay out of harm's way and make the right choices. It is their direct internal communication with their souls. If we sabotage their trust in that little inner voice, we open the doors for them to look to external voices for guidance and direction.

Here are some simple tips to help children develop this special, innate power.

Modeling the Use of Our Own Intuitive Powers

We might say something like, "I have a hunch Aunt Sally needs a visit from us. Let's go see her after church this Sunday." If the hunch proves right, we could let them know how glad we are that we "listened to our heart."

Encouraging Them to Follow Their Own Hunches

If they feel they shouldn't go to a sleepover because they have a bad feeling about it, we can support their choice instead of telling them not to worry, everything will be all right. We can also encourage them to ignore remarks from others that belittle or ridicule this remarkable ability.

When dealing with moral issues, I ask my children to live by the motto: "*If it feels wrong, don't do it.*" Bad moral decisions are always accompanied by a sense of uneasiness that they must learn to bring up to a conscious level and heed.

Teaching Children How to Strengthen Their Intuitive Powers

We can train our children to consciously use their intuition. Suppose Caroline can't decide which of two books to do her book report on. We can ask her to close her eyes and visualize, or imagine, giving the presentation first on one, then the other. She will probably get a better feeling about one. When she makes her choice with intuition as an aid, she'll be right more often than wrong and will learn through these successes to trust her inner voice.

I'll often ask my children to tap into their intuition with these techniques:

- To problem solve yes or no questions, I ask them to close their eyes and visualize some sort of ball. Then I tell them to ask the question. If the ball floats up, the answer is yes; if the ball sinks, the answer is no.

- For questions with multiple short answers, I ask them to tell me the first choice that comes to their minds when I clap my hands. Then I ask the question and call out, "1, 2, 3, 4, 5," CLAP. Whatever they have as their first image is called their "flash answer" and is probably the answer their intuition is indicating.

If the question has a more complex answer, I ask them to lie down and close their eyes. I then tell them to take some slow, deep breaths. I describe some peaceful setting they're in, like a lovely beach or a flowery meadow. When they're relaxed, I ask them to descend, in their mind's eye, a small flight of steps leading to a long hallway. On either side of the hallway are numerous closed doors. Behind one of those doors lies the most suitable answer to their question. I ask them to go to that door and open it. When they've done so, I ask them to describe the images they see.

It sometimes takes patience to put it all together, but the point is that they're given the message that intuition is real, powerful, and useful.

Playing Intuition Games

Intuitive games can be a blast for the family. We love to use color flash cards and take turns guessing the colors on each. Initially, our scores were no better than 50 percent, but believe it or not, they improved with practice. We do the same thing with stock quotes, the color hat the chef at Benihana's will wear, the time the mail truck will come, etc.

Keeping an Intuition Journal

An intuition journal helps children sort and interpret intuitive impressions. If they know they must write these impressions down, they're more prone to pay attention to every little signal that flits across their brains. And in the act of writing down their intuitions, they will automatically focus on details like textures, smells, colors, and complex feelings. At the end of the day or week, they can review which "hunches" materialized. Over time, children will learn to pick up patterns in their intuitive signals according to time of day, where they were, what they ate, what their emotional state was, etc. If they keep this journal religiously, in a short time they'll become more skilled in picking out which signals feel true and which are just false alarms.

Teaching Children How to Receive Intuitive Signals More Clearly

Meditation is an excellent way to help children listen to their inner voice. One simple method can be done as an entire family. I ask my children to get in a comfortable position, close their eyes, and become a passive spectator of their own thoughts and impressions. When images flit across their consciousness, I ask them to merely notice them. They must not alter these impressions by categorizing, interpreting, elaborating, predicting, sorting, labeling, or defining them. After a while, children become skilled at having undistorted intuitive signals at their disposal—enabling their intuitive prowess to soar to new heights and their self-direction to become more rooted and true.

Teaching children to develop, trust, and rely upon their intuition is an important way to strengthen their inner directedness. With this internal communication fortified, their dependence on making choices based on reactions to external influences diminishes. The stronger our children's internal focus, the more powerful their spirits become.

Four

TEACHING CHILDREN EMPATHY

> *He who wishes to secure the good of*
> *others has already secured his own.*
> *—Confucius*

EMPATHY AND "BENEVOLENT SELFISHNESS" are
two intertwined traits that make up the heart of the self-
directed. Empathy is "the vicarious experiencing of the
thoughts, feelings, and attitudes of another." For self-directed
children to respond—not react—to external influences, they
must be able to understand, or empathize with, them fully.

Selfishness, as conventionally defined, is "concern pri-
marily with one's own interests." Sounds bad, doesn't it? True
selfishness, however, is actually a wonderful trait, because
honoring those self-interests requires being moral. For
instance, if our child cuts in front of his friends at the water
fountain, he may get his drink quicker, but he has broken his
integrity. Or suppose a man donates to a local charity. His
motives could be "good selfish" because giving makes him
feel good inside. Or his motives could also be "bad selfish." He

might have made the donation so members of the community would respect him more. But this is not selfishness. This is greed. Will he feel good about it inside? Nope. Will people really respect him more? Doubt it. Has he avoided tarnishing his character? Absolutely not.

When self-directed children have a high sense of empathy, they examine the misfortunes of another until they develop a deeper understanding for that person's situation. Once they've done this, they will respond through "benevolent selfishness." Let's go back to the water fountain. If a self-directed child was one of those pushed aside, she might think, "I know where this is going. Everyone in line is going to get mad and pick on him. I know how *I* would feel if my friends picked on me." (Empathy.) "I can't let Sammy go through that. I'd feel like I let him down. I'm going to take him aside and talk to him. If he loses friends, I'd feel bad about myself all day long." (Benevolent selfishness.) You see how watching out for her own feelings benefits everyone in that situation? If she had reacted instead of responded, she might have said some ugly words or helped turn his peers against him. In that situation, no one wins.

Where does self-sacrifice fit into the concept of benevolent selfishness? Aren't there times when we must sacrifice ourselves for others? No way. Suppose I'm a young, single mom with three kids under the age of six. Should I scale down or postpone my career and social life to provide for them? Absolutely! I love them so deeply that I want to avoid the pain I'd feel to see them suffer. But as they become older, do I work eighty-hour weeks so that they each can have TV sets in their rooms? No, because indulging them is not good for them. As they become older teens, do I work two or three jobs to put them through college? Heck no! Not if they can get financial aid or scholarships. Do I take out loans to help them buy their first car or house? Certainly not! Why should I deny them the pride that comes from earning things on their own? I would probably develop a sense of resentment rather than love. So self-sacrifice to avoid our own pain is noble. Self-sacrifice to uphold our image or abide by a distorted sense of duty is cruel, to ourselves and those it's meant to help.

Here are eight steps to helping children develop empathy and benevolent selfishness.

1. TEACHING CHILDREN HOW "BENEVOLENT SELFISHNESS" WORKS

When children are old enough, we can explain the difference between selfish and self-righteous or greedy. Teaching them to follow the motto, "If it feels wrong inside, it's good for no one," can help them keep their motives sincere and pure. We can help them understand this distinction better by talking about the "selfish" acts we engage in, what motivates us to do them, how these acts do *not* harm others, and how the benefits to ourselves spread to those around us. We can also help them analyze the motives behind their own acts toward others. Do these motives allow them to keep their morals intact? Are their actions truly good for them in the long run? Do their actions help, rather than harm, others? Could any ulterior motives be involved that make their acts less angelic than they appear?

2. HELPING CHILDREN UNDERSTAND OTHERS BY USING THE "EMPATHY TRIAD"

We can help children develop a deeper understanding for others if we teach them how to assign empathy-triad levels to those with whom they are in conflict. The triad consists of *happiness, inner strength,* and *outlook at that given moment.* Suppose Sarah has a problem with a friend (Megan) who's jealous every time Sarah makes a new friend. If Sarah's parents have taught her how to use the empathy triad, here's what she'd do: First, she'd compare Megan's happiness level to her own. Surely, Megan can't be happy at that particular moment if she wigs out at the prospect of sharing her friend! Then she assigns levels of inner strength. Megan, in this particular circumstance, displays an insecurity that proves she has less

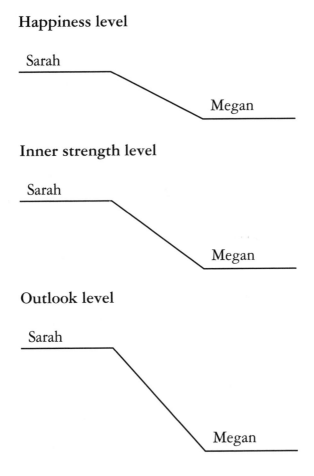

Happiness level

Sarah

Megan

Inner strength level

Sarah

Megan

Outlook level

Sarah

Megan

inner strength than Sarah. Finally, Sarah compares the outlooks for both Megan and herself. Megan is putting herself in the precarious position of losing a friendship. Wasn't that just the thing she was trying to avoid in the first place? And if the friendship collapses, she's going to feel pretty down for a while. Sarah, on the other hand, is in a strong position, because she knows that no one has the right to deny her a new friendship. So we have the triad level assignment shown on page 80.

One look at this balancing act, and it's pretty clear to Sarah who's in a better position to respond rather than react in this conflict. Understanding her position of strength will give Sarah the confidence that will allow her to feel empathy towards Megan ... to develop an understanding that is free from resentment, frustration, and anger.

3. Helping Children Develop Empathy through Service

Through bringing relief to someone who is suffering, children can come to understand the depths of that suffering. For instance, they can hand out blankets and hot tea to homeless families on a particularly cold winter's day. Or perhaps they can help a recently widowed neighbor by mowing her yard and taking her trash cans out. By performing these acts of compassion, our children can't help but think about the unfortunate lot of those they help. When they do, they're sure to think about how it would feel to be in those other shoes. As children grow older, we might try encouraging them to find their own special niche where community service is concerned.

We can also help them apply this sense of charity and compassion to their friends and family members. If a teammate strikes out in the last inning to lose the baseball game, maybe a smile or warm pat on the shoulder is enough to lift his spirits. If a sibling is crying over a lost book report, our child might offer to help in the search. Whether at school, in the family, or in the community, acts of service teach our children about suffering, and this, in turn, teaches empathy.

Again, when our children help others, it's important to ensure their motives are pure and moral. One of the most effective ways of ensuring the sincerity of actions is through anonymity. If their acts of service are anonymous, it is impossible to harbor motives like greed, self-righteousness, image improvement, or other forms of secondary gain. With anonymous service, there is no doubt that their motives are to feel good inside and, therefore, to lift their souls.

4. HELPING CHILDREN USE INTERNAL DIALOGUE TO DEVELOP EMPATHY

As parents, we can try to show our children how to hone internal dialogue to perfection in many ways. Some examples follow:

- When our children are faced with people they don't like or are at odds with, encourage them to try to find something good, however miniscule or trivial, in that person. If they're too mad to come up with anything more than "his socks don't stink as much today as they did yesterday," it's OK to throw a few ideas their way.
- If they still can't see anything worthwhile in that person, ask them to close their eyes and imagine him or her as a cute little newborn baby or as very ill or sad.
- Still stumped? Ask them to see their enemies as children with their own burdens. Everyone has baggage of some sort. Remind them that even those they despise are no exception. As Mary

Wollstonecraft Shelley aptly put it, "No man consciously chooses evil because it is evil; he only
mistakes it for the happiness he seeks."

- Ask children to mentally place themselves in
  their adversaries' shoes.
- When we are angry with someone, we often mistake what motivates them, assuming that person
  did something to intentionally hurt us. But their
  behavior usually has less to do with us than we
  think. For instance, suppose Thomas is playing at
  Jeff's house and suddenly announces, "I'm bored.
  I want to go home." Jeff gets angry, because he
  thinks Thomas is calling him a total bore. So he
  reacts with, "Fine, go ahead, but you're not my
  friend anymore. I'm not going to ask you over
  again!" But if Jeff took a moment to think,
  "What's this all about?" he might ask Thomas,
  "Why do you want to go home now?" He might
  find that Thomas is homesick, hungry, or tired. We
  can teach our children to ask questions so that they
  more fully understand the behavior that annoys or
  enrages them. With knowledge, of course, comes
  understanding. And with understanding comes
  true empathy.
- Ask children to look back at prior experiences,
  when the tables were turned. For instance, in the
  example above, has Jeff ever wanted to go home
  early while playing at a friend's? Was he ashamed
  to admit being homesick or not feeling well?
- Express aloud your own empathetic internal dialogue. For instance, "Daddy looks so tired after coming home from work. I bet he'd feel so much better

if someone brought him his slippers and newspaper." Afterwards, we can help them see what a powerful effect their empathy had: "Did you see how happy Daddy was that someone took the time to make him feel comfortable? He sure feels loved now."

The purpose of all this inner talk is powerful. It guides our children to understand rather than blame and to use reason to override negative reactions like defensiveness, hurt feelings, and negative judgments.

5. HELPING CHILDREN DEVELOP EMPATHY THROUGH ROLE PLAY

Whenever children have a hard time empathizing with someone, role-playing can perform miracles. Suppose Shelly gets angry any time her friend Jill invites Eliza to her house for a sleepover. Here's what Jill's mom might say to help Jill feel empathy for Shelly:

> Jill's mom: *"Shelly and you seem to be having trouble getting along. What's going on?"*
>
> Jill: *"Oh she's the most annoying person in the world. She gets so mad when I invite Eliza over!"*
>
> Jill's mom: *"Hey, maybe we can play a game. I can pretend to be you and you can play Shelly. Maybe we can figure out a way to handle this."*
>
> Jill: *"I don't know what you're talking about, but OK. I'll try anything."*
>
> Jill's mom: *"Okay, here goes. You first."*
>
> Jill as Shelly: *"I heard you invited Eliza over. How can you stand her? I mean, she's so rude to everyone. You know she tells everybody at school that you don't stand a chance at making the swim team this year."*

Jill's mom as Jill: *"You sound angry about me inviting her over. Are you afraid that will mean you and I won't be as close to each other?"*

Jill as Shelly: *"Well, yeah I guess. It seems like you spend more time with her than with me."*

Jill's mom as Jill: *"I can understand how you would feel that way. I guess I have invited her over a lot, because we just became friends, and we're trying to get to know each other better. But you'll always be one of my very best friends. You and I go back all the way to first grade!"*

Jill as Shelly: *"I wish I could be sure of that."*

Jill's mom as Jill: *"Tell ya what, why don't you come camping with me and my family this weekend. And I don't see why you can't join Eliza and me today. Maybe we can all roller-blade after school."*

Jill as Shelly: *"OK. That sounds great! I'm sorry I came down on Eliza so hard."*

See how the main objective was fulfilled? Jill sought first to understand Shelly's real intentions rather than assume they were evil and assess blame.

6. USING "I MESSAGES" TO TEACH CHILDREN EMPATHY

When we use "I messages," we send a loud and clear signal: "Understand how I'm feeling right now, please!" I hope this process jumpstarts the cascade of internal dialogue that makes children consider what we are going through and what they should do to make things better. Let's look at an example.

Dad: *"Hey, Tim, you forgot to rake the leaves after you cut the grass yesterday."*

Tim: *"So? Bob invited me to the movies. You can't expect me to miss that!"*

Dad: *"But I had to rake them up myself before the garbage truck came around. I felt angry, because it took so much time that I missed being able to meet my pal Henry for our usual Saturday afternoon round of golf."*

Tim: *"Oops, sorry. I guess I'll try to think of that next time. Maybe I can help you finish painting the garage today so you guys can play golf tomorrow, instead."*

Dad: *"Thanks, that's very thoughtful of you. It makes me feel better to know you care about the way I feel. I'll call Henry and see if he can reserve a tee off time."*

In this example, the "I messages" were successful in helping Tim realize how it would have felt to have been in his father's shoes (empathy), and when he understood the inconvenience it caused, Tim did the right thing to make himself feel better (benevolent selfishness) by finding a way to make amends.

7. MODELING EMPATHY

Voicing our own internal dialogue is an excellent way of modeling empathy for our children. Suppose Aunt Emma has the flu. You might talk out loud to yourself to show your children how you empathize with her situation, what you wish to do about it, and why: "Poor Aunt Emma is sicker than a hound dog! And she always bakes pies for the church bingo game on Fridays. I just know she'd feel bad about not being able to do it, and that'd just tear my heart out. By golly, I'm gonna crank those pies out for her right now. Wanna help?" And when someone's upset you: "That checker at the grocery store was so short with me today. She's usually so nice! I wonder if anything's wrong. I'll bet money her feet are killing her. Next time, I'm going to be especially nice to her. Might even give her one of the magnolia blossoms from our garden."

We can then show them how we act upon our empathy. Our actions speak a thousand decibels louder than our words. Again, anonymous actions hold the most powerful lessons.

8. TEACHING CHILDREN EMPATHY BY NOT CRITICIZING THE UNFORTUNATE

I don't know if it's cultural or instinctive, but humans commonly pick on the weak or hurt. It might be some strange-looking guy in the crowd, an elderly driver going twenty miles per hour on the freeway, someone stuttering during an interview on the six o'clock news, or an obese friend. Criticizing people with imperfections sends our children a message that the shortcomings of others are intentional and exclusive to everyone else but us. They learn to chide others for not correcting those flaws, even when the flaws can't be changed, and to react negatively to imperfect people rather than respond with empathy and understanding.

If we work hard to raise empathetic children, they'll develop a sense of inner strength that will protect them against the external influences beckoning them away from the proper choices. Consider empathy as one more vaccine against external direction.

Five

DISCIPLINING TO PROMOTE
INTERNAL DIRECTION

> *Respect the child. Be not too much his*
> *parent. Trespass not on his solitude.*
> —*Ralph Waldo Emerson*

WHAT IT MEANS TO DISCIPLINE IN A WAY THAT PROMOTES
INTERNAL DIRECTION

Our children may come into the world as perfect miracles, but
we still have to teach them how to manage themselves among
others. To teach them the rules of civil behavior in a way that
doesn't make them externally directed or break their spirits,
we need to remember that our job is to guide them as mentors, not control them as dictators. Our discipline must reflect
the nature of this role.

If I had to boil the main goal of this type of discipline
down to one thing, it would be as follows: The way we discipline should motivate children to comply with clear and reasonable rules of behavior, and they should agree to those rules
only after they've analyzed them through internal dialogue.

That internal dialogue should help them conclude that they will behave a certain way because it's the right choice for them, not because they want to avoid punishment. So we can try to use discipline techniques that will get them to use their sense of reason to examine their behavioral choices and weigh all the potential consequences these choices might produce. But, first, we need to clarify the difference between punishment and discipline. Punishment is an attempt to control children on a personal or subjective level. Since it's tainted with disapproval, it attacks our children's self-worth instead of addressing their behavior, prompting them to distrust their internal dialogue and, therefore, react to external stimuli. Discipline, on the other hand, is more objective and non-degrading. Its purpose is to guide and teach, rather than to control. Since discipline does not reflect upon our children personally, it doesn't undermine their self-worth and allows them to contemplate their behavior internally.

Parents often render punishment when angry or frustrated, sometimes when they're stressed by events that have nothing to do with their children. At other times, it occurs when they think their child's behavior is a personal slight against them. For these reasons, punishment is usually illogical, judgmental, and it often fails to fit the crime. On the other hand, discipline is logical, nonjudgmental, and it usually suits the behavior it targets.

Let's look at some examples that highlight this difference. When Tommy cheats on a test, swatting him and banishing him to his room without supper is punishment. His mother and father are probably outraged by what his actions do to their reputation as parents, so they take the offense personally. Discipline, on the other hand, would be if Tommy had to write up a full confession for the teacher, or if he's forced to repeat the test or receive a failing grade, or if he's required to stay in his room and study the material until it's mastered. Discipline must be directed at the behavior instead of the child, properly suit the offense, and be delivered without unpleasant emotions. Most importantly, discipline must encourage our children to use their reasoning skills so that they can consciously evaluate, correct, and prevent their mistakes.

In this chapter we'll look first at twelve prerequisites that are the foundation for a discipline strategy that promotes self-direction in children and then, later, at eight specific ways to discipline children to encourage self-direction.

THE TWELVE BASIC REQUIREMENTS OF SELF-DIRECTED DISCIPLINE

1. Rules our children can agree with

Rules that support the family's values and principles are a necessary part of discipline-guideposts that help our children function successfully in the world. After all, they don't live in a vacuum. They must learn to consider the rights and feelings of other people while still safeguarding their own self-interests. The rules that should be established and enforced are *those that prevent children from inflicting any kind of harm on themselves, their surroundings, and others*. It's as simple as that. All other rules need to be tossed, because they'll just act as outside influences that provoke an externally directed reaction. Chris, age nine, says, "When my parents are strict, that doesn't mean they're mean. They just want me to follow the rules. I like to have rules, 'cuz I want help in being good."

The most important characteristics of the rules we set are reasonableness and clarity. If our children don't understand or agree with the purpose and meaning of our rules, they won't incorporate them into their reasoning process to decide if their behavioral choices should follow those rules. Suppose a family has a rule like "don't use the phone while Mom and Dad are out of the house." Perhaps parents have this rule to prevent their kids from gluing themselves to the receiver instead of watching over the younger siblings, but this reason was never properly conveyed. "Hey, when I say no phone, that's the law, no questions asked!" Even if the reasons were explained, this rule shows a lack of trust in the older children. A better stance would be to render the "no phone rule" as a consequence if and when they are negligent in their babysitting duties. So the parents go out, and poor Johnny remembers he promised to call his friend Brian to tell him what pages to study for the history test. Johnny thinks to himself, "Gosh, I promised Brian I'd give him those page numbers, but what about that rule? I better not call him because ... hmmm ... well, because ... why the heck can't I call him? Oh, yeah, now I remember, I'll be grounded from the phone for a month." Did he follow the rule for the right reason? Nope. He followed it because he didn't want to get punished—classic externally directed thinking.

Now suppose another family has a rule, "no wearing shoes in the house." Here comes eight-year-old Tommy after a scenic tour of the neighborhood ditch on his way home from school. So what's he going to think? Probably something like, "Yikes, look at my shoes. Mom and Dad don't want us to wear shoes inside the house, and I can see why now! If I forgot, I'd track mud all over the new carpets. Then Mom would probably make me clean it all up. Plus she'd be upset, and I sure wouldn't want to live with that." Tommy understood the rule and found it made perfect sense to him. He used this understanding in his internal dialogue to make the right decision for the right reason.

To keep these rules reasonable and clear, we might need to reexamine them periodically. As our children grow and circumstances change, so might these rules. We might wish to continually ask ourselves whether they're still fair, if they're still necessary and suitable, and if they still reflect the family's values and principles. Stephanie, age thirteen, says, "Sometimes parents don't change the rules as we get older, and when we try to talk about this, they aren't willing to listen or compromise. It's like 'that's the rule, kid.'" And again, I cannot stress enough how crucial it is that these rules and boundaries have continuing relevance and meaning.

2. Respect for our children

When we aren't respected by another, we can't possibly fully respect that person, because we don't feel understood by them.

To preserve what is truly extraordinary in our children, we must genuinely respect them. They really do deserve it. And children raised by those who respect their feelings, ideas, opinions, and actions are ones who grow up with the ability to create changes that will benefit humanity. Why? Because these are children who learn to respect themselves. This self-respect strengthens their resolve to look inward to make their decisions—to be self-directed.

To show respect for children, we should accept two givens. First, children are our spiritual equals. Second, our role is not to manhandle them into becoming the people we want them to be. I can't tell you how often I've seen parents treat their children with a disrespect that they would never show adult strangers. Parent and child differ only in size, experience, and knowledge—characteristics that are neither inherent nor permanent. In short, we must show our children the same respect that we would expect others to show us. We need to send them the message that what they have to say is important and should be heard.

3. Consistency and follow-through

Being consistent disciplinarians is crucial to raising self-directed children, too. Consistency is perhaps the biggest challenge we parents face, but without it, our children develop internal dialogue patterns directed by outside influences: "Is this the time Mom's gonna crater when I whine and plead for her to take me out of time-out? Hmmm. Have to come up with a good plan to make her give in." When our discipline is sporadic, their internal dialogue will be, too.

But if we stick to our guns, they'll have internally directed internal dialogue: "I better take this time-out calmly. She'll just say she won't start the timer until I'm quiet. I've tried every trick in the book, and *nothing* works on her. She must be pretty serious about that rule to not play soccer in the house. I can see why, since her favorite lamp busted. From now on, I'm playing outside."

Equally important is that parents are consistent with each other. Of course, being completely different people, we all have different ideas about child-rearing. But it's worth it to develop a discipline program with which both parents are happy. A united front prevents one parent's sabotaging or undermining the other, fodder for parental manipulation by our clever kids. When children pick up on parent-parent inconsistencies, they exhibit externally directed thinking: "Mom says I can't ride my bike to the store to spend my allowance money. I know Dad thinks she's over-protective, so I'm gonna ask him." On the other hand, when parents are on the same page, their children might think in a more internally directed way: "Gosh, that rule about riding my bike alone to the store must be important for a reason. My folks are really sticking together on that one, so how can I win? I can see why they feel that way, really. What if I get lost? Or maybe a car will run off the road and . . . oooh I don't even wanna *go* there. I'll just wait until one of them can take me."

4. Modeling our own good behavioral choices

It's important that we try our best to obey the same rules we expect our children to obey, because not doing so confuses them about the meaningfulness of those rules. This confusion then motivates them to engage in externally directed thought patterns like, "Gosh, Dad curses like a rapper. How come I can't even say words like 'idiot' and 'stupid'? It's not fair. Those are useful words! Hey, I *do* have a younger brother to deal with, here!" Here's another example: "Boy, I can't believe Mom told Mrs. Bevins that she can't bake brownies for the bake sale at school because she's sick with the flu! She's all dressed up to play tennis with Aunt Pauline! Maybe when she tells us we shouldn't lie, she means little white lies are OK. Does telling my teacher that Fido peed on my book report count as a white lie? I bet it does."

In both these examples, the children used external factors to arrive at a decision that is morally wrong. "If it's OK for my folks to bend the rules sometimes, it's OK for me to do it, too." More importantly, they used their parents' rule infraction to justify wrong choices. That just adds another line to the web of self-deception they're weaving.

Now, let's look at an example of modeling that creates internally directed thinking: "Mom says she wants us to use our words instead of hitting each other. She's never laid a hand on us, so I know she really believes in that rule. Hey, I don't like being hit, so why should my little sister? I'm going to talk to Annika about how I feel when she steals my Barbie clothes—instead of pummeling her." Here, through a completely self-directed internal dialogue, she uses her mom's consistency to help her examine the significance of a rule. She decides to obey that rule, because her behavior is morally wrong, not because she's told to.

5. Keeping cool

Every one of us has a breaking point, even conscientious parents like you who love their children enough to read books like this one. After all, there are only so many "But Mommm's" and "No, I don't want to's" that a human being can take before we lose control. Nevertheless, we need to try to maintain our self-control as much as humanly possible. One "I wish you were never born," "I'm so ashamed of you," "You'll never amount to anything," or slap across the face can have a permanent and devastating effect on our children's self-image and outlook. Sure, this is bad stuff, but what's it got to do with raising self-directed children? Lots. When parents lose their cool, their children typically shut down attempts to analyze their own behavior internally, because they're getting messages from those they love and trust that their ability for self-scrutiny is flawed. Knowing this effect, we might wish to think before we speak or raise our hand in anger. And we must avoid making justifications for losing control with our children.

Here's what some children say about their parent's losing control:

Abi, age twelve: "Kids don't like being screamed at or hit, because it means the parents aren't listening to them, and it makes them get mad at their parents."

Erik, age ten: "When kids get yelled at, it makes them feel like they want to cry, because they feel bad about themselves."

Stephanie, age thirteen: "Like, some parents yell at their kids all the time instead of helping them figure out what to do about their problem. That's really wrong. And when they hit their kids, it doesn't teach them a lesson. It just makes them mad!"

Whenever we do have trouble keeping our cool, when we're tempted to yell, scream, or slap, we might try separating ourselves from our children until we have a chance to cool off. We can use that time to analyze our feelings. Are we really out of control because Timmy tried to flush his toy truck down the toilet to watch it twirl around and around? Isn't that just the innocent curiosity of a child at work? Will blowing up at him do any good? Or are we just frustrated because our computer crashed for the fourth time this week? Once we've had a chance to think things over, we can take a great big breath, reflect on the moments of closeness we've had with our children, remember that they are learning and growing, and realize the harm that would come if we change ourselves from Dr. Jekyll to Mr. Hyde.

Suppose we do the inevitable and go ballistic. Whenever *I* do, I try to apologize without placing conditions on why I did what I did. For instance, when I tell one of my kids, "I'm sorry I lost my temper with you," I'll leave it at that. No comments like, "but you know how I hate being interrupted when I'm on the phone." What's a self-directed kid likely to think when we apologize for losing it? Probably something like, "Gosh, Mom treats me just like a regular grown-up. It was brave of her to say she's sorry, so I know she must really love me. I feel bad about interrupting her while she was talking on the phone. I'll try not to do that again. I'm going to say I'm sorry, too, so she'll feel better." Compare the two. Ranting and raving makes our kids project their thinking externally to

"I hate my parents. They're such ogres." Keeping our cool or apologizing when we don't makes our children think about the bad choices they made and ways they should correct them. That's what self-direction is all about.

6. Addressing the behavior, not the child

Even the most dedicated parents slip up and lash out at their children with verbal assaults like, "Your room is a mess! Why do you insist on living in a pigsty?" But, attacking children personally instead of addressing their *behavior* leads them to believe that every mistake is a reflection of their self-worth. Michelle, age thirteen, says, "When parents say rude stuff like 'you're such a slob' or 'you're so fat, stop eating so much,' it makes kids feel sorry for themselves instead of getting them to take care of the problem. If I believed that stuff, I'd feel like I was such a rotten person." And after all, how can children be self-directed when they don't think very highly of that "self?" How can they have faith in any of the internal dialogue that "self" creates? Instead, they'll tend to place their trust in external influences for which they have more respect.

Some children react to these attacks by counterattacking, making the parent out to be the "bad guy." Others use these insults to characterize their identities. But when children can't separate their identity from their behavior, they no longer see their problems and decisions objectively. Once this objectivity is lost, making conscious changes in their choices becomes difficult, perhaps even impossible.

We can teach our children that they are not their choices but, rather, the creative force behind them. We can show them they have complete power to change this force in any way and that it is the conscious drive to make decisions, and not the outcome of the decisions, that builds their identity and sense of worth. Outcomes, after all, are part of their past and can't be changed. We can change only what lies in our future. So, if the outcome of our children's decision is not good, we might try to explain that this decision doesn't make them inherently bad. We can tell them that even good people can make bad choices. A few examples: Suppose Timothy has sloppy table manners. He smacks loudly when he chews and reaches over everyone's plates with his grimy, unwashed paws to grab the last biscuit. Dad yells out, "Timothy, you are the biggest slob. I swear, I can't take you out in public. You're disgusting!" These remarks address Timothy's worth as a person. He's labeled as a pig, which he either takes as the gospel truth and thinks less of himself or doesn't believe and retaliates against his father with some insolent remark. Either way would represent external direction. Now if his dad says something like, "Son, in our family, we believe in showing respect for others at the table. That means washing up, chewing with a closed mouth, and asking to have food passed," then Timothy is forced to examine his behavior, its repercussions on others, and ways he can correct it. In other words, internal direction. His dad's remarks addressed his behavior fairly and politely, so there'd be no reason for Timothy to retaliate.

7. Letting our children be the rightful owners of their problems

One of the cardinal rules of raising self-directed children is never to let their behavioral problems become more important to us than to them. Our children must always be the sole owners of these problems. Otherwise, they will fall back on external direction.

How do we get ourselves caught in this little trap? Almost everything that draws us in involves one simple detail: we feel a higher sense of urgency concerning our children's problem than they do. Sometimes, we take their naughtiness too personally, as if they're doing it just to upset us. So we resort to yelling or nagging. Other times, we're afraid our parenting skills fall short. So we do their chores when they refuse or forget, bribe them to be nice in the grocery store, and let them slide when they throw us an insolent remark. Sometimes, we just don't feel as if our children are capable of behaving well. So we rescue them by cleaning up after them, soothing the feelings of a sibling they've teased, or doing some of their homework when they say it's too hard and they'd rather watch TV.

Once we rescue them, our children gladly relinquish ownership and, therefore, their inner contemplation of their problems, because they can plainly see that these problems are more important to us than to them! And after all, kids won't tackle a tough problem if they don't feel it belongs to them.

If we can be aware of who's feeling more urgency concerning our children's behavior, we can step back from the problem. Sometimes a mantra helps. I like saying to myself, "This is not my problem; it's his (or hers)." After a while, our children will figure out that we aren't gonna buckle under to pressure and let them off the hook, so they'll give up and try to think of ways to solve their behavioral problems on their own in a self-directed way.

8. Minimizing the blabbering

Another parental faux pas is talking *way* too much. We lecture, direct, explain, negotiate, wheedle, coax, beg, insist, demand, warn, and interrogate. How can kids reflect inwardly about their decisions with this kind of distraction? They can't. They simply tune us out until they eventually become parent-deaf. Those children who don't ignore our ceaseless prattle are the ones who join in by talking back, getting angry, playing passive-aggressive games like pouting, playing not-so-passive-aggressive games like slamming doors, or finding other ways to manipulate us into shutting up. The last thing they'll do is think, "Mom's so upset about me not cleaning under my bed. I guess those dust bunnies are looking pretty scary. I'm going to run up to my room right away and make it spic-and-span!" In our dreams!

One eleven-year-old child sums it up well: "When my mom sits there and goes on and on and on about what I'm doing wrong, I just start thinking about something else, like Nintendo. It's just boring!" So let's try a little more silence. That way, our children can examine their actions internally as every self-directed child should. Later on, I'll show various ways of distilling our discipline strategies down to a near whisper. And we all know that a whisper gets everyone's attention.

9. Using more positives than negatives

It's so easy to get caught in the trap of relating to our children through conflict alone. If we do, our parent-child relationship becomes one of antagonism rather than joy. It doesn't help when our vocabulary overuses words like "no," "can't," "stop," and "don't." Using these words to excess means that our role as mentor to our children is tenuous at best: we use these words to put out fires rather than to encourage and guide them. Words like these don't offer them a way to find the right choice. This style of parenting is *reactive* instead of *anticipatory*. Parents choose it because it's more expedient, and it doesn't require them to analyze and predict a child's behavior. Some parents can almost do it in their sleep! One of the mothers saw a videotape of herself on Christmas continually telling her kids to stop touching things, don't fidget, stop whining. She couldn't get over how she "sounded like a real nag," and "none of the kids were very happy that day." Children who experience this negativity don't bother with internal dialogue. They just react externally by thinking about how much they can't stand their parents.

So how can we break this pesky habit? We might start by trying to become aware of it. We can make a mental note of every "no," "can't," "don't," "stop," and other negative expression and, each time, examine our motives. Are we trying to dominate our children? Are we just trying to maintain some sort of order? We need to learn to first stop and think: what's the worst that could happen if we were to say "yes," "you may," "please do," or "go ahead"? If we think before we react, we can have fewer battles with our children, and view them through their strengths rather than their imperfections. This approach helps us like our children more, so they become a joy rather than a chore.

When our children aren't at odds with us all the time, they not only enjoy us more, they become less "parent-deaf," too. Once we reduce the antagonism, it becomes easier to create a more positive environment for our children. Children react to negativity and respond to positivity. One ten year old says, "I like it when my parents stay happy when they discipline. I don't like it when they get all mad and cranky."

There are several ways to achieve positive discipline. First, we can avoid throwing past mistakes in their faces. Doing this only shames them and, again, teaches them to evaluate themselves in terms of what is wrong with them instead of what is right and good. Instead of focusing on the mistake, we should focus on solutions. By doing this, we encourage our children to use their powers of reason to analyze our suggestions so that they can either accept or reject them. And whenever we focus on solutions instead of the problem when we discipline our children, it teaches them, likewise, to focus on solutions.

Another way to keep things positive is to not qualify positive remarks. An example: "Wow, you cleaned up your room nicely, *but* you forgot to get some of the things out from under your bed." We must do our best to allow positive statements to stand alone, unmarred by accompanying criticisms.

A third way to keep discipline as positive as possible is to point out what our children did right. For example, my son Erik often has trouble finishing his morning routine. The one thing he often neglects is his hair. Instead of saying, "Erik, your hair is a mess! Why can't you ever keep it combed?" I point out some of the things he has accomplished well: "You're almost ready, Erik. You've put on nice clean clothes, you've finished your breakfast and put away your dishes, and you've brushed your teeth and have your backpack all ready. All that's left is running a comb through your hair." In the second example, he focuses on all of his successes and, through his process of reason, he can make the choice to add one more success to that long list. In the first one, he focuses on what a rotten kid he's been or what a cranky tyrant his mom is.

Another way to create a positive milieu is to encourage children to help themselves. If our child has trouble in math but is playing video games the day before a big exam, we can point out ways he can help himself: "It would help to use this spare time before dinner to go over your multiplication facts. Do you want me to call them out to you?" This slight parental nudge encourages our children to engage in internal dialogue to think about ways in which they can help change their undesirable behavior to desirable behavior.

10. Not ignoring misbehavior

Neglecting our children's misbehavior only honors the "step aside" part of the "guide, then step aside" rule. When children whine, beg, pester, quarrel, or throw tantrums, ignoring them simply encourages them to persist. Many parents ignore problems because they can't handle them, don't want to be inconvenienced, or have bigger problems of their own! Some parents use ignoring as a conscious discipline tool, especially for whining and other annoying behavior. They'll make taunting remarks like, "Is someone talking in here? I guess not. All I hear is a horrible whining sound." This does little to get children to think about their behavior and to reason through a change. The last thing they'll think is, "Boy, my dad is not paying any attention to this. Maybe I should stop this nonsense and be a big girl!" What they're more likely to think is, "My daddy hates me. He doesn't pay any attention to me. He loves Sarah more than me. I hate him, hate him, hate him! I'm going to run away. *Then* he'll be sorry." Here, the child directs her attention to external influences (her dad) rather than looking inwardly for solutions to her misbehavior.

One child says, "When my mom ignores me on purpose, I get so annoyed. I can't stand it. It's like, I know what she's up to. She can't fool me or anything. So I get so mad I say something mean and stomp off."

11. Not using external influences to change children's behavior

It is convenient to use outside sources to help us discipline our children, but this technique is like holding up a big sign that reads, "Look to the outside world for answers to your problems!" The most common external influences parents use are bribes and threats. Threatening to take a toy away or withholding a privilege promotes external direction. So does invoking a higher authority: "Wait until your father gets home!" is one of the all-time favorites in this category. My specialty in years past was using Santa Claus as the heavy. "Do I need to call Santa? Honey, what's that hot-line number to Santa, again? Annika is refusing to get ready for bed, and I think he needs to know this." And of course I make sure she thinks I'm really talking to the big man himself. I'd even go so far as to offer her the phone and say, "Annika, do you want to tell him about the poor choices you've been making?" Unfortunately, it worked like a charm. My kids were always angels one month before Christmas. Eventually, however, these statements prove that our authority can be undermined. Boy, does this ever open up the floodgates of manipulation the whole year round! Not only that, what happens when they stop believing in Santa?

Here's a suggestion for those times we're at the end of our rope. Look your little mischief maker squarely in the eye and ask, "If you were a parent, what would you do with a kid who was behaving the way you are?" You'll be surprised at some of their great ideas! Sometimes, they come up with harsher consequences than we would have!

Our children should learn to modify their behavior and make choices because it matches their values, not because it matches someone else's, or because they are afraid not to, or because they don't want to incur the wrath of some mythical authority figure.

12. Not rescuing children from the consequences of their misbehavior

One of the most common parenting misconceptions is that it is our job to make our children happy. So many parents shower their children with gifts, sweets, rewards, and praise. They over-protect and over-guide. They sugarcoat their children's mistakes and failures. All of these practices rob children of their ability to find their own happiness. They never learn how to fully express themselves, because it's all done *for* them. This is external, not internal direction.

It is extremely easy to over-involve ourselves in our children's behavioral choices: cleaning up their spills, picking up their dirty clothes, doing some of their math problems, and so on. When I find myself over-involved, I stop and remind myself what my parental role really is: *We must guide, then step aside*. When we're over-involved, we're really just guiding, without stepping aside. In fact, at the extreme end of this spectrum, we're not even guiding them. We're railroading them down a path to external direction!

So, we must do the bare minimum necessary to ignite our children's internal assessments of their problems. Then we should sit back and observe what happens.

But let's face it, sometimes parents are wimps. They bail their children out so their children don't have to suffer the consequences of their horrible behavior or so their behavior isn't a bad reflection on them, as parents. They might, for instance, make excuses: "Johnny's having a tough time behaving in school. It's just that we're going through a move and his dad has a new job. He'll be fine when things settle down." Sometimes it's unnecessary intercessions: "Don't pick on Sam! Don't you even remember that he has a heart murmur!" This "rescue ranger" parental attitude sends a bad message to children: we don't have faith in them to handle their own problems. If they're to become self-directed, this inner faith is crucial! This attitude also rescues them from having to use their reasoning skills, which takes an enormous amount of conscious effort on their part!

Another way parents occasionally behave like wimps is that they give in too easily with their children. For instance, when David shoves his little sister and we banish him to time-out, if he whines and cries long and loud enough, Mom might throw up her hands and give that famous "second (or third, or fourth, or fifth) chance." One child says, "If I beg enough, my mom always let's me have my way. I wear her down, I guess. It's really easy to make her feel sorry for me!"

Idle threats really add to the wimp factor, too! Jon, age twelve, says, "I know when my mom and dad mean business and when they don't. And they usually don't!" We make it even easier for them to see through us when we threaten the impossible, "If you don't straighten up right now, I'm leaving you behind. You can stay home alone and fend for yourself while the rest of us enjoy our summer vacation!" Never, never, NEVER threaten a consequence that you can't deliver.

If we try to follow these twelve rules, chances are that our children will find it natural to use internal direction to figure out their choices, assess the consequences of those choices, and decide how to correct bad choices. The common thread in all of these rules is that we must give our children all the right reasons to behave. In the self-directed, those reasons always come from within.

EIGHT DISCIPLINE TECHNIQUES THAT ENCOURAGE SELF-DIRECTION

Read on and I'll show you my favorite practical techniques to discipline children in a way that preserves and even encourages self-direction. These eight techniques have one thing in common—each stimulates children to analyze both the choices they are making and the potential consequences for themselves and others. It's a good idea to mix these techniques up, so that your discipline program retains a freshness that will keep your children on their toes. I also suggest that, from time to time, you reread this section, as well as the previous one, to refresh your memory.

Let's take a look at my favorite eight techniques.

1. Use questions

The technique of using questions is more important for teenagers, but it also works for younger children. In a nutshell, parents teach children to make better choices by asking them questions rather than delivering the usual onslaught of criticism, nagging, and didactic lectures. These questions provide a framework for our children's internal dialogue as children reason out their choices and come up with decisions on their own. For instance, if Jimmy calls his younger brother a stupid, brainless dweeb, we should first avoid rushing to the "victim's" rescue by raking Jimmy over the coals. Later, we can ask Jimmy, "How do you think your brother feels when you say things like that to him?" "How would you feel if someone said those things to you?" "What can you do to make him feel better?" We also need to make it clear to Jimmy that our questions are not rhetorical and that we expect a response. If we get one, great! If not, believe me, the cogwheels are turning in his little brain. Here are some other examples:

If our daughter tracks mud on our freshly mopped kitchen floor after softball practice, we can ask her, "How do you think I feel when I look at this mess on the floor right after I worked so hard to clean it?" "What's our rule about wearing shoes in the house?" "What do you think you can do to make things right?"

By the way, it's fine to help children come up with answers to our questions if they need it and if we think that they'll be receptive.

No finger pointing should be involved in these questions. No criticism or shaming. And, we must also be careful not to interrupt, "give a better answer," assume an angry tone of voice, or express these questions in a way that might be construed as forms of hostile criticism. The purpose of our questions is not to belittle, provoke feelings of shame and guilt, vindicate our own feelings of exasperation, or punish our children in any way. If we remember to voice these questions calmly and respectfully, our children will have no excuse to react through retaliation, a classic externally directed response.

The only purposes of our questions are to encourage our children to examine and acknowledge their poor choices, to invite them to discover ways to make amends or rectify the consequences of those choices, and to figure out ways to make better choices. This technique, when carried out with the child's self-respect and dignity in mind, can be a powerful tool that not only helps develop skills in problem solving, but also validates and strengthens us in the important role we have as our child's guide.

2. Describe the problem impartially and give specific information

Maintaining our objectivity will help our children keep their minds on their own mistakes instead of what they think are ours. This objectivity can be achieved by using impartial descriptions or by giving specific information concerning their misbehavior. Both are good substitutes for evaluations, which tend to be more subjective, inflammatory, and hurtful. These substitutes don't attack our children's self-worth or make them react blindly, while evaluations like criticism and ridicule do. Most importantly, both techniques help children consider the ramifications of their actions.

Describing the problem impartially would be like saying, "I see it's already six o'clock and you haven't started your science project," instead of "What on earth are you doing! It's already supper time, and you're sitting there in front of the television! Your science project is due tomorrow! I am so sick of your procrastinating! I hate having to remind you to do your homework day after day!" The first is informative and objective. The second is accusatory and subjective. One is brief and calming. The other takes more time and effort and creates antagonism between parent and child. Imagine a child's response, both internally and externally, to each of these quite different approaches!

Another example of this technique is mirroring feelings back to the child. Suppose Max and his friends were excluding another child. We might say, "I see Robert feels left out, since you two excluded him from your Secret Agent club. He's looking pretty glum over there. He must feel like nobody cares about him." Because these remarks are not the least bit accusatory, they don't attack Max's self-worth.

Giving specific information also provides children with the additional data they need to consider a situation internally. Such information would include saying, "Feet belong on the floor" when our child has her feet up on the table. That's much more effective than saying, "Laurie, how many times do I have to tell you to keep your filthy shoes off my table?" When we tackle a behavioral problem by describing it or giving information about it, our children are left to reflect upon their actions and make conclusions and decisions on their own. Furthermore, by maintaining our objectivity, we retain a sense of calm, we avoid hurtful power struggles, and we further fulfill our mission to be our children's greatest guide.

3. Give limited choices

Another way to discipline so that our children tackle their behavioral problems through self-directed reasoning is by giving them choices. My three favorite ways to provide choices are the "this or that," the "if-then," and the "when-then" techniques. These three, although simple and easy to carry out, go far in helping parents avoid those counterproductive negatives like "no," "don't," "can't," and "stop." Stephanie, age thirteen, says, "When my parents tell me what to do all the time, I just stop listening. It's like, I think 'Why do I have to listen to you? Leave me alone. I can figure these things out for myself!'"

Here are examples of the "this or that" technique: Let's say our child is begging to have sugary Poptarts instead of the healthful suggestions we offered her. Before she gets a chance to become emotionally attached to something she's not allowed to have, we can say, "What would you like this morning, corn flakes or oatmeal?" She might be less compelled to challenge the rules if she feels empowered by having a choice. And we don't have to be the "heavy" by telling her, "No, you most certainly cannot have that for breakfast!" If bedtime wars are a sad way of life, we don't have to fight over whether or not they go to bed when they're told. We can give them a choice instead, "It's time for bed; which do you want to do first, read a story or brush your teeth?" Most struggles with children involve their thirst for power and attention. Giving them choices shows them that we respect their ability to make decisions and that we are willing to give them a reasonable part of the power and attention they want. This show of respect helps them contemplate these choices with internal dialogue rather than react to inflexibility, thereby becoming externally directed.

Some examples of the if-then and when-then techniques follow: If our child is throwing a fit about putting her shoes on to go to the park, we should try not to blow up and say, "Forget it. There's no way I'm taking you to the park when you act like that!" Instead, we can calmly tell her, "*When* your shoes are on, *then* we can go to the park." Suppose our child is doodling and daydreaming instead of doing his homework. We can tell him, "*If* you finish your homework, *then* you can go out and play."

These three techniques are highly effective in motivating children to think about their predicament and correct it on their own through the use of their internal dialogue.

4. Be a minimalist

I have to admit, in other areas of my life, I've adopted the "more is better" attitude. My dogs are fat, my houseplants are drowning in their own mildew, my trees are pruned to sad, meager little stumps, and my boys' hair is flush with their scalps. This same philosophy often spills into our over-disciplining children. As I've mentioned earlier, the more we yak, the less they're able to contemplate their behavior inwardly.

How can we apply the minimalist approach to discipline? Through simple and quiet forms of communication like one or two word remarks, facial expressions, or gestures. Suppose Alex takes his shoes off in the middle of the foyer where others can trip all over them. If we simply say, "Alex . . . shoes," he's reminded to focus his attention internally on his bad choice and use internal dialogue to find ways to correct it. Suppose Nancy is going on her second hour of gossip on the telephone. We can simply say, "Nancy . . . enough," and sweep our index finger across our necks to give that universal "cut it off or else."

The less we say, the less our risk of annoying, insulting, over-controlling, or degrading our children. And chances are, we won't say something that can be misinterpreted. They'll usually regard gestures or solitary words as friendly but firm reminders. Like all of these other techniques, minimalism encourages children to think about what they're doing wrong so that they can correct it. The result—fewer externally directed power struggles in our relationship with our children.

5. Use humor

I love humor. It's a wonderful and under-used tool that is capable of defusing the most explosive situations. If we use our imagination, our children can *laugh* their way to making better choices. For example, we can conjure up our best Italian accent and play the part of a goofy waiter to get Thomas to stop being so wishy-washy when he chooses what he wants for lunch. We can tell Megan that the jacket fairy is on vacation when she throws her jacket on the floor after coming home from school.

Humor promotes self-direction for several reasons. First, it shows our children that we refuse to fight with them, so they have no reason to retaliate. This atmosphere leaves them free to engage in internal dialogue concerning their misbehavior. With humor, we also make it clear to them that since we're not going to wig out and jump down their throats, it's obvious that their problem is not more important to us than to them. Finally, humor defuses explosive situations so our children save face while they correct their behavior in a self-directed way.

This technique shouldn't include mocking. Imitating their whining, crying, or tantrums will only infuriate them and make their behavior worse. Other than that, the only other stipulation is to have fun with it. Be creative. Be zany and wacky. Chances are everyone's spirits will be uplifted. And, maybe, just maybe (no promises, now!), you can quit your day job and give Seinfeld a run for his money.

6. Use self-directed time-outs

A great deal of controversy surrounds time-outs. Some believe that banishing children to a time-out sends them the externally directed message that they are so terrible that they must be removed from present company. Others think that it's a non-degrading, effective means of discipline and certainly preferable to yelling and hitting. My personal belief is that children should only be separated from a group if reasonable attempts to have them correct their own behavior within that group have failed. More important, if that separation must occur, time-out shouldn't be an exile but a "regrouping station" or "thinking corner" to give children either an opportunity to create the internal dialogue necessary to assess and correct their behavior, or a logical consequence to protect the rest of the group from their misbehavior.

Removal should be done calmly and politely, so they won't be tempted to focus externally on how mean and unfair we are. After a short time, we can try to help them examine the events that led to their time-out. Then, we can teach them how to find alternative solutions to the problem as well as ways to prevent it from happening again. Let's analyze one situation where a time-out could be used to promote internal direction.

Jimmy bites his best friend Brandon on the arm out of sheer frustration. The first thing we can do is show him that we understand his feelings, *"I realize that you were so frustrated with Brandon that you bit him"* (an "impartial description").

Then we firmly state the rule that we expect him to follow, *"Biting is not allowed, Jimmy"* ("giving specific information"). Next, we ask him to come up with an alternative solution. If he draws a blank, it's OK to help him out a little: *"If you don't like something that Brandon is doing, then maybe you can use your words to let him know how you feel."*

After that, we need to deliver a logical consequence: *"Jimmy, I want you to sit here by me until you cool off. I'm worried that you might still be angry enough to make the same mistake."*

Finally, we can have Jimmy make amends: *"Now, I want you to come up with something that you think would help take care of Brandon's feelings."* If he refuses, he'll just have to sit out longer to ensure another fracas won't occur.

Very likely, a series of interactions such as this one would suffice. Through this dialogue, Jimmy learns that his feelings are not only understood but that he is permitted to express them, as long as he does so without hurting anyone. He also learns how to use his reasoning skills to come up with alternative solutions and discovers that all of his actions have consequences. In the end, he's given the opportunity to right his wrong. Therefore, Jimmy is taught how to conduct himself with others without being separated from them for an extended period of time.

Suppose we had chosen an "externally directed" time-out as our first approach by saying something like, "Jimmy! You march right over to that bench and sit down for ten minutes. I don't want to hear another word from you!" Jimmy probably would have used that time thinking, "Mommy isn't being fair! She likes Brandon better. She didn't hear him calling me all of those names. I hate Brandon! I'm never playing with him again!" This response certainly isn't what we want, because here, Jimmy has evaluated his predicament as an unjust punishment, turning us—the judge, jury, and executioner—into an external influence that incites reactions from him that will dictate his next course of behavior, as if we are pulling the strings on a puppet.

If the first approach fails because Jimmy is so hysterical or enraged that he can't even listen to what we have to say, we can say something like, "Jimmy, you seem to be too mad to think right now. I want you to sit by me on this bench and give yourself time to cool off. When you're not as mad as you are now, maybe you can give some thought to what just happened between you and Brandon and what you might plan to do about it." If the situation is beyond that and we see the little veins sticking out in his neck, we can use the time-out as a "protective corral," by saying something like, "Jimmy, I need you to sit here by me so you won't be tempted to hurt Brandon again. You're so angry, I'm afraid you might do something you'll feel sorry about later. When I feel comfortable that you won't hurt one of your friends, we'll talk about what happened, and you can play with them again." If you need to modify the time-out for those children who refuse to stay put, you can restrain them in your arms and say something like, "I have to stop you until you learn to stop yourself." Both these examples entail using time-out as a logical consequence. Regardless of which self-directed time-out we choose, the first approach can be attempted again when Jimmy's calm and coherent.

Some parents' frustration threshold is so low that time-outs are appropriate as a first line of defense. The same for families with a large number of children. When you have a bunch of kids all going off the deep end at once, it isn't practical to sit down and have a dialogue with each of them. One of the pluses in these circumstances is that removal of the child to a "regrouping station" gives these parents a time-out of their own, allowing a period for *them* to cool off and think about what they should do next. In summary, the time-out discipline strategy does work for *some* situations and *some* parents. However, it shouldn't be used as a substitute for parental modeling, words of guidance, or logical consequences. Rather, this strategy should be used as either a chance for children to quietly contemplate their misbehavior and find workable solutions or as a logical consequence that separates them from the rest of the group (parents included) so they can't harm the members of that group in any way.

7. *Use the level system for teenagers*

My favorite discipline strategy for children over twelve is the three-level system. With this technique, your teen wakes up every morning on a level-three status, with full privileges. If any of ten different infractions are committed, like defiant behavior, dishonesty, or abuse of privileges, he or she is demoted to level two. At this level, all social privileges are denied. This means no visits with friends, no online chatting, and no telephone. If another transgression occurs, it's down to level one, which is like a teen time-out, really, because they are not allowed to engage in anything pleasurable. This includes watching TV, listening to music, taking a nap, eating snacks, having dessert, playing with "their stuff," and playing video games. They're pretty much limited to bathing, doing their schoolwork, completing their chores, eating at regular mealtime, trimming their toenails, and picking the lint out of their belly button. Boring maybe, but it does stimulate them to internally examine the consequences of their actions, an examination that then paves their road to self-direction. After all, the infractions and their consequences are pretty clear and fair, and there's no externally directed parenting, like yelling, so our teens can't react with an externally directed counterstrike.

I also like the fact that the slate is wiped clean the next day, because week- or month-long groundings that multiply as their transgressions mount are too difficult to keep track of. Eventually, these lengthier punishments leave teens feeling frustrated and defeated. They adopt the "why bother" attitude and peg us as the bad guys, which leaves no motivation for them to contemplate the error of their ways. So, by overwhelming them with seemingly endless "teen imprisonment," we unwittingly promote external direction. For an in-depth look at this level system, please refer to page 275.

8. Render logical consequences

The central focus in a strong and effective discipline program should always involve natural and logical consequences. Natural consequences are those that need no parental involvement. Going hungry during lunch would be a natural consequence if a child repeatedly forgets to bring lunch to school. A logical consequence is one that does require parental involvement. For example, if our children are making fun of one of their siblings, we shouldn't allow them to participate in whatever the family is doing. It is logical, because this exclusion protects the rest of the family from possible verbal abuse. Logical and natural consequences are highly effective discipline tools because they encourage children to use both self-monitoring and internal dialogue to assess their behavior and its effects. They're pressed to use their reasoning skills because the consequences make sense in the context of their behavior. They'll feel that they are getting what they deserve, and this fairness gives them no other choice but to examine their behavior and make whatever conscious decisions are necessary to avoid repeating it.

Other forms of discipline like nagging, reprimands, lecturing, and criticism give children excuses to bypass this internal dialogue and reasoning altogether. Instead, they'll tend to focus their attention outward, putting all their energy into evaluating how unfair, uncaring, impatient, mean, scary, or ridiculous we're being. To avoid this external focus, we need to deliver consequences with kindness and respect, then step aside and have faith that good will result. Some of us might need to close our eyes and hold our breath, but these consequences must be given from the position that we are not their adversaries. Above all, we are their guides and teachers, and no matter what, we're always on their side.

For the reasoning process to work, consequences must have meaning. One discipline mistake parents commonly make is using illogical consequences as a tool for discipline. In other words, consequences that don't fit the crime. When they give illogical consequenses, their children focus all their anger and attention on the parents and the injustice they have to suffer, rather than on their own poor choices. If we ground our child from watching television for a week because she smarted off to us, that wouldn't have any logical connection as far as she is concerned. Telling her that she'll have to eat dinner up in her room alone so that the rest of the family won't be subjected to her insults would make more sense. Even grounding her from socializing with her friends would be more logical if we tell her we're worried that she might make the same bad choices with them as well. (Of course, most children wouldn't dare treat their friends the way they do their family, but we can create our own logic for this consequence by assuming aloud that they might. In other words, we can stretch the logic when doing so helps.) We can let her know she can try to make a better choice again tomorrow. It's important to give children a chance to make amends and to prove that they can correct their inappropriate behavior. Giving them a chance to correct and make up for their mistakes sends the message that we have faith in their ability to choose wisely and to manage themselves and their own destiny, skills that are characteristic of the self-directed. This attitude allows children to feel confident about analyzing the consequences they receive through their internal dialogue. So it makes them comfortable with being self-directed.

How we discipline and encourage our children is probably the most crucial factor in whether they become self-directed or externally directed as adults.

Six

Helping Children
Rebound from Failure

> *Good people are good because they've*
> *come to wisdom through failure.*
> *— William Saroyan*

I FIRMLY BELIEVE CHILDREN inherently accept their failures if they think they won't be judged by others. I asked several of the children interviewed if they'd have any problem shooting hoops in an empty gym, even if they shot less than 50 percent. Every single one of them said they wouldn't be the least bit uncomfortable, but if someone were watching...now that'd be an entirely different story. Each one of them claimed they'd be uncomfortably aware of their misses and would probably stop trying altogether.

No matter how self-directed our children become, the sad truth is that not everyone else in the world is. There are externally directed people ready to pounce on every little mistake our children make. So, over time our children learn to fear the ridicule or reprimand that comes along with failure.

They learn to use external evaluation as a means of self-assessment instead of using their mistakes as information that will help them internally consider future choices.

Failure has been interpreted by society as a less than perfect outcome instead of what it really is—a stepping-stone to success, another outcome in our quest for a goal, an opportunity to learn. As far as our personal growth is concerned, just as much is gained by our failures as by our successes, often more. Society's distorted interpretation of failure is responsible for today's commonplace reluctance to make choices. This apprehension then leads to "decision paralysis"—or the habitual choice *not* to choose. The unhappy result is often anger, frustration, cynicism, or apathy. Those who fear failure fear taking risks and facing unknown adventures, ideas, experiences, and people. This fear creates a population of underachievers (those who are afraid their choices will result in failure) and perfectionists (those who are afraid that making a lesser choice will make them less acceptable). Such a race becomes afraid to think, because the product of their thoughts may produce failures, which will weaken their sense of worth. Instead, they rely on others to do the thinking for them.

As parents, we can raise our children to both welcome and learn from the mistakes they will surely make, instead of being shattered by them. We can teach them to contemplate their mistakes so that they can grow, instead of allowing those mistakes to generate external reactions that will make them wither. Here's what some of the interviewed children had to say about mistakes, about failure, and about how they handle both.

Michael, age nine: "If I try something and it doesn't work out, sometimes I don't even finish it or try again, because I worry that I won't get it right ever."

Kimberly, age ten: "I hate it when my mom puts my spelling tests on the wall when I get a hundred and she throws away the others, even when I just get one crummy thing wrong. It makes me think she only likes me when I'm perfect."

Here are some internally directed suggestions that might help our children develop good skills to recover from defeat.

DISCUSSING OUR OWN MISTAKES WITH OUR CHILDREN

We should discuss our own mistakes with our children, why we made the mistakes, how we are responsible for them, and what solutions we intend to find. For example, we can say something like, "Oh boy, I guess I shouldn't have been so short-tempered with my friend. I guess I took my bad mood out on him. I think I'll go over and apologize." This statement shows our children that we aren't afraid to admit our mistakes, we accept full accountability for them, we *can* find an appropriate solution, and we refuse to let it degrade our self-worth. After correcting the mistake, it's a good idea to express any feelings of relief we might have, so that our children can understand how powerful it is to confront and handle our blunders without hesitation. It's also helpful to try to convey a good attitude about it when discussing our mistakes, because an attitude of guilt, shame, disappointment, resentment, or sorrow will only make our children fear their mistakes more, and that fear makes failure loom large as an external influence.

NOT DENYING OPPORTUNITIES TO EXCEL AS A CONSEQUENCE FOR MISBEHAVIOR

We must never deny our children something at which they excel as a logical consequence for misbehavior. Suppose, for instance, that your daughter is the number one player on the lacrosse team, and she gets a lot of inner strength from this success. It would be a mistake to punish her by refusing to let her play in the next game when she goofs around with her friends and comes home late from practice one day. It's natural and common for parents to do this, because they feel it's a highly effective tool of punishment to deny children something they treasure deeply if they're disobedient. For this reason, many people grow to become adults who never follow through or achieve their goals, because, as children, the things they enjoyed were used against them, in a form of externally directed punishment. They no longer use internal dialogue to analyze actual or potential mistakes, so they no longer accept challenges.

SHARING LESSONS WE'VE LEARNED FROM OUR OWN MISTAKES

As embarrassing as it may be, it helps children if we tell them what we've learned from our *own* bad choices and what the consequences of those choices were. We can candidly discuss prior drug experience, poor study habits, regrettable sexual relationships, and so forth. We should divulge the consequences we've had to endure as well as the positive learning experience garnered from these mistakes. The fact that we expose our mistakes to our children shows them that we aren't ill-at-ease with mistakes and are willing to confront and correct them. Children also learn that there are positive lessons to be learned from any mistake.

TEACHING THE VALUE OF FAILED ATTEMPTS

It's important to teach children that there isn't a limit to the number of times they can try something. If they need to make forty-five attempts to get the basketball in the hoop, so what?

They can't worry about what others will think of them with each consecutive mess up. In fact, we can teach them that trying again and again is a measure of perseverance—an attribute characteristic of the self-directed. After all, each failed attempt just means they've cast one more stepping-stone in the water to get to the other shore. We might even want to tell our children something like, "You're one more step closer to success" when try after try winds up in defeat. But to prevent remarks like this from ringing hollow in their ears, we need to help them discover everything they've learned from each of their attempts. If, for instance, your child falls when he's learning to roller-blade, maybe he learns that he needs to tighten the straps around his ankles. If he falls another time, maybe then he realizes that he needs to loosen his upper body muscles more, and so on.

TEACHING CHILDREN TO STRIVE FOR PERSONAL EXCELLENCE, NOT PERFECTION

So many children are ashamed when they can't achieve perfection. We can reduce their shame in several ways. First, we can teach them that we all have different strengths and weaknesses in this world of multiple intelligences. We can't possibly expect everyone on a football team to play quarterback. Not exactly ideal for the team, really. We need good linebackers, receivers, fullbacks, cornerbacks, and placekickers, too. Second, we can encourage our children to seek personal excellence over perfection. *It's all right for them to be imperfect.* We are all works in progress, parents included. So our job is to urge them to continually strive for personal growth: this means they should try improving over their own past, doing their best to reach a goal, and raising the bar for that best each time. This self-betterment should be driven for the sake of their own satisfaction rather than for the approval of others. Moreover, its pace should be governed by their own agenda, not others'. Third, we need to show that we are happy when they do the best they can do. This means we mustn't only post their perfect schoolwork on the refrigerator door. It's a good idea to showcase their less-than-perfect work around the house, too, especially if it involved a great deal of effort. Doing these things will help our children develop a confidence in forming their own personal standards of excellence instead of feeling as though they must conform to the standards set by others.

Using Mistake Contests

I find it extremely helpful to ask children to write down every single mistake they've made from the moment they crawl out of bed until dinnertime. In fact, we can write down our *own* little list, too. Then, at the dinner table, each person describes the mistake from which they've learned the most. After everyone is finished, the entire family can decide which one was the best and why. Hey, how often can you win a prize for goofing up? Again, this contest will raise the level of comfort our children have with their own mistakes, because it exposes the positive side of those mistakes. This cozy relationship with goof-ups paves a smoother road for examining them with internal dialogue so they become blessings rather than burdens.

Downplaying Past Failures

Many parents rub their children's noses in their mistakes or repeatedly bring up past failures. I suppose some do this because they feel embarrassed about those mistakes, too. Perhaps it reminds them of similar mistakes they've made. They might think something like, "Timmy failed algebra! I'm such a rotten parent. I probably should've hired a tutor for him. Now he's going to be a math bonehead just like I was." Parents' own feelings of failure can be so burdensome that they feel they must punish their children for making the mistake. The more such parents focus on the child's role in the disaster, the less responsible they believe they'll feel. Other parents rub their children's noses in their failures because they think it will help keep them from repeating the mistake. Oh, how deluded they are. Sure, they won't repeat the mistake, because they probably won't ever take on that risk again. These children grow to view mistakes as external factors from which they must cower and hide. They never dare to explore their failures with internal dialogue, because doing so would be like opening up an old wound and pouring a bucket of salt over it. The sad result—children who are underachievers, some assembly by parents required.

Teaching "Failure Tolerance" by Not Over-reacting to Mistakes

Although often difficult, especially when we feel frustrated ourselves, it's important not to get totally bent out of shape over our children's mistakes. If we want our children to develop "failure tolerance," we need to actually downplay their mistakes. In fact, unless they bring up mistakes for discussion, their mistakes usually don't need to be brought up at all, unless the situation is potentially hazardous. Our kids are with it enough to realize a mistake has been made and have probably already experienced natural consequences. Parental interference might just interrupt them from delving into healthy internal dialogue that is so vital to their self-direction. If they do seek our advice or solace, we can simply let them know how remarkable they are for even trying and point out the good that came of it, including the things they did well within their failed attempt.

Encouraging Mistakes

We might even wish to go so far as to *encourage* mistakes in our children so that they perceive mistakes more as positive opportunities to grow than as something that gnaws away at their self-worth. Children must learn to stare adversity in the face and think, "What can this teach me? How can this help me grow?" They will then develop self-confidence, pride, and a sense that they can do anything they want. I go so far as to encourage my children to make small failures early on in areas that aren't terribly important to them. For instance, one of my sons enrolled in a tumbling class when he was five. He was awful at it and he knew it! But, since not being the tumbling champion of the universe wasn't the end of the world for him, he got a chance to experience and recover from defeat without becoming emotionally devastated. Doesn't that sound more like a success to you?

Encouraging Independence

We'd be surprised at our children's capabilities. Many parents have no clue as to the depths of their own children's potential, so they expose them only to endeavors that promise certain success, and they butt in to help with those that pose any significant challenge.

It's important to have faith in our children either to succeed or handle their defeats graciously. We can start by encouraging them to do things on their own whenever possible and by inviting them to try challenges in which they might fail. We should resist taking over for them when they struggle, and avoid sheltering them from endeavors we think are too challenging, because doing so sends the message that they are inept and cannot manage without our help. When two-year-old Sarah pours a cup of milk and starts to spill, Mom shouldn't grab the carton out of her hands to finish the job. She should let her spill! Then she should point out the parts of that task that Sarah did manage well and ask her to clean up the mess. In fact, whenever children are having trouble in any undertaking, I find it extremely effective to point out what they are doing well rather than where they are falling short. That way, they begin to focus on their successes rather than their failures.

Bottom line, we need to have confidence in our children. They really are capable of more greatness than we think. They are born into this world with self-confidence. If we have faith in them, they will retain this self-confidence and will not perceive the prospects of failure as an external influence from which to shrink.

TEACHING HOW TO SEPARATE FAILURES FROM SELF-WORTH

Our children can be taught that there is a difference between failing at a task and failing as a person. We can start by letting them know how much they should value the fact that they've tried.

When my sister, a devout tennis player, loses a match, she says, "I didn't lose. I just ran out of time before I found a solution." I love this philosophy, because it focuses on effort rather than result, and it implies a sense that we can accomplish anything we want, given enough time and elbow grease. It also suggests that there are solutions to every problem. We need only persevere long enough to find them. These messages help our children define failure as something separate from them personally. They define it as something they experience, something from which they can learn, something they can resolve, and something that results from their choices rather than from their identity or personality.

ACCEPTING SUFFERING AS A GOOD THING

We often protect our children from their own failures because we don't like to see them suffer. But this sheltering harms them by turning mistakes and failures into external influences rather than fodder for internal dialogue that could further their own personal growth. We must allow them to suffer so that they can learn to handle it. In fact, there is nothing we can do to prevent them from suffering occasionally in their lives. Suffering, while inevitable, helps them develop tolerance, confidence, and compassion. I remember observing my son's class in action in a small room with a one-way viewing window. His class of ten second graders was quite different from the public school from which he was transferred, because each child had some form of learning disability, varying from mild to severe. Most had struggled all of their young lives with constant defeat, teasing from other children, and the scorn of teachers who hadn't understood their condition well. What I saw was truly remarkable. The children were exquisitely compassionate with one another. If one of them was having a hard time with something, the others would help out and congratulate him for his hard work and for everything he did well in the task. One little boy struggled to complete an in-class math assignment. After he finally finished it, the others purposely walked by his desk, patted him on the back, and told him what a good job he had done. The level of tenderness, caring, and understanding was well beyond what I'd seen in a group of "normal" children, much less in a group of adults. By the end of the observation period, I actually felt grateful for my son's struggles, because I began to see that his suffering could teach him to become compassionate and understanding.

We must try to remember that suffering can be a wonderful gift for our children. We must have faith that they can handle it without withering; give them our unconditional love and acceptance and assure them that they can reap the good that suffering has to offer. We can also do everything we can to guide our children to understand why they suffer, what benefits they can gain from it, and how they can eventually free themselves of that suffering instead of falling victim to it.

Seven

HELPING CHILDREN HANDLE
REAL-WORLD INFLUENCES

> *Adversity is the first path to truth.*
> —*Lord Byron*

THESE ARE INDEED SPECIAL TIMES in which we live. Certainly we have advantages now that we've never known before. I, for one, ain't knocking no-scoop kitty litter. But sometimes I think that society's technological advancements have outstripped its gains in moral development and plain ol' common sense. In the process, we've lost the proper order of our priorities, our commitment to values, our collective dignity and self-respect, our autonomy, and, in the end, our freedom to exercise our free will without uncertainty or fear.

The time has come, now, for us to fight against every negative external influence that might steer our children off their self-directed course. Here are some of the worst influences we may have to confront and conquer.

DRUGS AND ALCOHOL

One of our biggest fears, as parents, is that our children might either be sucked into that dreaded drug and alcohol nightmare or be victims of others who have. And our fears are justified, because our children will most definitely be exposed to this influence. Will they make the right choices through internal direction, or will they buckle under the formidable weight of external influences such as peer pressure? That's the question we need to address.

Why do children fall into this trap in the first place? Andrew, age thirteen: "Peer pressure gets kids into drugs and booze, but sometimes they're just curious about how it'll make them feel. Like, you're at a party, right? Someone might say 'you want to try this?' and everyone's watching you, waiting for your reaction." Anonymous, age fifteen: "There are tons of reasons kids get into trouble with drugs and alcohol. First, they know it's not allowed, so that attracts them, and they want to look cool and grown up. Some just want to get wasted because they're sad or feel like losers. Maybe they feel useless to everyone." Here are eight possible reasons why children do drugs or alcohol:

1. *Feeling powerless*
2. *Peer pressure*
3. *Exploration of inner awareness*: When the false identity some children assume to satisfy society doesn't fulfill them, they use artificial means to discover who they truly are.
4. *Façade fatigue*: Some children are so tired of maintaining a façade to gain acceptance from the outside world that they're looking for relief.
5. *Escape from pressures*: Others seek escape from the spinning hamster wheel that takes them nowhere.

6. *Cry for help*
7. *Revenge*: Some children punish their parents and others who have made them conform to rules that make no sense for them.
8. *Curiosity*

If we're raising our children to be self-directed and if we're giving them all of the unconditional love and support they need, it's unlikely they will resort to drugs or alcohol. Here are some suggestions to help keep them safe:

- Parents need to model a drug-free lifestyle. No sense preaching about the dangers of PCP while smoking a joint. Remember, things have to make sense and be meaningful for children's internal dialogue to be clear, effective, and useable.
- Alcohol must also be used sensibly and sparingly, if at all. Parents shouldn't come home plastered from the dinner party at the Joneses'. They shouldn't suck down a brewsky while cruising down the interstate. Again, double standards confuse children to the point that they don't even bother trying to assemble internal dialogue to explore their choices. And in that void where their internal dialogue should be, external influences will most certainly set up shop.
- It's a good idea to role-play peer pressure situations with our children. They'll eventually be offered drugs, alcohol, or both. So, we want them to work on making their good choices through internal direction. We want their own choices to be rehearsed enough to become automatic.
- We can prohibit our children from watching movies or television programs that portray substance abuse

as a normal, if not fashionable, way of life. We don't want them to get the idea that drugs will make them look cool. This modeling just encourages them to view drug abusers as their pathfinder down that bumpy road of external direction.

- We need to discuss drugs and alcohol with our adolescent children before they get their information elsewhere. Questioning can stimulate them to develop their own internal dialogue. Here are some sample questions:

  "Why do you think kids your age take drugs and get drunk?"

  "What kind of physical, emotional, and mental problems do you think drug use can bring on?"

  "What kind of legal trouble can these kids get into?"

  "How do you think you'll react when someone tries to get you to experiment with drugs or alcohol? What will you say to them?"

  "Do you think it's a sign of strength or weakness to refuse these kinds of offers?"

  "Do you have any friends that will support your decision to abstain?"

  "How would your friendship change with someone who either experiments with drugs and alcohol or tries to pressure you to?"

  "What will you do if you see someone you know doing drugs or getting hammered?"

  "How will you handle any curiosity you might have on how drugs or alcohol make you feel?"

- If our children do make a bad choice, we need to give strong logical consequences that have a lasting impact. We can remove their driving privileges.

There's nothing like getting around on a dorky pair of roller skates to convince them we mean business. We can forbid them from socializing with their friends for an extended period. We're talking months here, people, not days or weeks. If they protest bitterly, tough cookies. We can just tell them that we're not willing to take a chance on trying to figure out with whom they seem to be making their bad choices, so all friends are taboo until they pull their act together. Our children will understand the fairness and appropriateness of these consequences, even if only deep down in the innermost recesses of their minds. And if we also make it clear that we have faith in them to make better choices in the future concerning substance abuse, they will respect us for our toughness and reflect internally on what fork in the road they should travel down next. If we balance that toughness with equal amounts of love and understanding, they'll be OK. At the same time, we might need to examine our relationship with our children. Are we giving them enough unconditional love and support? Are our rules and boundaries clear and fair? Do we enforce them consistently and logically?

VIOLENCE AMONG CHILDREN

Why do children resort to violence? The children I interviewed consistently cited *the frustration and anger that comes from not fitting in* as the most powerful reason. This desire all goes back to the simple fact that human beings have two principal urges—*to survive* and *to belong*. Often, these urges go hand in hand, and when violence is perceived as a way to survive or a way to belong, we got trouble. To understand what we can do as parents and as members of the community, we need to understand the external influences that contribute to youth violence:

1. *Poor modeling from parents and others around them*
2. *Violence portrayed in movies and television programs*
3. *Poor impulse control*
4. *The lack of a meaningful role within the pack:* Many children consider themselves like society's appendix—totally dispensable. Sometimes acts of violence make them feel more powerful—as if they're screaming: "Here I am, you bozos! I'll show you I'm good for something!"
5. *The need for attention*
6. *Fear of others who are different:* Uniting against "enemies" who are different gives members of the pack that sense of belonging. Negative group consciousness enters, stage left.
7. *Negative group consciousness:* "Conformity" violence committed against a common enemy, whether another race or another gang, is the frayed thread that binds a violent group together.
8. *Loss of power when society ignores them*
9. *Lack of accountability*

Can we do anything to protect our own children from succumbing to violence? Here are some internally directed ways we can help improve the odds in our children's favor:

- We can limit our children's exposure to movies or television programs that contain violence.

- We can help our children develop self-control by being consistent disciplinarians and develop impulse control by making them wait for the things that they want.
- We can discuss the issue of violence with them. Questioning will help them develop their own internal dialogue. Role-playing scenarios involving potential violence can also help our children rehearse the internal choices that they do eventually make.
- We can exercise self-control. No hitting, spanking, shouting, screaming, slapping, yelling, name-calling, and so on. We can model delayed gratification in our own behavior.
- We can teach our children to resolve their conflicts peacefully. They must learn that violence is NEVER an acceptable solution to a problem!
- When our children commit acts of violence, logical consequences should be rendered.
- We must instill values like responsibility, accountability, reverence for life, kindness, self-discipline, and patience in our children. These values supply them with important pieces of information to which they can refer while constructing the internal dialogue that will help them make peaceful choices in their lives.

MODERN TECHNOLOGY

We have built our highly advanced, technological society on a bed of external direction, and someone has put way too many quarters in the mattress vibrating machine. Unless we counteract this wild ride with some self-direction, we're headed for some loose fillings.

Since external direction is behind the greed for profit and since this greed is a big part of what drives society's "progress," we've allowed for a certain amount of collective irresponsibility and lack of accountability. For this reason, we have worldwide predicaments like deforestation, the destruction of the ozone layer, nuclear warfare, the pollution of our waters, and the replacement of imagination and creativity with passive entertainment.

Technology, through its advances in communication, has exposed us to so much more data. As a result, our children are bombarded by, and therefore vulnerable to, more external influences than ever before. Passive electronic entertainment like computer video games, Web crawling, and chat rooms are used by many parents as electronic babysitters: "Tommy's quiet up in his room playing Turok on his Nintendo. Hooray! That gives me plenty of time to pluck my eyebrows and do a pedicure. He'll be fine." Yep, and he feels just fine checking out those porn sites, too!

One interviewee says, "Man, if my parents *ever* knew some of the places I go on the Internet, they'd freak. It's like, major heavy X-rated stuff. I just lock my door and cruise away. They have *no* idea, and I'm keeping it that way, thank you very much. You're not telling them, are you? Isn't this confidential? I don't wanna get busted or anything." Funny guy. Clueless parents.

But don't hurl the Sega out the window just yet, because technology can be a boon rather than a burden. We just need to teach our children to use it responsibly—in accordance with their values and with the long-term welfare of humanity in mind. They need to think rather than react.

There are many ways to raise our children to have a healthy and responsible relationship with advancing technology.

Helping them develop internal dialogue about technological responsibility

We must raise our children to understand that technology should be used only if it's not at the expense of something or someone else. Through question and answer, we can assist them in applying their own internal dialogue to the subject.

"What do you think are appropriate uses for the computer for you personally?"

"How much time do you think kids your age should play computer or video games?"

Delivering logical consequences for technological irresponsibility

Always be aware of where kids are going on the Internet. If you have to hover over them, so hover already! When we find out they've broken the rules, they should be given logical consequences, like losing computer privileges for a certain time. Again, this consequence gets them to consider their choices internally. The same goes for other technologically irresponsible actions like electronic game overuse, littering, and so on.

Encouraging children to support technologically responsible causes

We can encourage children to support causes that advocate and defend the interests of our planet, particularly when these interests are endangered by the greed, shortsightedness, and indifference that technology sometimes creates:

"What do you think about the way your leaders are handling environmental issues?"

"What are your feelings about electronic entertainment replacing other creative, more active forms of entertainment?"

"Do you have any interest in supporting any technological or environmental causes?"

Humanity and technology can have a harmonious, symbiotic relationship if coupled with a commitment to moral values and spiritual concerns. Such a relationship is possible if we encourage our children's sense of global accountability.

THE HURRIED LIFE

Over-scheduling ourselves programs us to focus only on external things like errands and scheduled activities, a focus that eventually alienates us from our inner self. And when our children follow our lead, they don't develop and practice their reasoning skills. It's a lot quicker and easier to react than to think and respond.

Why do we create such a life for our children and ourselves? Lots of reasons, again all pretty lame. First, it takes every spare moment and then some to rack up that long list of accomplishments that'll guarantee us a spot in the winner's circle. Second, there are so many options for us now. A hundred years ago, playing "kick the can" meant you hit the high times, where entertainment was concerned. Now, we have almost every conceivable way to pleasure our bodies and minds. Unfortunately, we still have that same old twenty-four-hour day. And, believe me, we fill just about every second with trivial things. One of the casualties of this time war, then, is meaningful time spent with our children—time discussing values, ideas, memories, and feelings, and time helping them come up with their own choices and ideas through internal dialogue. Children find their jam-packed schedules overwhelming. One thirteen year old says, "When I have too much to do, I get really stressed and don't do my best in school." Let's look at some ways that guarantee our children the time they need for internal direction.

Debulking the daily schedule

First, we can try not to over-schedule their day. I see so many children stressed out from days that are jam-packed with soccer practice, Kumon math, Tae Kwan Do, ballet, etc. Kids need time to sit and think if they're to become self-directed.

Developing a deeper relationship with our children

The hurried life we lead with our children often makes our relationships with them more superficial. But a deep bond is essential to helping them become self-directed. The closer they are to us, the more respect they'll have for us, and that allows us to more effectively guide them. Furthermore, a closer relationship gives us more contact—more time to teach them how to develop and use internal dialogue. So, they might have to give up their piano lessons or softball practices. Replace them with playing catch in the backyard or discussing our thoughts and philosophies with them.

Another way to become closer is to make ourselves more available to them on their terms. If they ask us to read them a story when we're busy reading the paper, we need to ask ourselves, "What's more important here?" Of course, this technique doesn't mean we must snap to attention and shout, "Sir, yes sir!" for their every demand, but we just need to stop and think about their feelings before we angrily or absentmindedly shoo them away.

Slowing down the pace

One way to slow down the pace is to limit the times we say "hurry up." I, for one, have cut mine from 2,340,900 to 105 times a day. Pretty good for starters, eh? How can we expect our children to contemplate their choices when they're pummeled with these words?

We can also encourage everyone (including ourselves) to speak more slowly and calmly. Children need gaps in the conversation and relaxation in their own communication style to develop internal dialogue.

Taking more time for discipline

Sometimes our lives are so hurried that there's no time for consistent discipline. But discipline is crucial to the development of the internal dialogue that will help our children make self-directed choices in their behavior. Consistent discipline takes a conscious, if not exhausting, effort on our part, especially if our lives are overly full, but it's vital to raising self-directed kids.

Avoiding the creation of vicarious lives for our children

Sometimes, we live our children's lives for them for convenience' sake. After all, we can do things a whole lot faster. It's easier to clean up their breakfast dishes when the school bus is coming down the street than to teach them to manage their time more effectively by making them complete their responsibilities, even if it means they have to miss the bus and walk to school. But our children need to experience their own choices and consequences if they are to learn how to develop internal dialogue.

Consumerism vs. Simplicity

Instead of striving to merely *be*, many have chosen the route of consumerism to satisfy our desire to *have*. The belief is that, in order to be happy, we have to collect as many "things" as we can. And the fact that society reveres those with the most toys helps encourage this mentality. Here's what some children say about the pressure to purchase.

"If you don't have the best and the people you hang out with do, you feel like you're going to be made fun of and rejected."

"Fitting in is the big thing behind spending money and being spoiled. You spend big bucks to try to look like one of the popular people so that's who you can become."

How can we raise our children to be driven by simpler, more spiritual things, so that they learn to treasure inner influences over external ones? Here are some ways.

Teaching our children that people are more important than things

We need to make our children feel loved and secure no matter what. If they accidentally break our favorite vase or spill grape juice all over our carpet, that's a great time to let them know that they are more important than whatever was damaged—those things are replaceable; our children aren't.

De-emphasizing material goods by reducing the number of gifts for our children

Early in my parenting career, I worked so many long hours as a doctor that I felt guilty about not having enough time for my children, so I'd compensate by showering them with gifts and special treats. They quickly came to expect this and became very spoiled. When I made the decision to stop this behavior of mine, I was worried about their reaction. But, you know what? They did fine! In fact, they're happier, because they sense that I value them more than things. Too many gifts are a drag on children's morale, because they really do want to contribute and give instead of being on the receiving end all the time.

De-consumerizing birthdays

When my children have their birthday parties, I insert a note in the invitations that reads as follows:

> *"No gifts are necessary, because the pleasure of your company is gift enough for me. If you really want to give me something, please bring an unwrapped used or new book for me to donate to our school library."*

I was nearly thrown into a state of shock when my children didn't whine and moan at this suggestion. In fact, they were all for it. And when they carried those books to the librarian, they nearly exploded with pride. Later, to help them reflect internally on this activity, I asked them how giving made them feel compared to receiving gifts. Each one preferred giving to getting. We can teach our children that birthday parties are to see that their friends have a wonderful time, not to "hit the jackpot."

Understanding that our children don't have to have things to be happy

We can try to have faith in our children to be OK about doing without the latest trends or fashions. Here are some ways to get around the "gotta have it" phenomenon that forces our children down a road of external direction:

- Where clothing is concerned, our obligation is to cover our children's bodies, not decorate them.

- We can teach our children how to create something new from something old, instead of letting them rush out to buy the latest and greatest.
- We can also help them find ways to create and enjoy simplicity with free pleasures like a backyard picnic, or playing soccer in the cul-de-sac with friends.
- We can encourage them to reflect on how the joy they get from these kinds of experiences compares to buying or receiving a new toy.

Helping them reflect on their purchases

When our children give in to their temptations to buy a new toy, we can wait a couple of weeks and then ask them if they still enjoy it as much. I doubt if they do. In fact, it has probably collected an inch of dust in their closet already. Through this guided internal reflection, our children can learn about the ultimate dissatisfaction that immediate gratification brings them.

Modeling simplicity in our own lives

We must make it clear to them that status, material goods, and money are not the important things in our lives. Children from families fortunate enough to attain financial security or affluence must understand that material goods are a by-product—not the cause—of happiness and are something to share and enjoy with others.

SEXUALITY

Today, thanks to the media, sex is often about power, domination, and image. In other words, *sexuality has become an external influence*. This influence has caused our young people to focus more on body image and less on good character and sound morals, because their sex appeal is just another of the many prerequisites that they must satisfy to gain the approval of their pack. Here are some remarks from our interviewees:

> *"We see things about sex on TV and we think that's how life is and that's what we're supposed to do. Peer pressure is a big reason, too."*

> *"I think curiosity and peer pressure are behind the whole sex thing. I mean, if you're curious about how sex feels and all and your friends crank up the pressure, that's all the excuse you need."*

Here are ways to assure healthy, self-directed sexuality in our children.

Teaching our children what sex is really all about

We can teach our children that sex is the ultimate expression of love between two souls. Make it clear to them that, in this way, sex is natural and beautiful. It's not about external, passing factors like image, power, and control. We can also teach them that sex isn't a means of escaping boredom and that it doesn't represent a way to seek pleasure through the five biological senses alone.

Defending modesty

Modesty should be defended as something that enlivens eroticism rather than suppresses it. We can encourage our children to retain their modesty because it can buy them the time they need to make wise internally directed choices about their sexual behavior. As their parents, we can encourage them to show modesty in both behavior and dress.

To help them develop the internal dialogue they need to make the right choices, we can use questioning:

"If kids your age don't try to turn on their sex appeal, how do others react?"

"What do you think when you see some of your peers consciously try to look and act as sexy as they can? What does this do to the sexual relationships this behavior eventually brings about?"

"Do you think that the pressure to be sexually appealing does any harm or good to relationships with the opposite sex?"

"Do you think your peers try to be sexually attractive because they want sex? If not, what are the real reasons?"

Role-playing can also be used to help them discover ways to overcome obstacles such as peer pressure involving sex or ridicule regarding their modesty.

Developing friendships with the opposite sex

Being able to make and sustain healthy friendships with the opposite sex enables children to see others as people rather than as sexual objects, and they'll be less inclined to perceive the opposite sex as depersonalized external influences to which they must react.

Modeling good expressions for sexuality

It's important to model affection and closeness with our partners in the presence of our children. We shouldn't go out of our way to hide our romantic hugs, those times we've danced to slow music in the kitchen, our warm kisses, and those long looks of intimacy.

Teaching children the risks of sexual irresponsibility

We need to educate our children about the disadvantages and dangers of sexual irresponsibility by stimulating them to analyze its risks internally, through questioning:

> *"What do you think you would do if you got your girlfriend pregnant?"*
>
> *"Whose responsibility would that child be?"*
>
> *"Where would you live?"*
>
> *"How would you be able to complete your schooling, while you financially support another mouth to feed?"*
>
> *"What can happen if you engage in unprotected sex?"*
>
> *"What would you do if you came down with a sexually transmitted disease?"*

The best time to do this sort of questioning is before it's needed. Otherwise, our teens will view our questions as an attack on their current sexual behavior.

Discussing our own past sexual choices

I know this one can be a toughie, but it's important to discuss our own past sexual choices—our regrets, the pressures involved in our bad choices, and so on. Exposing our own internal dialogue helps them develop their own. And they don't have to re-invent the wheel by repeating the mistakes we've made.

Preventing our children from watching movies and television shows that tout a warped sense of sexuality

We must prohibit our children from watching movies or television programs where the heroes and heroines are revered for their sexual prowess and precocity. A better alternative: Jane Austen or Charlotte Brontë books and movies, and other sources that reveal and laud modesty and sexual responsibility. Our main objective is not to make our children asexual. Our objective is to get them to make choices about sexuality through internal dialogue rather than reacting to the external pressures of others. They must be taught to look beyond society's distorted perception that sex is a force that feeds upon power and control. They must look past the pretense to see what sexuality is really about. Once they consider true sexuality, our children can grow up comfortable with their own sexuality and the physical and spiritual pleasures it offers.

BODY IMAGE AND THE PERCEPTION OF BEAUTY

The beautiful people. These are the people that get the jobs and the nod of approval from society. Image is what our externally directed world responds to the most. Here are some of the things our interviewees had to say on the subject:

> *"The girls really put pressure on us guys to have great bods and all. People make fun of you if you're short or fat and things like that."*

> *"The most stressful thing I'm up against is looking good. I see people who have everything going for them, physically. They look great and all. And they're laughing and having a great time. It just makes me want to be like them."*

But, most of us are far from "physically perfect" according to society's definition. And since our children realize that discrepancy, their self-esteem and confidence take a real beating. If we don't feel accepted by the pack, how can we achieve that sense of belonging? Because of this externally directed focus, we're faced with problems like bulimia, anorexia, and other disorders that go along with having a distorted body image and a rigid perception of beauty. This relentless pressure to comply with society's definition of physical perfection is one of the reasons that teen depression and suicide rates have skyrocketed. So what can we do, require everyone to wear brown paper bags on their heads? I don't think so. Let's consider more practical, internally directed solutions.

Fighting back against the media that promote unattainable images

We need to hold the media at least partly responsible for propagandizing our children into focusing on their physical flaws and struggling for beauty at the expense of character. Why not protest against this together—loudly? That means canceling subscriptions to magazines that deal almost exclusively with ways to be more physically beautiful, boycotting TV stations that hire only the best looking newscasters, watching talent shows rather than beauty contests, and so on.

Discouraging our children from wearing designer fashions

We might want to discourage our children from being seduced by trendy fashions in order to fit in with their peers. Children need to dispense with as many external influences as possible, and being coerced into believing they have to dress a certain way is one of them they can do without.

Teaching our children where true attraction comes from

Have you ever met a gorgeous person whom you couldn't stand or a homely person you were quite fond of? Of course, to both! We can discuss this with our children, teaching them that true attractiveness comes from a person's self-expression, creativity, self-acceptance, and ability to show love, affection, and intimacy. By making observations or asking questions about their own peer group, we can stimulate internal dialogue on this subject:

> *"What is it that you find so appealing about Mary (your child's 'homely' friend)?"*

> *"You don't seem to get along very well with Mike (a physically attractive friend)—what is it about him that rubs you the wrong way?"*

> *"How important is it to you that your friends are nice looking, physically?"*

> *"What traits do you most value in a friend?"*

> *"What would you rather have, an unattractive friend with high integrity or an attractive one with lower moral standards?"*

Not defining others by their physical characteristics

For example, instead of saying, "Who's that fat guy in your class?" we can say, "Who's that boy sitting on the second row next to Mary?" When we define people according to their physical attributes, our children will get the message a person's physical appearance is a huge portion of their identity. Once this belief is internalized, it will serve as a strong external influence.

Complimenting the character, not the exterior

For instance, instead of saying, "Jane, you're getting to be so pretty," we can say something like, "I really respect the fact that you're so dedicated to your schoolwork."

Not criticizing or ridiculing someone's looks

I see people critiquing others' looks all the time, especially in that safe six-foot radius around their television sets. "Wow, that old lady has so many wrinkles, spackling compound is her only hope!" These people feel empowered by taking others down a notch or two, but doing so in front of children teaches them to place more importance on external rather than internal characteristics. Once our children realize that they don't have to accept society's definition of beauty, our children will no longer be enslaved by the appearance of themselves and others. When they're freed of these shackles, our children can begin to nurture the real beauty that lies within them and see the inner beauty within others—a wonderfully inherent ability in the self-directed.

THE WINNER-LOSER MENTALITY AND COMPETITION

In our efforts to win at all costs to gain the pack's acceptance, we actually separate ourselves from other members of the pack. The collective result—a disunited and contentious society. We wind up not giving a second thought to the pain and suffering of others, because we often see their loss as our gain. Jessica, age thirteen, says it all when she makes the comment, "I think everyone should know that there's more than one understanding to things. People should allow for more of a gray zone. There's just too much pressure to be on the right side of the black and white thing, and it makes us not like each other as much." Here are some ways we can cultivate a win-win attitude in our children:

- We can teach our children that they don't always have to be superior within a relationship, a conflict, or some other type of interaction with another. In fact, it's better to strive to be effective rather than superior.
- Let them know it's OK to say, "I don't know," instead of insisting on being right all the time. We can model this same behavior. That means we don't need to be afraid of being wrong or not knowing all of the answers. Gosh, how much fun could *that* be?
- We can try not to reward or encourage competition. We can stick with cooperative games that let everyone win and that have no opponents. We can even encourage our children's schools to replace competitive games with cooperative ones, both in health fitness programs and intramural activities.
- We might keep our children out of competitive sports until they are old enough to handle defeat. They need to be mature enough to see failures as temporary events that are completely disconnected from their self-worth.
- If our children engage in competitive sports, we need to help them define winning as facing adversity and challenge well, instead of as defeating the opponent or having the highest score. A real "win" is when they did their best, when they showed improvement, when the entire team cooperated, and when they had a great time.
- If they compete, they should do so with their own past performance, so that they reach for personal growth by cultivating traits like perseverance and self-discipline.

- We don't want to motivate children by setting up contests like, "Let's see who can get ready for school the quickest." I know this approach is tempting, because it works so darn well, but it only encourages them to see everyone around them as a potential opponent.
- We can show children that a win-win attitude means they try first to understand the other person's position and then find a way to strike a compromise. Role-playing such situations can be helpful here.
- We can teach our children the arts of negotiation, cooperation, compromise, and other win-win tactics. They need to know that they can arrive at a win-win solution for any conflict, and these tools will give them the keys to this understanding.

If we can raise our children to adopt this non-adversarial attitude, they can grow to change society from a collection of opponents to a collection of friends. Once we achieve this cooperation, we'll have a populace committed to a common good. Looking down the road to self-direction, harmony would be the rule, rather than the exception, and the problems of the present would soon become lessons from the past.

Conclusion

*For I dipt into the future far
as human eye could see, Saw the vision
of the world and all the wonder
that would be.*
—*Alfred Lord Tennyson*

THE KEY TO CHANGING our externally directed world into a self-directed one is in choosing the right road. We need to teach our children to rely on reason to analyze those influences that come from outside themselves rather than to react mindlessly to them. We need to teach them to achieve their sense of belonging to the pack by finding roles through which they can contribute rather than taking the unconscious route of conformity or fighting.

And the high road is easier travelling than you think, once we all change our perspective. The fact that our children are born free-spirited and self-directed gives us a huge head start. All we need to do is to teach them to respect the existence of others and the world they live in rather than controlling or dominating them into living in the way that society wishes.

We're so entrenched in external influences that this change will take the most profound level of commitment and patience. All I ask is that we each try to do the best we can every day. We need to be constantly aware of the ways we influence our children in our words and in our actions, asking ourselves at every turn, "Am I encouraging external or internal direction?"

Specific Child-
Rearing Challenges

HOW TO HANDLE THEM TO
ENCOURAGE SELF-DIRECTION

The best way to make children good
is to make them happy.
—Oscar Wilde

HERE ARE SOME INNER-DIRECTED SUGGESTIONS
that will help with some of the most trying child-rearing dif-
ficulties we may stumble upon. All of these approaches are
designed to preserve your children's ability to rely on internal
dialogue instead of external influences to assess and correct
their behavior. Using this section as a ready reference will
help you raise a self-directed child, even if it means carrying
the book, tattered and tear-stained, to the market, in the car,
or at home. There are *some* challenges that, I hope, you will
never have to face, but others will be as inevitable as a pimple
on prom night.

To get to self-direction, there are a few universal caveats
for every one of the situations that follow. First, our children
need to understand and agree with both the need for the rule
and the consequences for breaking it. Only when they come

to agree with our rules, through their own internal dialogue, will they become self-directed. Second, look to your own parenting strategy as the possible source of some of the problem. Are you over-controlling or over-protective? Either trait can elicit an externally directed response, as your children react to an unhealthy situation. Third, remember for all these parenting challenges how important it is for you, as the parent, to model the right behavior. If you're expecting your children to act one way and you act another, the double standard will throw a monkey wrench into their whole internal dialogue machinery.

And lastly, don't forget to laugh.

ACCIDENTS

WHY THEY DO IT

Children break, spill, and knock over things as though it's a national pastime. Part of the reason for these accidents is they haven't quite figured out the relationship between their bodies and the space around them. And sometimes, their reflexes are inappropriately quick, making them difficult to manage. Occasionally, though, children will have accidents to manipulate, annoy, or take revenge, but this motive is exceedingly rare.

LOGICAL CONSEQUENCES

Have them clean up their own spills and pay for those things they break. If they have to do tasks above and beyond their usual chores to earn extra money, so be it.

SOLUTIONS TOWARD SELF-DIRECTION

Make observations that are nonjudgmental: "It seems like your glass of milk was resting on your place mat. Maybe that's why it tipped over." "Throwing a ball in the house is not safe for the indigenous lamp population."

If they're new at whatever task backfired, observe what was good. "Everyone spills sometimes, Timmy. But did you see how you got the carton of milk out of the refrigerator by yourself? After you clean up, let's give it another try!"

Use humor: pretend like you're a news anchor holding an imaginary mike to your mouth and say, "This just in, folks: an earthquake registering 6.5 on the Richter scale has just been reported with the epicenter located on the breakfast table at the Medhus's house."

Use minimalist techniques: "Tommy, milk." Point to the mess.

Use questioning to get them to think about their actions: "How do you think I feel about having syrup all over the floor?" "What do you think you can do now to make things all right?"

Give choices: "If you clean up that milk, then you can try pouring another glass again."

If they have an "accident" on purpose, whether to manipulate or show their anger, they should also be given a time-out to rethink their motives.

AGGRESSIVE PHYSICAL ACTS
WHY THEY DO IT

Children resort to physical aggression for many reasons. Some aren't quite mature enough to think about the consequences and control their impulses. Some are more skilled non-verbally than verbally, so they don't know how to handle conflicts with words, especially in the heat of the moment. Some children can't handle feelings that overwhelm them, especially anger and frustration.

LOGICAL CONSEQUENCES

They should be removed to another place to cool off. Once there, guide them through an appropriate reasoning process. Show them that you understand their feelings: "I know how angry you must have felt when Jimmy took your turn in line. It's OK to feel angry, even with one of your friends."

Teach them empathy: "How do you think Jimmy felt when you bit him?" "How does it feel when someone bites *you*?"

Help them find alternatives: "What words can you use next time to let Jimmy know he's making a bad choice?"

Teach them to make amends: "What can you do now to make Jimmy feel better?"

If they persist in using aggressive acts as a means of resolving their conflicts, tell them, "I'm afraid you might make the same bad choice again, so Jimmy has to go home now."

Let them know that you have faith in them to make better choices: "Maybe you and Jimmy can play together tomorrow when we go to the park. I know you'll choose to use your words next time."

SOLUTIONS TOWARD SELF-DIRECTION

Use questioning: "James, what are the rules about hitting in our family?" "What do you need to do next time instead?" "What do you need to do to make your sister feel better?" This questioning helps them develop their own internal dialogue later on.

Give impartial descriptions and information: "Hitting is not allowed in our family." "Sarah looks like she was really hurt by that kick."

Some children benefit from learning relaxation techniques like breathing exercises and meditation. These techniques allow children to cool off enough to think about the consequences of their actions.

Give limited choices: "When you stop pulling the cat's tail, then you can play with her again."

Occasionally, children with speech/language disorders can have trouble with aggression. If you think your child may have such a disorder, ask the teacher to make a referral to the school speech/language pathologist.

ALCOHOL, DRUGS, AND SMOKING
WHY THEY DO IT

Children resort to substance abuse for many reasons, all of which I've discussed in chapter 7.

LOGICAL CONSEQUENCES

The consequences should be harsh and nonnegotiable. For instance, they can be subjected to a three-month period where they're not allowed to go out with their friends: "John, you're making too many terrible choices when you're with your friends, so I'll have to remove you from them until I feel comfortable that you're ready to make more responsible decisions."

Take their car away for three months. They can spend a couple of weekends volunteering in a halfway house for teens recovering from substance abuse problems or in other community service projects that deal with this same issue.

SOLUTIONS TOWARD SELF-DIRECTION

Have your child and the rest of the family get appropriate counseling if substance abuse is more than a one-time experiment. Investigating family relationships and uncovering depression or other psychiatric illnesses may be vital.

Use examples. I love to point out the veteran smokers with emphysema dragging their oxygen canisters behind them in the grocery store, with long green tubes connecting them via their nostrils. Or how about that drunk singing show tunes at the bus stop? Pretty hip, eh?

Use questioning: "What are the rules about smoking in our family?" "Why do you suppose we have that rule?" "What do you think when you see Aunt Sally smoking?"

"When you make better choices and stop sneaking alcohol at parties, then we'll feel more comfortable about giving you back your car."

ANIMAL CRUELTY

WHY THEY DO IT

Sometimes children are so overwhelmed with affection for their pets that they inadvertently squeeze the stuffing out of them, so to speak. Some are just curious to see what happens when they kick, prod, or hurl Kitty across the room. On rare occasions, children have a psychiatric illness that causes them to have sadistic urges.

LOGICAL CONSEQUENCES

Take the animal away from your child. If they can't play with their pets gently, they shouldn't be allowed to enjoy the benefits of playing with them at all.

If the behavior persists, give the animal to someone who'll take better care of it.

Ask your local SPCA if your child can volunteer for a weekend or two.

SOLUTIONS TOWARD SELF-DIRECTION

Ask them how they think they'd feel if someone treated *them* the same way. Let them know what could happen to the animal if they keep subjecting it to cruel treatment.

Use impartial descriptions and information: "Brownie looks scared and sad after being treated that way." "Being rough with animals is cruel and is not allowed in our family."

Use the when-then approach: "When you can treat your hamster more gently, then you can have her back."

Give your child a choice: "Jane, you can either treat the dog more gently or we'll have to give her to Aunt Sally, who I know will treat her with more respect."

Ask your children what they were feeling at the time and help them find alternative ways of expressing that feeling.

Annoying Habits (Nose-Picking, Nail Biting, Etc.)

Why they do it

Almost everyone has annoying little habits, but when our children do, it drives us nuts. So, we nag and nag and nag until the whole ordeal becomes a huge power struggle that keeps the habit alive and kicking (or picking, as the case may be). Some children develop these habits because of stress, some develop them because they have a physical condition like a tic disorder, and some develop them just because.

Logical consequences

If your children engage in a disgusting habit like nose-picking, remove them from the group: "Other people don't like to watch someone eating their boogers, Adam. You'll have to leave the room to spare them the anguish."

Solutions toward self-direction

Never chide or nag your children to get them to stop. Give choices instead: "Debbie, it's OK to pick your nose with a tissue as long as you do it in private."

Use impartial descriptions and information: "Picking your toenails is a nasty habit. We don't allow that in public, much less at the table."

Use questioning: "Frank, how do you think it makes others feel when they watch you eat your boogers?"

Use minimalist parent techniques: "Harry, nose." Point to your nose and say your child's name: "Janie."

Use humor: "Spring cleaning, Thomas?" "Finding anything interesting?"

Ask your children what motivates them to bite their nails, incessantly clear their throat, and so on. Is it because they're nervous? If so, maybe the source of that nervousness is something you can help them with.

ARGUING DISRESPECTFULLY WITH PARENTS

WHY THEY DO IT

Arguing inappropriately is often a way for children to test their limits or let off steam. Some feel over-controlled and argue to rebel. Most are still inexperienced in finding respectful ways to settle a conflict.

LOGICAL CONSEQUENCES

When your children argue disrespectfully with you, ask them to leave the room. You don't need to be subjected to any unnecessary rudeness.

SOLUTIONS TOWARD SELF-DIRECTION

Give choices or observations: "Brandon, it looks like you're angry at me for telling you to clean up your room. How do you think I should have handled it instead?" "It makes me feel angry and frustrated when you talk to me that way." "Tom, you can either tell me why you're so angry in a respectful way, or you can leave the room and try again when you've had a chance to cool off."

Use questioning: "What are our rules about arguing disrespectfully?" "Why do you think we have those rules?" "How can you get your point across without breaking them?" "What do you need to do to make amends?"

Use humor to defuse the tension: place a sign on your forehead that reads, "Kick me. If it's good enough for our little Johnny, it's good enough for me."

BAD GRADES

WHY THEY DO IT

First of all, it's not the grades that are important here. What is worrisome *is* that it might be an indication that children have lost their enthusiasm for learning and whatever effort this involves. Many things can cause our children to have this problem: depression, procrastination, unappreciated learning styles (a kinesthetic learner being taught purely by auditory instruction), the fear of being branded a nerd, and the fear of failure.

LOGICAL CONSEQUENCES

Children should never be disciplined for making bad grades unless their poor scholastic performance is caused by bad choices: staying up and talking on the phone instead of doing their homework, going to a party instead of studying, etc. If this is the case, they shouldn't be allowed to engage in any of these distractions until their homework is completed.

SOLUTIONS TOWARD SELF-DIRECTION

Give choices: "James, if you finish your math in time, you might have time to go to the movies with Billy."

Give impartial descriptions and information: "I see you're watching TV instead of working on your book report. I'm wondering what will happen if you don't turn it in on time."

Use minimalist parent techniques: "Bobby ... science project!"

Use humor: attach a sign on their school books, "Lonely and ignored by current owner. Please play with me."

Use questioning: "Tommy, is that term paper due this week?" "What do you need to do to avoid running into problems with this assignment?"

Know what kind of learners (visual, multi-sensory, auditory, kinesthetic, etc.) your children are. Help them "learn how to learn" in their own style and give suggestions to their teacher along these same lines.

Teach your children how to handle defeat early on. Give them small feats that won't be totally devastating for them if they fail. Point out whatever they do well in that accomplishment, no matter how small or trivial it seems.

Let your children know that you love them regardless of the grades they make. Teach them that the knowledge and skills they attain and their continued love of learning are the only things that really matter in the end.

BATHING HASSLES IN YOUNGER CHILDREN
WHY THEY DO IT

Let's face it. Our younger kids can always find *something* more important to do than bathing, at least from their perspective.

LOGICAL CONSEQUENCES

Let your children know that bathing is not a choice. But deciding if Daddy or Mommy shampoos their hair, choosing whether story time or bath time comes first, and so on are choices they *can* make. If they still pitch a fit when bath time comes around, they should lose their right to make those small but important choices. Furthermore, they'll lose their bedtime story since they decided to fill that time with their whining, begging, and other measures of resistance.

If they refuse to take a bath, they won't be allowed to subject the public to their negligent hygiene practices. This means not going over to Trent's house to play, not going to the movies, not joining you on your errands, and so on.

SOLUTIONS TOWARD SELF-DIRECTION

Give choices: "Do you want to brush your teeth or bathe first?" "When you've cleaned up, then you can go with me to the grocery store."

Use impartial descriptions and information: "Dirty children aren't allowed in the grocery store." "We believe in cleanliness in our family."

Use questioning: "What are our rules about bathing?" "What would be the consequences if you never took a bath?"

Use the minimalist parent approach: "Howie . . . bath time now!"

Use humor: Pretend you don't see your child and say to your parenting cohort in crime, "Have you seen Larry? I can't find him. All I see is a wiggling lump of coal in the middle of his room."

BEDTIME HASSLES
WHY THEY DO IT

Most children resist going to bed because they don't want to miss any of the action happening with the rest of the family. Sometimes, they enjoy waging a great big power struggle, because that means they get more of your attention.

LOGICAL CONSEQUENCES

If your children don't finish their "pre-bedtime" routine in time, like brushing their teeth, taking their bath, and putting on their pajamas—guess what! There won't be enough time for a bedtime story. (Be sure to always find enough time to tuck them in and kiss them, though.)

If your children get to bed late, they'll be tired the next day, and you can capitalize on their sleep deprivation by creating logical consequences. "Jane, you look exhausted after not getting enough sleep. I guess you won't be able to go to Mirel's party today after all."

SOLUTIONS TOWARD SELF-DIRECTION

Give choices: "Would you like to go to bed at 7:30 or 7:45 tonight?"

Use questioning: "What are our rules about getting ready for bed?" "So, what do you need to do now?"

Use impartial descriptions and information: "It's important to get enough sleep every night to feel good the next day." "I guess we won't be able to go to the park tomorrow, since you won't have had enough sleep tonight."

Use humor: "The sleep fairy is twitching. She has a nervous breakdown when kids don't go to bed on time."

Never fall for the "one more glass of water" routine. My five year old used to come up with all sorts of excuses: "I have one more question." "I need to go pee-pee." "I need to go poo-poo." "I'm thirsty." "I forgot to hug you." "I forgot to give you a kiss." If the original routine is followed to the letter, everything else is just a stall tactic. Bedtime means they must remain in their rooms until morning. Trust me, they won't die of thirst or hunger, and they won't drown in a puddle of pee in their sleep.

BED-WETTING

WHY THEY DO IT

Most experts view bed-wetting as a sign of an immature neurological system or perhaps a type of sleep disorder. Recent medical research, however, has found that many children who wet the bed may have a deficiency during sleep of an important hormone known as anti-diuretic hormone (ADH). ADH helps to concentrate urine during sleep hours. Testing of many bed-wetting children has shown that these children do not show the usual increase in ADH during sleep. Children with enuresis, therefore, often produce more urine during the hours of sleep than their bladders can hold. If they don't wake up, the bladder releases the urine, and the child wets the bed.

If they've been dry all night for a long period of time and *then* begin to wet their bed, you need to consult their physician, because this could be an indication of a physical or emotional problem.

LOGICAL CONSEQUENCES

Give your children the responsibility of removing the wet sheet from their beds, washing the sheets, and replacing them with new ones. They might need some help with this task, depending on their age, but even children as young as four or five can manage the lion's share of this task.

SOLUTIONS TOWARD SELF-DIRECTION

Again, never ridicule or punish your children for bed-wetting. They simply can't help it, and you're just asking for years of professional counseling bills for them if you make it an issue of shame. Other than the logical consequences mentioned above, there are no self-directed solutions to this problem. The condition is largely physical and maturational. Internal dialogue is important only in their handling bed-wetting without stigma rather than in stopping it altogether.

BEGGING

WHY THEY DO IT

Some kids know that if they beg long enough and in a voice that would make the cat lose all of its fur, they'll get their way.

LOGICAL CONSEQUENCES

It's important that you don't take on the sense of urgency that your children create when they beg. "Ho hum" should be your attitude here. Many consequences will work well. For instance, if your children beg to go to the park when you've already told them you have a meeting to attend, that's it for their park-going days for a week.

It also helps to send them from the room you're in. You don't have to be subjected to the irritation. They can be annoying in their *own* space.

If you offer them some treat, and they beg for something better, the original offer becomes null and void.

SOLUTIONS TOWARD SELF-DIRECTION

Unless it's obvious, give them an explanation for not acceding to their wishes. This information is important for them to generate the necessary internal dialogue in the future.

Using questions can help them develop this internal dialogue: "What are the rules about begging?" "Why do you think we have those rules?" "How can you handle things differently next time?"

Use impartial descriptions and information: "Begging is the one sure way people will not get what they want, in our family."

Use choices: "When you stop begging, then I can listen to whatever reasonable grounds you think you may have for getting what you want."

Use humor: "Uh-oh! I think I hear the begging police" (make police-car siren sounds—don't worry, it gets better with practice—then say the following in a serious, authoritative voice): "Pull over lady. I have a report from neighbors of a violation of the penal code 246.7 for incessant begging. Are you aware of your rights?"

BIRTHDAY HASSLES

WHY THEY DO IT

Some children act up during their own birthday party, because they're just so overwhelmed with various emotions—excitement, anticipation, frustration, disappointment, and so on. Children act up at other kids' birthday parties because they're quite obviously not the center of attention.

LOGICAL CONSEQUENCES

If your children can't behave well at a birthday party, whether it's for them or for another child, take them away from the party. Take them home, if you have to. Tell them you can't allow them to spoil the day for everyone else.

If your children don't show thanks for a gift, even after a gentle reminder, that gift should be immediately taken away and either returned or donated to a needy and more appreciative child.

SOLUTIONS TOWARD SELF-DIRECTION

Before your children go to another child's party, discuss how they might feel about someone else's getting all of the attention.

Give information like, "The purpose of birthday parties is to show our friends and families how glad we are to have had another great year together." So, it's their responsibility to see that all of their guests have a good time.

Allow your children to help plan their own party. They feel empowered when you give choices: "Do you want a chocolate or vanilla birthday cake?" If they're a guest, help them find some way to contribute to make the party more fun for the guest of honor. For instance, maybe they can make up a special party game.

Instead of gifts from the guests, ask them to bring a used or new book to donate to the school library, or something similar. Your children should be the ones to decide what sorts of items to donate, and *they* should be the lucky devils who get to hand over the presents in person. When they do, they will feel so proud that their altruism will become addictive. Afterwards, ask them questions: "How did it make you feel to give those books to the library?" "How do you think Mrs. Godfrey, the librarian, felt about your generosity?" Add impartial descriptions like, "Those books will make a big difference in your school library. I'll bet lots of kids will enjoy checking them out year after year."

BLAMING OTHERS (LACK OF ACCOUNTABILITY)
WHY THEY DO IT

Most children don't want to appear inadequate in front of other people. And they certainly don't want to be ridiculed, criticized, or punished for their mistakes.

LOGICAL CONSEQUENCES

First of all, never set your children up to lie. More about that later under "Lying." If you suspect them of doing something wrong, have them correct it or make amends in some way. For instance, if you find your garage walls covered with tempera paint, hand each of your children a bucket of water and a scrub brush and tell them, "It's all yours." Even if the innocents have to use a little elbow grease, they'll have bigger biceps to show for it. In other words, "it ain't gonna hurt 'em!"

Have your children take care of the feelings of those they unfairly blamed for their own mistakes.

SOLUTIONS TOWARD SELF-DIRECTION

If your children don't accept the blame for a mistake they've made, tell them flat out that you weren't born yesterday. This candor stalls any attempts for them to create rationalizations that, in turn, could progress to self-deception.

Use impartial descriptions and information: "We believe in being accountable for our actions in our family." "I remember you promised Josh you'd take over his paper route this week."

Provide choices: "When you can accept responsibility for your actions, then you will be given the privileges that go along with a higher level of maturity."

Help your children develop the inner dialogue they need to avoid blame-shifting. Questioning is perfect for this: "Didn't you promise Josh you'd take over his paper route this week?" "What do you think is motivating you to blame him for not getting it done today?" "How do you feel when someone falsely accuses you?" "What can you do to make things right?"

Let your children know that it's OK to make mistakes, but once they do, they should focus immediately on a solution rather than find someone else to take the rap.

Admit your own mistakes and shortcomings freely to your children. You can't possibly raise them to be accountable for their actions when you aren't accountable for your own.

And doing so will help them feel more at-ease in dealing with their own mistakes through internal dialogue.

Point out those times when your children *do* show a sense of accountability: "Mary, I bet you're so proud that you recognized your mistake and found a way to make it all better. I don't know many grown-ups that could do that!" (Sadly, this is true.)

Give your children age-appropriate tasks for which they can be responsible. If they fail at the task, point out everything they did well, in spite of the end result, guide them in correcting their mistake, and encourage them to keep trying. Children who learn to recover from defeat are generally highly accountable individuals.

BODY PIERCING, TATTOOS, AND OTHER BODY EMBELLISHMENTS

WHY THEY DO IT

Body image is so important today. And children will do nearly *anything* to distinguish themselves from the crowd through their outward appearance. It's as if they're wearing a flashing neon sign around their necks that's saying, "Notice me, dammit! I'm special!" Unfortunately, half of their peers are wearing that same darn sign.

Of course, there are cultural issues involved. And there's the matter of personal taste. But if you're the least bit skittish about your children making permanent alterations in their external appearance, here are some suggestions.

LOGICAL CONSEQUENCES

If your children follow the stipulations and limits you set forth, regretting their decision will be consequence enough. Read on.

SOLUTIONS TOWARD SELF-DIRECTION

I'm a firm believer in self-expression, but when the consequences of their self-expression are permanent, children should be allowed to act only after certain conditions have been met. For example, impose an age limit of fifteen years. You can veto alterations to certain parts of their bodies, like nipple studs (ouch!). To ensure they have the opportunity to feel the consequences of their decision, require them to go through a dress rehearsal. If it's a tattoo they want, they need to wear a temporary henna tattoo first. If it's an extra piercing on their earlobe, have them wear magnetic studs for a few months first. If they still want to go through with it after this waiting period, let 'em go for it! (But make *them* foot the bill!)

Explain the risks of these procedures. For instance, tongue piercing can cause a serious infection, but it can also alter dentition. The constant pushing of the stud against the back of the front teeth pushes them forward. Might get mistaken for Mister Ed or Trigger if they're not careful.

Model to your children the importance of embellishing what's *inside*. Questioning works well here: "How important is a person's exterior appearance nowadays?" "Do you think this emphasis is good or bad?" "Do you sometimes feel pressured by this trend?"

If you can think of any trends that were popular in your day and old-fashioned now, point them out. And if *you* have any tattoos or body piercings, let your children know how you feel about making a decision with lasting consequences. "I was really excited about getting a tattoo when I was your age, but now, I'd give anything to take it off. I've outgrown it years ago and am totally sick of it."

BOREDOM

WHY THEY DO IT

Children today seem to expect every single second of their lives to be filled with the most stimulating entertainment possible. After all, there are lots of options! Couple this glut of options with the fact that most parents think their number one job is to make their children happy, and the result is the never-ending struggle to spare our children inevitable moments of boredom.

LOGICAL CONSEQUENCES

Let your children either learn to make the most out of their quiet moments or fill them with their *own* ideas for entertainment. Never try to save them from frustration by fixing their boredom for them. This is not your job. But teaching them how to handle that frustration is.

SOLUTIONS TOWARD SELF-DIRECTION

When your children come up to you and whine, "I'm bored. There's nothing to do," use questioning like, "What are you going to do to solve that problem?" Better yet, tell them it's good to be "bored" on occasion, because it gives them time to recoup, reflect, and exercise that rusty inner thinking mechanism between their two ears. They can think of it as a "Richard Simmons Aerobics Hour" for their inner voice.

Try to convey a sense of empathy: "I know how you feel. I feel bored from time to time, too." (Would I give *anything* to remember what *that* feels like again!)

Buy only toys that stimulate their creativity and call for active participation, not ones that passively entertain kids into zomboid states. Also limit your children's exposure to other passive forms of entertainment like computer and video games and television. Toys should be designed to help them develop internal dialogue rather than external reactions.

BORROWING THINGS WITHOUT RETURNING THEM

WHY THEY DO IT

Children get busy and forget. Some just don't think about the effect they have on others. Some don't care. Some lose or break whatever they borrowed and hope that if enough time goes by, the object will be forgotten.

LOGICAL CONSEQUENCES

If your children break or lose an item they borrowed, help them find ways to make amends, like earning money to pay for a new one or coughing up whatever it takes to repair the damages.

If your children forget to return something they borrowed, they certainly shouldn't be allowed to borrow that item again for a while. Maybe they could make amends by letting the loaner borrow whatever he or she wishes in return. They could even be required to pay a small interest fee in either money or deeds.

SOLUTIONS TOWARD SELF-DIRECTION

Have clear family rules and boundaries on this subject. First, there should be no "borrowing" without asking. Second, while objects are under their care, the borrower is responsible for whatever happens to the items borrowed, regardless of any "extenuating circumstances" (translation: lame excuses). Third, a mutual agreement should be made on when the borrowed item should be returned.

Use questioning: "What are our rules for borrowing?" "What do you need to do to make things all right between you and your sister?" "How does it make you feel when someone borrows your stuff without your permission?"

Use impartial descriptions and information: "I see you borrowed Tommy's bike without his knowledge. I bet he'd be pretty upset if he found out."

Never get involved with borrowing incidents involving your children and their friends or siblings. Let them find ways to work out any conflicts on their own. If they never get their item back, they learn not to lend anything to that person in the future and the other person learns that to be trusted, you have to be trustworthy.

BRAGGING

WHY THEY DO IT

Children brag to try to convince other people that they're better than they really think they are. Somehow, their self-esteem has taken a beating in the past, and they're struggling to repair it.

LOGICAL CONSEQUENCES

When your children brag, they'll get whatever consequences they deserve from those who have to put up with it. Tell them how most people might react, though, so that they'll have something to think about when their friends roll up their eyes and walk away.

SOLUTIONS TOWARD SELF-DIRECTION

Teach your children to find ways to appreciate who they are and discover their *own* inner sense of worth. Eventually, these thoughts may become incorporated into their internal dialogue.

Ask your children questions to stimulate their internal dialogue: "How do you feel when someone else brags? Don't you find it annoying?"

Use impartial descriptions and information: "Johnny seemed to wrinkle up his nose when you were talking about all the karate awards you won. It may have made him angry."

"In our family, we try to make our friends feel good about themselves, instead of trying to prove that we're better."

Role-play bragging scenarios with your children, first with you, then with them, playing the braggart. Again, this will help them develop internal dialogue about bragging.

BRUSHING TEETH AND OTHER PERSONAL HYGIENE ITEMS

WHY THEY TRY TO GET OUT OF DOING IT

Hey, they've got better things to do, what can I say?

Do you really think washing up before dinner or brushing their hair gets their adrenaline going? Does clipping their nails make their spines tingle? I seriously doubt it. If so, you probably have a very boring family.

LOGICAL CONSEQUENCES

If your children don't comb their hair or bathe regularly, they'll find out about it from their friends, eventually. Let them know how *you* feel about the way they look and smell, but never nag them.

No one comes to the dinner table without washing hands first. No cleany, no eaty. As for dental hygiene, it's not that easy. If they won't brush their teeth on their own, brush for them. If they're seventeen years old, they might squirm at the idea of you brushing their teeth while their blind date waits at the door.

Uncut nails will become annoying and deadly, unwashed hands will stink and gross them out when they pick their noses, and their clothes will walk out the front door on their own if they don't do their laundry. In other words, personal hygiene habits usually have a built-in consequence system that works pretty well.

Teach your children why hand washing and teeth brushing are so important. Bring up some disgusting pinworm story or the specter of dental implants—if you're desperate.

Use impartial descriptions and give information: "It's already 7:00, and you haven't brushed your teeth yet."

Use choices: "If you've finished washing your hands, then you can come to the table to eat."

Use humor: Put a sign near the toothbrushes that reads something like, "Wanted, new home for neglected toothbrush." Look in their mouths and feign dismay, saying that the little sugar bugs are excavating a vacant lot on one of their molars so they can put up a new shopping mall there.

If your children don't brush their hair in the morning and look like a cross between Don King and a pekinese, who cares? Sure, they might get a barrage of nasty critiques from their peers, but we hope that they'll make their decisions based on their *own* opinions. If it becomes important enough, they'll start combing, trust me. If they just forget to "do their do" but hate looking like a bed-head every morning, help them remember in a nonjudgmental way: "Lukas, you've gotten ready for school so quickly. Let's see. You're dressed, you've eaten, you've brushed your teeth, and you have your lunch made. All you need is to comb that hair of yours a little, and you're off!"

BULLYING

WHY THEY DO IT

Some bullies feel so powerless and unaccepted that they must grab on to whatever power they can by controlling, intimidating, and threatening. Many of these children feel they have no meaningful niche among their peers. Still others have not been raised with limits or been given consequences for their aggressive actions.

LOGICAL CONSEQUENCES

If your children bully other children, they shouldn't be allowed to play with others until they're prepared to make better choices. When you separate them from the rest of their group, let them know your reasons. Any bullying should be followed by having them make amends with their "victims."

SOLUTIONS TOWARD SELF-DIRECTION

Teach your children how to resolve conflicts without aggression. For instance, role-play situations where first you and then they play the bully. Also try role-playing different scenarios involving friend-to-friend interactions. This process might include asking to share a toy, accepting "no" for an answer, or sharing a bench at the school lunch table.

Help your children discover ways that they can have a meaningful role within their group of friends or among family members. For instance, you can take your child and a few of his best friends to the movies. Tell him, in front of the others, that since there are so many children for you to take care of in a busy public place, his job is to make sure everyone treats each other nicely. His other friends can have assignments, too, like keeping everyone together in one place, making sure they're quiet during the show, or writing down the concession stand orders.

Questioning can work well, too: "Do you think bullies earn more or less respect from their friends?" "What do you think motivates someone to bully someone else?" "How do you think most bullies feel about themselves?" (These questions should be asked during calm moments rather than when the child is bullying someone to avoid making the interrogation seem like a personal attack.)

Offer your child choices: "When you learn to stop bullying Jimmy, then you can have him over again."

Some children may need social skills training by professionals in a group setting with peers who have similar problems.

If your children are subjected to bullying by another child, let them handle it on their own, unless there are any physical threats involved.

CAR HASSLES

WHY THEY DO IT

From their standpoint, it's torture sitting in one place for an eternity. Our children are used to wide open spaces where noise travels unobstructed and the distance between siblings is under their full control.

LOGICAL CONSEQUENCES

Never start the car until everyone is buckled up. If someone unbuckles, pull over, safety permitting, and wait patiently until they belt up again.

If the noise or bickering level gets way out of hand, let your children know that driving with those kinds of distractions is dangerous. Then pull over when it's safe and convenient, and silently wait for everyone to settle down. Your children need to work things out between themselves, without any intervention on your part. If they don't pull their act together in a reasonable time, hi ho, hi ho, it's off to home they go!

Reverse time-outs work pretty well, too. If my children are going bananas in the car, I pull over, get out of the car, and wait quietly for them to settle down. They do, too, and quickly. When I look through the car window at them, I have to suppress my urge to throw back my head and laugh at their "Mom has really lost it this time" look.

Anyone who fights over or races to get the best seat has the last choice.

SOLUTIONS TOWARD SELF-DIRECTION

Use questioning: "What are our rules about car behavior?" "Why do you think we have those rules?"

Use impartial descriptions and give information: "It's dangerous to argue while someone is trying to pay attention to their driving." "Arguing about who gets to sit where is not allowed in our family."

Offer them choices: "When you stop fighting in the car, then we can go to the restaurant."

For repeat offenders, I set up a mock outing. Without tipping them off to my ulterior and highly sneaky purpose, I'll tell them to pile in the car for a trip to some place fun to which I couldn't care less about going. Seaworld, for example. Then I let them know that if they can't behave in the car, I'll turn around and go home, no matter what. The trip should be a little bit long, so there will be some time between that warning and your destination. And if they mess up, as they're bound to do, stick to your guns and go back home. Say as little as possible, despite their ranting, raving, crying, and pleading. If they *do* behave, point this out and ask them if the car trip was more pleasant when everyone behaved civilly. Repeating this "mock run" from time to time will keep the car monsters at bay.

CHEATING IN SCHOOL

WHY THEY DO IT

Children cheat to gain acceptance from their friends, teachers, and parents. Society places so much importance on winning and getting good grades that there's a lot of pressure to do whatever needs to be done.

LOGICAL CONSEQUENCES

If your children are caught cheating, they can do one or all of the following:

- Restudy the material until it's mastered. No play or leisure time until then.
- Apologize to the teacher.
- Accept a failing grade, even if they're the ones supplying the answers to someone else.
- Require them to be heavily monitored while taking tests, until the teacher and you feel comfortable that they won't cheat.
- Make them drop all extracurricular activities (football, karate, pep rallies, parties, and so on) until they show mastery of the subject without cheating.

SOLUTIONS TOWARD SELF-DIRECTION

Raise your children to understand that the grades are not the real goal. The knowledge attained and the perpetual thirst for learning are. Eventually, they'll internalize this concept as their own belief, which will then be fodder for internal dialogue concerning the subject.

Use questioning: "Why do you think some kids cheat?" "What do you think this accomplishes for them?"

Teach your children about the benefits of upholding their integrity through honesty and about how integrity is all tied into their overall happiness.

CLINGING TO PARENTS

WHY THEY DO IT

Children cling because they're trying to seek undue attention, or to manipulate, or because they're genuinely fearful. It's natural for younger children to go through clingy phases, especially when they're learning some new and scary skill, experiencing stress at school, or feeling sick.

LOGICAL CONSEQUENCES

If your children cling to you for undue attention or for other manipulative reasons, simply insist that they give you your space: "Caroline, I'm reading the paper now. You can sit in my lap when I'm finished." Don't make a big deal about it, because yelling and nagging may be just the attention they seek, even though it's negative. If they cling to your leg like a boat anchor, firmly peel them off and say, "I need to have my body to myself right now. I know you'll be perfectly fine on your own."

If your children cling to you out of fear, insecurity, fatigue, or illness, negative logical consequences aren't appropriate. They need you!

SOLUTIONS TOWARD SELF-DIRECTION

Help your children feel that their surroundings are safe. Don't scare them with statements like, "Never wander away from me again! I was so scared! Someone could have taken you away from me forever!" This fear only provides them with a reason to be externally directed.

Convey that you have faith in your children to handle themselves independently.

Give your children ample opportunity to accomplish various feats of independence early on, like making their own lunches or learning how to ride a bike.

Try not to do what they can manage for themselves. I've seen mothers feeding their eight or nine year olds their cereal, for God's sake! As if mothers don't have anything better to do with their time! They can come over to my house. I'll find plenty of ways to keep them busy!

Make observations when they act independently: "You tied your shoes all by yourself today, Ricky!" "Did you make your own breakfast just now, Brianna?"

Use questioning: "What is it that frightens you?" "What do you think might happen if you do that by yourself?"

Cliques

Why they do it

Many children find strength within a group. The exclusionary tactics of cliques make kids feel superior to others, because it classifies those who aren't "members" as inadequate or undeserving. Having both a common enemy and the same privileged status binds them all closer together.

Logical consequences

If you discover that your children are involved in cliques, they shouldn't be allowed to play with those friends until exclusionary measures are stopped. That means no parties, sleepovers, play dates, and so on.

Have your children and their friends come up with ways to maintain the group cohesiveness without excluding others. If they wish, help mediate and give suggestions.

Require them to make amends with whoever had their feelings hurt by the clique's exclusionary tactics.

Solutions toward self-direction

Role-play scenarios where your children play the child who is being ostracized.

Use questioning: "How would *you* feel if a clique excluded you from play?" "Can you think of a way you can maintain your friendships with these kids without hurting other people's feelings?"

Use impartial descriptions and information: "I see Tommy really got upset when you and your friends told him he couldn't play hide-and-seek with you guys." "We don't allow cliques in our family."

Use choices, too: "When you and Sarah can be friends without excluding others, then you can get together again."

Put your children in charge of transforming the clique into an open group: "Johnny, you're such a good leader. Can you help your friends find ways to play without making anyone feel left out?" When he realizes the benefits of disbanding a clique, he'll incorporate the experience for use in any future internal dialogue.

COMMITTING CRIMES
WHY THEY DO IT

Children commit crimes to satisfy their curiosity, to comply with peer pressure, to finance a drug habit, to feel powerful, to gain attention, to vent feelings of jealousy, or to get revenge.

LOGICAL CONSEQUENCES

Regardless of the crime, your children should feel the full extent of the legal consequences. Don't buy them out of the sticky mess, argue with the authorities, help them come up with excuses, or rescue them in any other way.

If you discover that your children shoplifted, make them return the stolen goods in person, accompanied by a sincere apology.

If you find that something of yours has been stolen, don't force a confession from your children. Instead, tell them that you expect it to be replaced within an hour or so, or the cost of the item will be divided among and docked from each child's allowance.

Have your children repay their victims in some way. If they vandalized the corner store, make them clean up the mess, pay the cost of repairs, and work weekends there (without pay) for a certain period of time. Of course, apologies given in person are always called for.

Make your children responsible for the costs of all legal fees, tickets, and fines. Hey, if they have to earn the money breaking up rocks in the backyard with an ice pick, so be it!

Remove anything used to commit the crime. If they got caught speeding or driving drunk, take away the car. If they shot someone's window with a BB gun, confiscate the gun.

Tighten up the reins. Make their curfew much earlier, don't allow them to leave your sight without adult supervision, drive them to school and take them physically to class, veto any associations with their current friends with whom they seem to be making bad choices, and so on. Tell them the reins will be loosened when *you* feel more comfortable that they'll respect the welfare and property of others.

SOLUTIONS TOWARD SELF-DIRECTION

Use questioning: "How do you think Mr. Parsons felt when you stole candy from his store?" "Do you think taking things from others is a sign of strength or weakness?" "What motivated you to do it?" "What do you plan to do to make things all right?"

If they have committed crimes in the past, have your children visit your local jail, sit in one of the empty cells, wear a pair of handcuffs, and speak with some of the police officers.

Use impartial descriptions and give information: "The Miller family is law abiding." "We do not tolerate breaking the law in our family." "It seems like getting caught for shoplifting really messed things up for you for awhile. You seem very down since that happened."

COMPLAINING

WHY THEY DO IT

Children complain to manipulate, to get attention, and to drive us bananas. Some complain because they feel over-controlled and don't think they have a voice in matters that are important to them. Others complain because it works. They get their way every time.

LOGICAL CONSEQUENCES

Once your children complain inappropriately, like, "I never get to go out with my friends. You're such a mean mother!" tell them they obviously don't have the maturity to voice their problems constructively and politely. In that case, they're too immature to go out alone with their friends.

SOLUTIONS TOWARD SELF-DIRECTION

Don't *you* gripe all of the time in front of your children, or speak disrespectfully to them. Otherwise, they'll internalize the assumption that these are acceptable forms of behavior.

Raise your children to understand that not everything works out as they expect. Teach your children alternatives to complaining by rewording what they say:

Sally: *"It's so boring in this family. I hate it!"*
Mom: *"Mom, can you help me come up with some ways to spend my extra time?"*

Use impartial descriptions and give information: "Complaining only irritates people. It's the last thing that'll get you what you want." "We don't allow complaining in our family."

Offer choices: "When you stop complaining, then I'll be able to listen to what you have to say."

Teach your children to focus on the solution, not the blame. Complaining often is their way of placing blame elsewhere.

Use humor: In your most official voice, say something like, "This is an announcement of the National Complaint Broadcasting System. The Webb residence has now been declared a gripe-free zone. All violators will be prosecuted to the fullest extent of the law."

Try to get them to communicate more cooperatively by approaching them with observations: "I notice you're complaining a lot. If you want me to listen, you'll need to speak to me more constructively and with a positive attitude."

Role-play situations where first you and then they play the complainer.

CRYING INAPPROPRIATELY

WHY THEY DO IT

Children cry inappropriately because they want to get their way, they're tired or sick, they're overwhelmed, they want our attention, they want revenge, they feel helpless, or they don't know a better alternative. Children also have different personalities. Some are just more sensitive than others are.

LOGICAL CONSEQUENCES

If your children cry without good reason, just tell them, "That is not a good reason to cry. If you insist on doing it, leave my space and go cry where you won't be bothering anyone."

SOLUTIONS TOWARD SELF-DIRECTION

Sometimes it helps to acknowledge their feelings: "You seem so angry. It's so hard when your friends are mean. But I know you're clever enough to figure out a way to make everything OK."

Teach them ways to handle emotions like frustration without crying. Role-playing can help out here.

Raise your children to be independent by not doing everything for them, by not rescuing them from every difficulty, by allowing them to do increasingly difficult feats over time, and so on.

Never feel sorry for them, show sympathy, or give in to their demands when their crying is a manipulative ploy. Otherwise, they'll cry in an effort to manipulate external stimuli. This is an externally directed tactic.

Use impartial descriptions and give information: "You're crying over not getting your way again. It didn't seem to do any good yesterday."

Whether the crying is appropriate or not, you can combine impartial descriptions with a statement that you have faith in them to handle their own problems (and that problem is *not* going to be more important to you than to them) by saying something like, "Hmm. Looks like you have a problem. What have you decided to do about it?"

CULT INVOLVEMENT

WHY THEY DO IT

Some children join cults to experiment with their own philosophies, to rebel against conformity, or to take revenge on an over-controlling parent. Others seek strength in numbers. And the identity that they can't seem to find within themselves is readily offered to them on a silver platter by certain groups. Cults often use mind control and other methods of persuasion to lure new members. Once initiated, children are given protection, a sense of belonging, and something in which to believe.

LOGICAL CONSEQUENCES

If your children become involved in a cult, yank them out of it, for goodness' sakes! Freedom of expression has its limits when there are safety concerns. Anyway, cults usually impose the expression of beliefs on children by coercion.

Tighten up the supervision. Make their curfew much earlier, don't allow them to leave your sight without adult supervision, drive them to school and take them physically to class, veto any associations with their current friends, with whom they seem to be making bad choices, and so on. Tell them that the reins will be loosened when you feel more comfortable that they'll make healthier associations.

SOLUTIONS TOWARD SELF-DIRECTION

Let your children know what you find so unique and special about them. Tell them that you're proud of them just the way they are and that you feel so fortunate to be their parent. It's important for them to incorporate these ideas to reinforce their sense of self and to lend strength to that inner voice that tells them they don't need to search beyond their own skin to find what they need.

Be sure you're not too controlling. Excessive controlling can make them externally directed, which, in turn, makes them look to conformity with other groups for a sense of belonging.

Use impartial descriptions and information: "In our family, we don't let groups make us trade our individuality for religious philosophies."

Use questioning: "What's the purpose behind this group?" "Tell me what you find appealing in its philosophies." "What motivated you to join?" "Were you ever made to feel uncomfortable?" Often, their alliance is so paper-thin that when you get them to think about the details, it all falls apart.

Work with your children to build healthy peer associations, like joining the neighborhood basketball team, taking up a new skill, or getting involved in church youth organizations. Again, this involvement gives them the self-confidence they need to rely on their own opinions of who they are rather than on the opinions of others.

CURFEW BREAKING

WHY THEY DO IT

Children break their curfew because they lose track of time, are naïve enough to think they can get by with it, are having too much fun to call it quits, want to be treated as if they're older than they really are, or want to rebel against being over-controlled.

LOGICAL CONSEQUENCES

No matter what type of curfew your children break (using the telephone or returning home), they should automatically have their curfew time shortened by an hour or two for one week to one month, depending on how badly it has been broken. You can bypass this consequence if there was a reasonable excuse or if it's their first offense.

For repeat offenders, take away telephone privileges or ground them from leaving the house at night, depending on what type of curfew was broken.

SOLUTIONS TOWARD SELF-DIRECTION

Don't impose overly strict curfews. A lot depends on how responsible your children are, where they plan to go, how bad the crime is in your area, and so on.

Use impartial descriptions and give information: "You're using the telephone past your curfew."

Use questioning: "Until what time are you allowed to use the telephone?" "Why do you think we have that rule?" "What time is it now?"

Give choices: "Lisa, you can abide by our phone curfew, or I can remove the phone from your room." "Bob, when you show more respect for our phone curfew, you can get your phone privileges back."

Use humor: stick a picture of a phone in the throes of exhaustion (tongue hanging out and all) on their phone when curfew time approaches.

CURSING AND OTHER FORMS OF INAPPROPRIATE LANGUAGE

WHY THEY DO IT

Some children use profanity because they've heard it from others or because they want to appear tough and grown up. Some use it to express anger or to enlist our help.

LOGICAL CONSEQUENCES

If your children swear, ask them to leave the room and return only when they can use words that are acceptable. If your children are young and don't understand the meaning behind the words, tell them, "We don't use those kinds of words in our family."

Your children should be required to make amends with whoever was subjected to their foul mouth.

SOLUTIONS TOWARD SELF-DIRECTION

When your children utter curse words, never show surprise. That might be just the external reaction they're looking for. If you slip up and curse, apologize to them.

Offer choices: "When you can use appropriate language, then you can go back outside and play with your friends."

Use impartial descriptions and give information: "I notice you're cursing more since you've made friends with Richard." "Cursing is a disrespectful way of treating others."

Acknowledge your children's feelings if anger or frustration motivates them to curse: "I know how angry you must be that your team lost the game, but I'd like you to express your feelings without using foul language." Help your children come up with alternative words. Role-play this whenever they're in a situation that incited them to curse.

Ask your children if they understand the meaning behind the foul language. Discuss how specific words can affect others, especially words with sexual or racial overtones. They need this information to formulate the most effective internal dialogue in making decisions regarding their language.

DAWDLING AND PROCRASTINATING

WHY THEY DO IT

Although all children occasionally forget or get distracted, many dawdle or procrastinate to get attention, to shun failure, to avoid making choices, to gain control back from over-controlling parents, or to get revenge. It's a passive-aggressive tactic that allows them to get away with their bad choices in an underhanded way.

LOGICAL CONSEQUENCES

Let your children suffer the natural consequences that are sure to bite them in the behind when they procrastinate. Don't bail them out of the "incomplete" they get on their school assignments. Don't drive them to school when they miss the bus.

If their dawdling inconveniences you, have them pay you back in time. "You didn't take the garbage out in time, so I had to rush out with it when I heard the garbage truck in front of the house. That took fifteen minutes of my time. You owe me fifteen minutes of hard labor."

SOLUTIONS TOWARD SELF-DIRECTION

Show complete disinterest in their many excuses for falling behind or failing to finish something. Delegating such problems to others allows your children to wash their hands of it and, therefore, avoid contemplating the task internally.

Follow up on the requests you make to your children. For instance, suppose you ask them ten times to carry out the trash, which is met with "Later, Dad" each time. Then, you forget all about it, and Mom winds up hauling it out instead. You've just proved to them that procrastination is an effective way to get what they want!

Use impartial descriptions: "You haven't completed your book report, and it's due tomorrow. I'm sure Mrs. Withers gives zeroes for incomplete work."

Give choices: "When you've done your homework, then you can go outside and play."

Use questioning, "What makes it so hard for you to get your work done?" "Do you have a hard time beginning the work or finishing it?"

DEFIANCE

WHY THEY DO IT

Children defy us because they have their own minds (gosh darn, don't you just *hate* that?). They want to test their limits and power. Some defy us to counterattack being over-controlled or over-protected, to take revenge, or to avoid doing something unpleasant. Some defy us because they feel unfairly treated. And some defy us because they've been raised in a permissive environment and can get away with murder!

LOGICAL CONSEQUENCES

Anything other than logical consequences will often make defiant children worse, because they see punishment as a green light to retaliate with even *more* defiance.

Here's an appropriate logical consequence for a defiant child: If Billy refuses to hold your hand when you cross the street, say, "I'm not going to be able to take you to the store with me right now, because you're choosing to be unsafe. Maybe we can try again later." If Jane refuses to get into the car when the family's going out for pizza, say, "OK, since you've chosen not to come with us, I'll take you to Ms. Harris's next door. She can sit with you until we get back." Remember to use your most convincing "ho hum" attitude so your children know that you don't intend to take on their problems.

SOLUTIONS TOWARD SELF-DIRECTION

Pick your battles. Don't say "no" to their every request just to "be in charge." Saying "no" to every request will just turn you into an external influence your children feel compelled to rebel against.

Don't over-protect your children. This also incites externally directed rebellion among the natives.

Always speak respectfully to your children, and try not to have the last word all the time. Again, you're just setting yourself up as an external influence . . . an emotional punching bag for your children.

Create meaningful discipline. *Never* use physical punishment. Invite cooperation. For instance, if your children usually refuse to do their chores, ask them to supervise their younger siblings with *their* chores while they do their own. Give them the feeling that you sincerely need their help. Even the general statement, "I'm having a hard time and would really appreciate it if you'd help me out by cooperating" works well. It gives them a sense of power. If children feel they are needed—that they truly have a way to contribute to the pack—they will be cooperative.

Give your defiant children choices: "Do you want to come here now and unload the dishwasher, or would you like to do it after you eat breakfast?" This also gives them the power they seek.

Use impartial descriptions and information: "You are treating me badly. It doesn't make me feel like being around you."

Try not to tell your children what to do. Instead of saying, "Do your homework right now," say something like, "What are you supposed to do now that you've finished your afternoon snack?"

Let them be leaders whenever possible: "Tommy, can you be in charge of deciding where we go out for dinner tonight?" "John, can you help your brother with this difficult math problem?"

DEMANDING

WHY THEY DO IT

Children make demands because, in the case of permissive parenting, it gets them what they want, and in the case of over-controlling parenting, it's their way of expressing rebellion and anger. Sometimes children make demands because they lack the skills necessary to satisfy those demands themselves. And some children just have bad manners.

We'll address five types of demands: demanding undue attention, demanding service, demanding immediate gratification, demanding indulgence (designer fashions, etc.), and demanding things (toys, candy, etc.).

LOGICAL CONSEQUENCES

Demanding undue attention

If your children demand undue attention, be sure that's exactly what they *won't* get. Let their request for unreasonable attention be *their* problem at all times. If you need to close yourself up in another room or take a walk outside, so be it.

Demanding service

Just don't do it unless they ask nicely and can't take care of their request themselves. Of course it's OK to do things for them, even when they're *able* to do them on their own, because that's just one way of showing them that we love them. But everything in moderation, folks. So when Johnny says, "Get me some cereal, now," reply, "I like helping you best when I feel eager to, and when you make demands like that, I don't exactly feel like bending over backward for you."

Demanding immediate gratification

If your children demand something right away, that should be immediate grounds for their *not* getting what they want. Let them know that if they had made their request politely and reasonably, their chances would have been a heck of a lot better.

If your children have a problem with immediate gratification with their personal purchases, impose a two-week minimum between their having a desire and satisfying it.

Demanding indulgence

If your children demand the best, don't give it to them, for goodness' sakes! Teach children the art and beauty of simplicity, and the value of money. Kids need to learn that they won't get everything they want in life.

Demanding things

If your children get the gimmes, take them away from the source of temptation. If you're at the toy store, toss 'em in the car and go home. If you're in the grocery store, out they go. If they make demands, ensure that they won't get what they want.

SOLUTIONS TOWARD SELF-DIRECTION

Demanding undue attention

Foster independence by giving children tasks that require a higher and higher skill level as they get older. Don't do everything for them.

Use questioning: "How do you think I feel when you want me to pay attention to you constantly?" "What can you do to take care of your own needs now?"

Use impartial descriptions and give information: "You seem to be wanting your brother to play with you all the time. He's getting frustrated, because he has things he needs to do on his own."

Use humor: Grab your throat, gasp for air, and make horrible gurgling sounds. Between your gasps, tell them there's a huge squid covering your face (them) sucking the life out of you.

Demanding service

Encourage them to take care of their request themselves. "The milk fairy is off today. See what you can do to help yourself out," or "You're such a big boy, I bet you can figure out a way to pour your own milk."

Train your children in skills that are age-appropriate. If you do things for them all the time, they'll never learn to do them on their own. Guide them to meet their own demands by using questions:

Tom: *"I want a glass of milk!"*

Dad: *"What do you need to do to get it?"*

Tom: *"But there's no more clean glasses!"*
Dad: *"What can you do with the dirty glass?"*
Tom: *"I can wash it, I guess."*
Dad: *"Great! Do you want me to help you get the milk out of the fridge, since it's so heavy?"*

Try using impartial descriptions and giving information: "We ask for things politely in our family." "You aren't asking for your request; you're demanding it."

Use humor: play the part of an exhausted servant, repeatedly uttering something like, "Yes sir, anything else, sir?" between gasps of air.

Demanding immediate gratification

If your children demand immediate gratification, teach them patience. Walk through the reasoning process with them. "Why do you want that stereo so badly?" "What if you find something else you want, and you've spent all of your money?" If they make the purchase, ask them later if they have any regrets, if they still enjoy it as much as they did at first, etc.

Use impartial descriptions and give information: "You just bought those roller skates last week, and you haven't touched them for days." "When we wait a couple of weeks before purchasing anything expensive, sometimes we wind up realizing it isn't what we wanted."

Demanding indulgence

Let your children know that your job is to clothe them, not to decorate them. If they want designer fashions, they'll have to cough up the difference.

Try questioning: "Is there a lot of pressure to have designer clothes nowadays? Is that really a good thing?"

Use impartial descriptions and give information: "There are lots of less expensive bikes that look really cool, and that extra dough could go to some other purchase later."

Teach them early on to be responsible and practical with money. I like the idea of giving teenagers a monthly allowance out of which comes everything but room and board. Haircuts, clothing, fast food meals, school supplies, gas, car insurance, movie tickets, etc.—all come out of their pocket. Trust me, they'll think twice about buying $120 tennis shoes.

Demanding things

Before you go anywhere that might tempt your children to come down with a severe case of the gimmes, lay down some rules in advance: "We're going to the toy store to buy a birthday present for your friend. If you ask me for a toy, we'll have to go home right away. Otherwise, we can spend a little extra time looking."

For them to stop making demands, you *must* stop giving in to them. Your giving, giving, giving is a dangerous external influence.

Use questioning: "How would you feel if someone always asked you to buy things for them?"

Give choices: "When you stop having the gimmes, then you can come shopping with me again." "If you refuse to stop begging for candy, then I will have to take you right home."

Try humor: "The magic genie no longer lives here. Your requests cannot be filled."

Use impartial descriptions and give information: "You always ask for candy in the checkout lane, despite the fact that I never give in." "We don't allow the gimmes in our family." "Begging for things is rude and annoying."

DESTRUCTION OF PROPERTY

WHY THEY DO IT

Children who go out of their way to destroy the property of others do so when they feel powerless, angry, or vengeful.

LOGICAL CONSEQUENCES

Children should be required to restore to its original condition any property they destroy. This means using a scrub brush to clean the graffiti on the wall, earning the money to buy a new vase to replace the one they knocked over with their ball, and so on. Encourage your children to apologize for their actions.

SOLUTIONS TOWARD SELF-DIRECTION

Try to understand your children's feelings: "You're so angry with your sister. I feel like that sometimes. But use your words instead of breaking the heads off of her Barbie dolls next time."

Teach your children better ways to express anger. Relaxation techniques like meditation might help. You can also role-play situations that would typically ruffle their feathers.

Use impartial descriptions and give information: "You broke my tape recorder. That upsets me. I've had it for a long time." "Breaking other people's things makes them very angry."

Use questioning: "What made you want to break Sally's CD player?" "How would you feel if someone broke yours?"

Offer choices: "If you insist on coloring on our new furniture, then I can't allow you to play with your crayons."

DISRESPECT

WHY THEY DO IT

Children show disrespect because they want to test their limits and explore the extent of their power over us. Some show disrespect because we model disrespect in our own behavior. Some use it as a way to rebel against over-controlling parents. And some do so because we've let them get away with it in the past.

LOGICAL CONSEQUENCES

When your children talk back, act disrespectfully, or show any other form of rudeness in their behavior, don't let them get by with it. Say something like, "I will not listen to your inconsiderate words. You'll have to leave the room and come back when you can behave nicely."

Have them make amends for their rude behavior.

SOLUTIONS TOWARD SELF-DIRECTION

Reword their disrespectful statements as in this example:

Richard: *"I hate it when you don't let me play outside late."*

Mom: *"I can't play out late, Mom? OK, thanks anyway."*

Try using impartial descriptions and giving information: "I noticed you didn't answer Mrs. Hardin when she asked how you were doing. She seemed offended by your lack of respect."

Offer choices: "You can either show respect to Tommy's parents, or not be allowed to play there anymore." "When you learn to show respect to the librarian, Mrs. Godfrey, then you can return to the library."

DRESSING HASSLES

WHY THEY DO IT

Some children use choosing their clothes as an excuse to create a power struggle. Some have problems with a heightened sense of touch. You know those little bumps on the inside toe line of their socks? They feel like Mount Everest to these kids. And their clothing is either too tight around the waist or too baggy. So they wear the one article of clothing they *do* like over and over, day after day.

Some wear crazy clothing combinations because they just haven't developed fashion sense. Other kids wear zany getups because they have their own unique fashion sense that no one else in the *entire* world seems to have.

LOGICAL CONSEQUENCES

If your children have dressing fits in the morning, don't make it your problem.

Let children wear anything they want as long as it's clean and appropriate to the weather. If they refuse, tell them something like, "Well, Harry, I guess you don't want to go out after all. It's unsanitary to wear something filthy, so you'll just have to stay home until you're ready to put on something that doesn't stand up on its own."

If your children choose an article of clothing at the store but then, two months later, say they'll never wear it because they hate it, have them pay for the original cost out of their own pocket.

SOLUTIONS TOWARD SELF-DIRECTION

Help your children develop their own fashion sense by looking through magazines together, modeling different styles in your own clothing, pointing out the creative combinations others wear, and so on.

Never make fun of their clothing choices. It's all a matter of opinion, and they certainly don't need their own fashion taste belittled such that they no longer trust in themselves. If their peers mock them for those choices, empathize with them, but remind them how important individuality is. What other's think about our external appearance should not shape our ideas about fashion.

Appreciate and respect your children's desire to be creative in the way that they dress. Don't make them change just because you're afraid other people might think you've got terrible fashion sense or are a bad parent.

Try giving your children choices if they have trouble deciding what to wear. "Do you want to wear your pink culottes or your blue jumper today?"

Don't nag your children to get dressed in the morning. They have to learn to develop their own "internal nagging mechanism." If they're late for school because they couldn't get dressed in time, that's something they'll have to reckon with.

Use impartial descriptions and give information: "I see you're not dressed yet. I wonder if you'll have time to eat breakfast before the bus comes." "Wearing filthy clothes is unsanitary."

Use humor: "That shirt you've had on for the last week is starting to develop a personality. Have you picked out any names for it yet?"

Involve your children in the decision-making when you buy them new clothes. Have them try each article of clothing on to be sure they approve of the way it feels and looks on their *bodies*, not just on the hanger.

EATING HASSLES

WHY THEY DO IT

Let's consider four categories: anorexia/bulimia, over-eating, craving sweets, and being picky. Recent scientific evidence implicates genetic factors as one possible determinant in eating disorders. But many children become anorexic or bulimic in satisfying the world's standard of beauty, as a form of self-loathing, or as a way to get attention. Children over-eat to satisfy feelings of sadness, frustration, or boredom. Children drive us nuts over sweets because they know we use sweets as control tactics (not to mention the fact that those Twinkies taste so darn good!). Children can be picky eaters because they can rope us in with their fussiness.

LOGICAL CONSEQUENCES

If your child suffers from anorexia or bulimia, take her to a professional who specializes in this disorder. If your child is an over-eater, limit the foods you keep in your house to highly nutritious ones. Monitor what he or she packs for lunch. Forbid sodas and sweets until a more healthful weight is reached.

Logical consequences won't work for children that go gaga over sweets. Removing its power to control is the way to go. See below.

If your child is a habitually picky eater, so what! His body is much smarter than *we* are and will tell him when to shovel it in. Never make it an issue. But by the same token, if he doesn't eat whatever's on his plate, he can forget about dessert. His next chance to eat will come with the family's next meal.

SOLUTIONS TOWARD SELF-DIRECTION

De-emphasize the importance of body image, and don't model this obsession in your own behavior.

Never use food to control, or it will become a strong external influence for your children. This approach means not withholding treats and sweets as a punishment and not using them as rewards or bribes. In the case of the sweet tooth, the best approach is to never start giving them sweets at all. If you're like me and the horse is already out of the barn, you can try a little trick that worked great for our family. I filled up one of my kitchen drawers with loads of candy and told my kids that they could dig in as much as they wanted as long as it was at least two hours before the next meal. When they'd come home from school, they'd be foaming at the mouth like rabid bats, clawing through the candy drawer and stuffing their faces almost before they could take the wrappers off. That lasted two weeks. Now that they know that their candy consumption is not a focus of my control, they couldn't care less. They go for more nutritious food items instead.

Teach your over-eater how to deal with emotions in ways other than eating. See if you can help them recognize the triggers that motivate them to dig into the Häagen-Dazs.

Get your picky eaters involved in the family's meal planning. Invite them to help cook and decorate the table, too. Even a three year old can contribute in some way.

FIDGETING

WHY THEY DO IT

Children *love* moving their bodies. After all, they haven't had them very long and aren't bored yet with the "let's see what this does" concept.

Many children are "kinesthetic" by nature. That means those little cogwheels in their heads turn better when they move their bodies. For instance, two of my children always had to twirl around in circles as I called out their spelling words. I'd have to take a Dramamine every Thursday.

LOGICAL CONSEQUENCES

So let 'em fidget, already. What harm can it do? This is a perfect example of the "pick your battles" philosophy. If you find it distracting, either stop what you're doing and watch them (it's highly entertaining, actually) or encourage them to go elsewhere.

SOLUTIONS TOWARD SELF-DIRECTION

Let your children know that there's a time and place for even the best of things, and teach them to be aware of places where their excessive movements might disturb others.

Use impartial descriptions and give information: "Fidgeting is all right only if it doesn't bother others." "Your fidgeting seems to be distracting those people at the next table."

Tell the sibling who isn't fidgeting something like, "Sally, you're sitting so quietly here in the restaurant. I know the couple in the next booth must appreciate that." Then, watch the others straighten up like magic. And remark on those rare times that your fidgeter does sit quietly: "Timmy, you're sitting so nicely at the table. It seems like we've been able to have nicer talks together when you behave this way."

FORGETFULNESS

WHY THEY DO IT

Children just have other things on their minds, sometimes. Not only that, if we do too much *for* them, they won't learn to handle responsibilities requiring them to remember things. And hey, everyone forgets.

LOGICAL CONSEQUENCES

If forgetting is a habit, let your children face the repercussions. For instance, if they forget to take their lunch to school more than two or three times during any given school year, stop bailing them out. Call the school office to request they don't lend your children any lunch money; you want them to experience a few hunger pangs. Their hunger pangs will help them remember next time.

SOLUTIONS TOWARD SELF-DIRECTION

It's all right to show them empathy: "Gosh, I'm sorry to hear you forgot your homework. I used to get so frustrated with myself whenever that happened to me."

Don't let your children use the ol' "I forgot" line as a way of getting out of things they don't like to do. This avoidance is just a rationalization ploy that then breeds self-deception.

Use humor: go up to your kid and, without saying a word, tie little strings on all his or her fingers.

Use questioning: "What can you do to help yourself remember your homework assignments?" "What happens when you forget to turn in one of them?" "How do you feel when this happens?"

Use impartial descriptions: "You don't seem to have any strategies to remember your babysitting commitments. Perhaps I can help you come up with some that worked for me."

Use choices: "You can try to come up with ways to organize yourself so that you don't forget your Girl Scout meetings, or you need to quit altogether."

Friend Hassles

Why they do it

Some friend hassles include fights, getting into mischief with friends, experiencing peer pressure, associating with the wrong crowd, and finding abusive friends. Kids get into these kinds of trouble because people are different. They have different beliefs and opinions, and when they're young, they tend to want others to go along with everything they say and believe. So friends fight. And because there's strength and pressure in numbers, friends tend to get each other into mischief. It takes children years of practice to figure out what type of friend they'll mesh well with from the standpoint of likes, dislikes, personalities, communication styles, and plain old chemistry.

LOGICAL CONSEQUENCES

If your children have the usual conflict with their friends, stay out of it. Don't come to their rescue. The spats themselves serve as a natural consequence.

If your children get into mischief with a certain friend or group, forbid the association for awhile. Say something like, "I can't let you hang out with Bobby until I feel sure that you're going to learn how to make better choices when you're with him."

If your children buckle under the stress of peer pressure, let them feel whatever natural consequences are sure to arise, and forbid the association for awhile. For instance, if they buy liquor with a fake ID, have them return it to the owner of the store with an apology. Never blame the peer group, though. Tell them they made bad choices *in the presence* of those friends, not *because* of them.

If your children pick friends that are mean, controlling, or abusive, let them handle it on their own rather than rescuing them. If their association causes more serious problems like engaging your children in activities that are illegal, immoral, or dangerous, intercede by forbidding the relationship. Who knows? Your children might even thank you for it.

SOLUTIONS TOWARD SELF-DIRECTION

Show empathy with statements like, "I know how much you value your friendship with Katie. It must have hurt your feelings when she teased you like that." Share your own friendship horror stories so that they know they're not alone.

Role-play scenarios involving peer pressure, arguments, ostracism, etc.

Verbalize how you work out any conflicts that might come up from time to time with your own friends.

Never criticize your children's choice in friends. If a friend is not right for them, they'll figure it out soon enough. Never interfere when a friend comes over to play but leaves out your child's other siblings. Again, have faith that they can all work it out on their own.

Teach them the finer arts of being a good friend, traits like taking care of their feelings and being loyal. This knowledge is important for the development of the internal dialogue necessary to make the right choices.

Never force your children to make up with their friends. If they ask for your help in mediating conflict resolution, that's fine.

Offer choices: "You can make good choices with Sally now, or choose to play with her when you can." "If you can't keep from breaking the rules when you're around Sam and Mike, then you'll have to find some friends around whom you can make better decisions."

Try using impartial descriptions and giving information: "We value friendships in our family." "We should all learn to value our own opinions and ideas even above those of our friends." "I see you and Josh are not getting along lately. You're resourceful; I know you'll find a way to make things right again."

Use questioning: "Why are you and Sarah not getting along?" "Can you think of any way that you could have handled your part in the problem differently?" "What do you plan to do about it?" In the case of peer pressure and mischief: "What are the rules about destroying other people's property?" "What made you feel you had to do what your friends told you to do?" "What do you think they would've said if you refused?"

Gang Involvement

Why they do it

Some children join gangs to rebel against conformity, to gain a feeling of power, to take revenge on an over-controlling parent, or to seek the sense of belonging they don't get at home. They seek strength in numbers bound together against a common enemy.

Logical consequences

If your children become involved in a gang, forbid that involvement, for goodness' sakes!

The logical consequences for gang-involvement mirror those for cults. See "Cult Involvement" in this section.

Solutions toward self-direction

Gang and cult involvement call for the same solutions. See "Cult Involvement" for details.

Have your ex-gang member give talks to local middle schools and high schools. They can also sign up for community service to fix some of the gang-related damages that have occurred in the neighborhood, like graffiti or broken windows.

Getting into Things That Don't Belong to Them

Why they do it

The grass is always greener in their parents' and siblings' rooms.

Logical consequences

Teach your children that others' personal property needs to be respected. If children break this rule, they should be made to compensate their "victims" in some way. If one of my children breaks my lipstick, we take their allowance and go to the store to buy a replacement. (Actually, all of my lipsticks are beheaded now. It must be a hard lesson to learn.) If they mess with a sibling's possession without permission, they pay something in return for the unauthorized "rental." Personal apologies are always warranted, too.

SOLUTIONS TOWARD SELF-DIRECTION

Use questioning: "Why did you find it necessary to go through your sister's diary?" "How do you think she feels about it right now?" "How would *you* feel if someone pried into your personal possessions?" "What do you intend to do to make things all right between you?"

Respect your children's private property, too. Don't get into *their* stuff without permission.

Use impartial descriptions and give information: "Getting into other people's things makes them angry." "It's difficult to trust someone who gets into personal property without permission." "I noticed you got into my bath salts without asking me. I'm going to find it hard to trust you for awhile. What are you going to do to earn back my trust?"

Try giving them choices: "If you continue to get into my makeup drawer, then I'll have to place a lock on that drawer at your expense."

Use humor: put a sign on their door that reads something like, "Come one, come all. Fire sale. All items must go. First come, first served."

GOING SOMEWHERE OTHER THAN WHERE THEY SAID

WHY THEY DO IT

Teenagers, in particular, think that they're more grown up than their parents think they are, and they feel as if they have to lie to be able to expand their responsibilities and privileges into the uncharted territory. Sometimes, though, they're just up to no good.

LOGICAL CONSEQUENCES

If your children go somewhere other than the place they told you they'd be, they shouldn't be allowed to go anywhere at all for awhile until you feel they've regained your trust.

SOLUTIONS TOWARD SELF-DIRECTION

Never punish your children when they tell the truth, because then they learn that the truth can be painful and must be avoided at all costs. Makes for some mighty sneaky kids. Don't be too controlling. Kids need to have the freedom to mess up and be less than perfect if they are to become willing to own up to their mistakes, both internally and externally.

Use questioning: "Is there anything I'm doing that makes it difficult for you to come clean about where you'll be?"

Use impartial descriptions and give information: "I found out you went to the ice cream store at midnight instead of staying at Josh's house like you promised. It's dangerous in that area late at night. You and Josh could have gotten hurt." "Lying makes it hard for people to trust you." "Telling the truth not only takes courage, but it gives you a sense of freedom and relief."

Offer choices: "When you show me that I can trust you, then you can have some of your social privileges back."

GROWING UP TOO SOON (MAKEUP, DRESS, DATING, SEX, ETC.)
WHY THEY DO IT

Children don't want anyone to think they're "babies." Wearing makeup, having a love interest, dressing seductively, and so on elevate their status in the eyes of their peers.

LOGICAL CONSEQUENCES

Create ground rules for what dress and behavior are appropriate for each age. Once you do, stick to them. No dating until they're fifteen, no makeup until they're thirteen, etc.

If your children break these rules, take the forbidden makeup away if they use it. If they have a boyfriend or girlfriend when they're too young, make their curfew earlier, suspend them from parties for awhile, remove their phone privileges, and so on.

SOLUTIONS TOWARD SELF-DIRECTION

Tell your children it's OK to be a child. I let my kids know that children have wonderful qualities that I'd love to see in more adults, like expressiveness, openness, and optimism.

Don't push it! Those kids will grow up soon enough. I see parents encouraging their fourth graders to have girl/boy dance parties. What are they thinking? And seemingly innocent comments like, "You look so grown up in that dress, Sally" make growing up ahead of schedule something your children think they should do to win your approval.

Let your children know that the message to be sexually appealing before they're ready for sex is flawed. Tell them that the overemphasis on sex in our culture is not about love, but about power, image, and domination.

Examine your rules. Are you being too strict with your limits? If my husband had his way, he'd forbid our daughters to date until they're thirty-five years old. Remember, rules have to make sense if our children are going to internalize and comply with them.

Talk to your children openly about sexuality. You want your children to feel completely free to talk about this subject. You might need to explain the sexual rationale behind certain types of makeup and clothing. Once an eleven year old understands the origins behind the use of blush, she'd probably think it's pretty gross and drop it like a hot potato.

If your rule is no premarital sex, don't then condone sexual irresponsibility by buying them condoms or putting them on the birth control pill "just in case" when they're fifteen. If it's not allowed, it's not allowed.

Talk about your own misadventures in trying to grow up too soon, including any regrets. Children can learn a lot from the experiences of others without reinventing the wheel.

Use questioning: "What do you think wearing lipstick without permission does to the trust between us?" "Is there anything I'm doing that makes it difficult for you to talk to me about the rules we have about these things?" "What do you plan to do to help me regain my trust in you?"

Use choices: If there are friends that continually coax them into doing things that are beyond their level of maturity, forbid the association. "If you can't make better choices when you're around Lisa, then I can't let you hang out with her anymore."

HELPLESSNESS

WHY THEY DO IT

Children put on the helpless act because they want our attention, they want to control or manipulate us, they want revenge, they want to get out of doing something they don't want to do, or they truly need our help.

LOGICAL CONSEQUENCES

If your children can really manage the skill, don't get sucked into their problem. Just say something like, "I see you're having trouble. You're a clever boy, though, so I bet you'll come up with a solution in no time."

Let your children experience the consequence: If they're too "helpless" to pack a school lunch, they go to school without it. If they're too "helpless" to go upstairs and find their sweater, they go to school as a human Popsicle. If they're too "helpless" to put on their shoes, say something like, "We can go to the park once your shoes are on. How much time are you going to need? If it's going to be longer than five minutes, I can pour myself another cup of coffee." Ho hum.

SOLUTIONS TOWARD SELF-DIRECTION

Never ridicule or punish your children for acting helpless. Doing so will make them focus on external factors for their choices.

If they genuinely need your help, don't let them whine those infamous four words, "I can't do it." Have them say something like, "I need some help, please." This way, they reflect internally on what they can do right, not what they can't do at all. So they focus on their partial independence rather than their complete dependence. Then, see if you can get them to do at least those parts of the task they *can* manage.

Foster independence in your children by letting them accomplish small feats early on. Don't do things for them that they can learn to do on their own.

Give them choices: "When you've found your jacket, then you can go outside and play in the snow." "If you finish cleaning up that mess, you'll have more time to play at Sally's house."

Use questioning: "What are our rules about buckling your seat belt?" "You were able to manage yesterday, what's different today?"

Use humor: When they act helpless, hand them a pair of crutches or a stack of bandages. Pick them up and carry them around, everywhere. As they giggle, tell them you feel sorry for helpless little jellyfish and can't help but come to their rescue. (Then insist they try the task again, of course.)

Homework Hassles

Why they do it

Children hate spending seven hours in school only to come home and face book reports, math problems, and geography projects. And the effect these homework hassles have on their parents becomes e-ticket entertainment that allows them to put off the drudgery. Some kids thrive on the negative attention. Occasionally, though, children wage homework wars because they're struggling in school.

Logical consequences

The worst you can do is plead, beg, nag, yell, and punish your children. If, by some unexplained miracle, such tactics work, it's because they don't want to be punished anymore, not because they want to fulfill their responsibility. Just keep that "ho hum" attitude alive and kicking, and let logical consequences take over, as in this example:

> Johnny: *"Mom, I hate homework! I'm not going to do it."*
> *(His ruse for trying to get you to help.)*
> Mom: *"I'm sorry you feel that way. If there's something you don't understand, let me know if I can help. Otherwise, you'll just have to take your problem up with Ms. Wadsworth in the morning."*
> Johnny: *"Oh fine, I'll do it! But I don't understand this one long-division problem. Can you show me how to start it?"*

The same thing goes for when they forget to bring home the things that they need to do their homework, when they fail to complete an assignment, and so on. Don't bail them out!

Give them choices: "When you've finished your homework, then you and Billy can go outside and play." "If you finish your homework by 5:00, you'll have time to watch your favorite show before dinner."

Use questioning: "What are our rules about finishing homework by five?" "Why are you watching TV instead?" "What do you need to do now to comply with those rules?"

Use impartial descriptions and information: "I see it's 4:30 and you haven't started your homework. It needs to be completed before supper." Or if they do their homework hassle-free, say something like, "I see you're finished with your homework already. That gives you more time to play before dinner!"

Use humor: act the part of a ruthless torturer, shine a bright light in their faces, and say something like, "Vee have vays of making you do your homeverk!"

ILLNESS (FAKING IT)

WHY THEY DO IT

Children fake illness to get attention and to get out of things they don't enjoy, especially schoolwork.

LOGICAL CONSEQUENCES

If you're certain your child is faking illness to get out of something, say something like, "You're perfectly fine, Lukas. Get dressed and eat before you miss the bus. It's a pretty hot day for walking to school."

SOLUTIONS TOWARD SELF-DIRECTION

Never reward your children when they *are* sick by buying them gifts or overdoing the kissie, huggie thing and so on. This doting makes them internalize the idea that illness equals love and affection, and it teaches them a manipulative tactic. External direction at its best (or worst).

Find out what your children are trying to avoid. For example, if they're having a hard time with one of their school subjects, discuss this difficulty with their teacher and set aside some extra time to help them master it. If there's a social problem like a bully who's teasing them, help them find ways to form a truce or resolve the conflict in some other way. Role-play the situation with them until they feel confident that they can work things out on their own.

Questioning also works: "You don't seem sick enough to skip school. Is there something you're trying to avoid? What will happen if you keep avoiding it—will the problem eventually go away?" "What can happen if you continue to miss school this often?"

INTERRUPTING

WHY THEY DO IT

Children interrupt because they haven't learned to be patient, they want to get our attention, they feel their importance is threatened when we focus on someone else, and, let's face it, we often let them get away with it.

LOGICAL CONSEQUENCES

If your children interrupt, tell them to leave the room until you're finished talking. Take them out bodily if you must, and then lock the door until you're finished with your conversation.

SOLUTIONS TOWARD SELF-DIRECTION

Let them know in advance when you have an important phone call, and ask them what they plan to do to keep themselves busy during that time. This preparation helps them internally reflect upon how to control their "urgus interruptus" reflex.

Role-play interrupting with your children. Ask them to talk about their day, and while they do so, talk to them about yours. It'll drive them crazy. Follow up by asking them whether they found it difficult to concentrate on what they were saying while you were talking.

Give them choices: "When I've finished with this conversation, I will be able to give you my full attention."

Use questioning: "What are our rules about interrupting?" "How do you think that makes me feel?" "How do you think the person I'm talking with feels?"

Use impartial descriptions and information: "Interrupting is rude. It's difficult to talk and listen at the same time." If they don't interrupt, say, "You didn't interrupt me this time when I was talking on the phone, so I was able to wrap things up quickly. Now we have time to have that picnic in the park!"

JEALOUSY

WHY THEY DO IT

By the time our children are eighteen months old, they start scoping out the relationships we have with other people. At twenty-four months, they get wise to the idea that these distractions might put limits on our availability. They think that there's only so much of us that can go around. Flashing red lights. Alarms. Whistles. Panic. And every time someone *new* enters that equation, they have to scramble to find a new role or niche.

LOGICAL CONSEQUENCES

It's one thing to feel jealous but another to act on it. If they hit, yell, or torture those they're jealous of, make them leave the room—or at least separate them from the other child.

SOLUTIONS TOWARD SELF-DIRECTION

Give children appropriate roles and contributions within the family so they feel that they belong. If a new sibling is involved, find a role that takes the older child's seniority into account. Don't compare your children to their siblings or peers, or they'll react to others as external influences through resentment and jealousy.

Teach them strategies to help dispel their feelings of jealousy. My favorite is to have them visualize the person they're jealous of as a newborn baby or an extremely old person. They can also try to find something good about that person.

Discuss those times you've had feelings of jealousy and how you chose to handle them.

Find ways to gain cooperation between your children and those of whom they're jealous. For instance, have them put up the Halloween decorations together, letting the one who's jealous have a supervising role of some sort.

Teach your children that we all have strengths and weaknesses. It's OK for Mary to be better at math and our child to be better at reading. Instead of being jealous of Mary's math prowess, encourage your child to help Mary with her reading and, in return, seek Mary's help in math.

Role-play situations that you know make your children jealous. The point of the exercise should be to learn that it's OK to feel jealous but not OK to act those feelings out in a hurtful way.

Give choices: "You can either behave nicely with Bobby, or we can have him go home and come back to play another day." Try questioning: "Why do you feel so jealous of David?" "Does acting on your jealousy make things better or worse?" "What kind of things can you think about that will help you handle your feeling of jealousy?"

Use impartial descriptions and give information: "Everyone has unique strengths. It's impossible to compare two people based on one particular strong point." "Jealousy can destroy friendships." "I noticed you felt envious of Mary's new party dress. Since she's your friend, maybe it would help you to think about how much joy she gets out of wearing it. I know you like your friends to be happy."

LAZINESS

WHY THEY DO IT

Children are lazy because they want to engage us in a power struggle, they want attention, they want to avoid something, or they're used to having everything done for them.

LOGICAL CONSEQUENCES

Let your children experience the natural consequences of laziness. If they don't do their laundry, they're stuck wearing stinky, dirty clothes in which they won't be allowed out of the house. If they don't clean their rooms, they'll have a hard time finding their belongings.

If your children balk at helping out in cooperative tasks, like cleaning up the dinner dishes, make them do the entire chore by themselves.

SOLUTIONS TOWARD SELF-DIRECTION

Give your children plenty of age-appropriate responsibilities early on. Don't take over a job that your children are too lazy to do. Make them finish it before they're allowed to do anything else. Show them how to make even the most tedious chores fun.

Let them know that the family genuinely needs their contribution to the household chores. "I need you to set the table so we can eat. I'm busy making the gravy, so that would really help me out." Afterward, tell them how much you appreciate their effort.

Provide information: "Working hard can make a person feel satisfied and valuable." "Not contributing to the daily family work responsibilities can make people feel unproductive and can make those around them resentful."

Make observations when they've done something they didn't want to do: "Look at that, you've mowed the lawn so well! I don't see any missed spots!"

LOSING THINGS
WHY THEY DO IT

Children lose things because they've got the attention spans of pygmy gnats. They leave their backpacks on the bus while they're talking to Josh about karate class. They lose their library book because the last place they read it was on the swing set in the backyard three very rainy days ago. And anyway, we all lose things on occasion.

LOGICAL CONSEQUENCES

If your children lose things all the time, the natural consequences will kick in as long as we don't jump to their rescue. If they lose one of their belongings, they have three choices: they can find it, buy a new one, or do without it. If they lose someone else's possessions, they also have three choices: they can find it, buy a new one, or get slam-dunked by a very angry ex-owner.

SOLUTIONS TOWARD SELF-DIRECTION

Show empathy: "I know how you feel. I lost my purse once, and it was so frustrating to go through the hassle of replacing all of my credit cards and my driver's license."

Use questioning: "Why do you think you frequently misplace things?" "Could there be some system you can use to keep that from happening so much?" "How does losing things make you feel?"

Choices work well when they lose possessions belonging to others: "When you are better about not losing things, then I'll let you borrow my books."

Use impartial descriptions and information: "You seem to lose things a lot. If you wish, I can share some of the tricks I use to help me remember where I put things." "There are lots of techniques you can use to keep from losing things."

It's OK to help them look for whatever they lost, as long as you never make finding it more urgent to you than to them.

LYING

WHY THEY DO IT

Children lie to escape reprimand, disapproval, rejection, ridicule, and shame. Some feel trapped or threatened, some don't want to disappoint other people with their bad choices, and some don't want to hurt the feelings of people they care about.

LOGICAL CONSEQUENCES

If your children are obviously telling a lie, let them know that you're not falling for it. Say something like, "I don't buy that story. Take care of your problem right away."

SOLUTIONS TOWARD SELF-DIRECTION

Never put your children in the position where they feel they have no other choice but to lie. For instance, if you find your two children near a wall freshly decorated with crayon scribbling, don't ask, "Who's responsible for this?" I mean, do you really expect one of them to eagerly jump forward to fess up? I don't *think* so! So, just make *both* of them take care of it by saying, "I want you both to take a bucket of water and a sponge and clean this up right away." By going about it in this way, you teach them to focus on the solution rather than on the blame. If the "innocent" ones protest, tell them they should have helped the other one stay out of trouble. Children need to learn to be responsible for taking care of others instead of having that "look out for number one" attitude that's so tragically commonplace today.

Use "I notice" statements instead of "Did you" questions. The latter just serve to catch them in a lie, especially if you already know the answer. So instead of asking, "Have you taken the trash out?" say, "I notice the trash hasn't been taken out. That needs to be done right away."

Show appreciation when they tell you the truth.

Use questioning: "Why do you think people lie?" "What can the consequences be for lying?" "What is the worst that can happen if you tell the truth?" "How do you feel when someone you trusted lies to you?"

Use impartial descriptions and give information: "Lying makes it hard to trust you." "You aren't being honest with me. Let me give you a few minutes to think it through, and we'll talk about this again honestly." "I don't believe in punishing someone for being truthful."

Make truthfulness part of the family identity: "We believe in telling the truth in our family."

MANIPULATIVE BEHAVIOR
WHY THEY DO IT

Children learn to manipulate when we give in to their demands—whether it's capitalizing on the parent-parent disagreements, "sucking up," whining, begging, or quivering their lower lip. Some use manipulation to seek revenge, and others will manipulate us when their requests are consistently denied for no good reason.

Logical consequences

Assure them that whatever they were trying to accomplish with such manipulative tactics isn't gonna happen—*because* of those tactics.

Solutions toward self-direction

Never give in to the demands of a manipulator.

Check your parenting style. Are you saying "no" just to dominate, control, or exercise your authority? If so, you're inviting external direction and manipulation.

Reword your children's manipulative statements using more direct language. When they say, "Tommy's mom is so nice. She gave him a brand-new skateboard! Boy is he ever lucky," you can say, "Mom, can you buy me a new skateboard?" Let them know that it's OK to be direct and that the worst that can happen is you'll say "no," whereas manipulative ploys will definitely mean their wants won't be fulfilled.

Use questioning: "What is it that you're *really* trying to say?"

Give information: "Being straightforward takes courage, and it helps people trust us." "Deception creates a lack of trust."

Use impartial descriptions: "You're not being direct with me. I like it when we can be open with one another."

Try offering choices: "Either be open and honest with me, or talk to me when you can."

Show your children that you're more willing to help them realize their goals when they ask for what they want in a sincere fashion.

If your children ask you for something that the other parent has already vetoed, say something like, "That's between your father and you. Leave me out of it." If, say, you tell your children to brush their teeth, and they come back with, "Daddy says I never have to brush my teeth on Saturdays," tell them, "I'm in charge right now, not your father." When you do have disagreements about child-rearing issues, don't argue about them in front of your children or sabotage the other parent's authority in any way. Children can easily adapt to different parenting styles and philosophies. In fact, it's healthy for them to come to the realization that people in the world *do* have different opinions about things, and that's OK.

MANNERS (THE LACK OF)

WHY THEY DO IT

Children show a lack of common courtesy because some are never taught manners, some are exposed to discourteous role models, and some just plain forget.

LOGICAL CONSEQUENCES

If your children don't say "please," then don't do as they ask. If they forget to say "thank you," then take whatever they should have been thankful for away from them until they do so. If they show bad table manners, have them leave the table until they can behave civilly.

If they show a blatant and purposeful lack of manners, ask them to leave the room until they can be more courteous.

SOLUTIONS TOWARD SELF-DIRECTION

Prepare a list of manners you want your children to adopt, and post it in an accessible place. Make sure they know why each one is important.

If they forget to say "please" or "thank you," then model it out loud for them: "Thank you for helping me with my homework, Dad." Keep repeating it until they say it, too.

Include good manners as a part of your family's identity.

Try using humor: If you have a rude pack of animals to deal with, try using your worst manners and see how this affects them. Slurp your soup, interrupt, reach over them to get the bowl of peas, eat with your fingers, and yes, you can even sneeze on their food and pick your nose. Desperate times call for desperate measures.

Use questioning, impartial descriptions, and information: "I notice you forgot to acknowledge Mr. Thomas when he spoke to you. Manners are an important way of showing respect. How do you think he felt?" "How do you think you'd feel if someone I was speaking with didn't bother to introduce himself to you?"

MATERIALISM AND CONSUMERISM

See "Demanding" (things, indulgence, and immediate gratification).

MEALTIME HASSLES

WHY THEY DO IT

Many children use mealtime as their main battleground for power struggles. It's often hard for them to behave when they're forced to sit still for an hour and fraternize with the enemy (their siblings) or keep from clowning around with their buddies (their siblings).

LOGICAL CONSEQUENCES

If your children are often late for dinner, let them miss it. If this habit is deeply ingrained, set them up to miss out on their favorite meals.

If your children play with their food, remove it and say, "Food is something we eat, not play with. When you're ready to eat properly, you may have it back."

When your children are noisy or rowdy at the table, you can remove them to another room to eat, and tell them they can return when they are ready to behave appropriately, or you can take your own plate and eat elsewhere. Either is effective, because children don't like it when the pack is separated.

SOLUTIONS TOWARD SELF-DIRECTION

Offer choices: "If you can't behave properly at the table, then you'll have to eat in your room."

Use impartial descriptions and give information: "Rowdiness is not allowed while we eat." "You're talking very loudly and haven't touched anything on your plate." "Dinner is finished in ten minutes." (If they're cutting up and are famished, they'll straighten up and eat quietly, especially if they've witnessed their full plates dragged out from under them before.)

Use humor: Quietly leave the table with your plate and eat elsewhere, or come back to the table wearing noise protection. You can also try sitting at the table with something noisy—your old saxophone, a drum set, pots and pans to clang together. They get the message when they're covering their ears.

Use questioning: "Do you think it's pleasant to watch people play with their spaghetti?" "What are the rules about being loud or rowdy at the table?"

Never get sucked into your children's power struggles. Kids who learn to manipulate others learn to manipulate themselves (self-deceit).

MESSINESS

WHY THEY DO IT

Some children are messy by nature, especially if they're active and curious, because these types of kids like to jump quickly from one activity to another. And let's face it, most of the time they feel like they have something better to do than to clean up after themselves. Occasionally, its rebellion against over-controlling or compulsively clean parents. Sometimes, they just have sloppy role models.

LOGICAL CONSEQUENCES

If it involves any place other than their own room, your children shouldn't be allowed to start their next play project before they've picked up after their last one.

If my children don't clean up, I grab a big trash bag, pick up the toys, and hide them in the attic for a few weeks. If they ask their whereabouts, I'll say, "Oh yeah, I remember seeing your train set the other day, and I nearly hurt myself tripping over it. I know I put it in a safer place. Hmm, let's see now. Where did I end up putting that dang thing? Oh well, give me some time, and I'll remember it *eventually.*"

If messiness is a *big* problem, maybe they just have too much stuff. Have them give some of their toys to the needy.

If your children's rooms look like the aftermath of an earthquake registering 9.6 on the Richter scale, close the door. If they can't find their belongings, tough luck. If they don't have any clean clothes to wear to school, too bad. If they break their toys when they step on them, ho hum.

SOLUTIONS TOWARD SELF-DIRECTION

Never nag, plead, beg, threaten, or bribe your children to clean up their messes. They need to develop their own internal nagging system. Never clean up their messes for them!

Use questioning: "What system can you come up with to get your surroundings in order?"

Try humor: Tape a sign on their door that reads "Condemned" or "Quarantined." Tell them the demolition crew is here to finish the job for them.

Use impartial descriptions: "Your room is messy. It must be really hard to find the things you need."

Give information: "Dirty clothes have never been known to walk on their own from the floor to the hamper."

Offer them choices: "When your toys are cleaned up, then you can go on errands with me." "If your clothes aren't in the hamper by the time I start the wash, they won't get cleaned—by me, anyway."

Make observations when they *do* clean up: "Wow, you picked up all of your toys already. That means you and Sarah have more time to play something else before her mother comes to pick her up."

MORNING HASSLES

WHY THEY DO IT

Sometimes those Monday mornings are just way too early. Like us, children have trouble getting out of their warm and cozy beds to get ready for the day.

LOGICAL CONSEQUENCES

If your children habitually oversleep and are old enough to manage an alarm clock, let them be late for school. Arrange for their teachers to make an issue of it when they finally do get there.

If your children have trouble getting ready for school, either let them get to school late or leave without them to take the other siblings or go to work. If they're late for the bus, make them walk to school or ride their bikes, safety, age, and proximity permitting. If you can't wait around for your kids to get their act together, because doing so will make *you* late to work, have them reimburse you for the extra time it takes you to drive them to school.

When my kids turn off their annoying alarm clocks and roll over to go back to sleep, I usually tell them, "It's late, but that's OK. I guess skipping breakfast from time to time won't kill anybody."

Never nag or yell. It just creates fodder for an externally directed power struggle between you and your children.

Never let on that their problems getting up and ready in the morning are more important to you than to them. Let them know that it's no skin off your back if they go to school late, in their pajamas, starving, moss growing on their teeth, and with hair making them look like the Wild Man from Borneo.

Use observations when they do all of their morning routine in a timely manner: "I see you've already eaten, gotten dressed, and brushed your teeth. Wow, now you have an extra ten minutes to watch cartoons!" If they forgot one part of their routine, you can say something like, "Look at you, Annika. You're dressed, you made yourself a great breakfast, and you brushed your hair beautifully. Now all that's left is brushing your teeth!"

Give information: "The bus comes in fifteen minutes."

Use impartial descriptions: "We leave in ten minutes, and you haven't eaten breakfast yet. I hope you have enough time. Lunch isn't until 1:00."

Use questioning: "It's 7:15. What time does the bus come?" "What do you still need to do to get ready for school?" "You're running behind. If you two keep fighting, what will happen?"

NEGATIVITY

WHY THEY DO IT

Some children are just negative by nature. Some learn it from negative and cynical role models. Some actually think their negativity makes them look tough or cool! Some children act negatively because they're stressed, sleep-deprived, depressed, or under-confident. And some are negative because they don't feel special within the family.

LOGICAL CONSEQUENCES

If your children seem to habitually voice negativity and pessimism for no good reason, tell them to leave the room and return only when they have something positive and uplifting to say.

SOLUTIONS TOWARD SELF-DIRECTION

Tell your children that you're willing to hear their gripes, but you need to hear the positive things going on in their lives from time to time, too. Teach them that life doesn't always deliver everything they expect, but how they handle what life delivers can make all the difference in the world.

Never rush to fix the problems about which your children are negative, just in case their dissenting remarks are ploys to get you to come to their rescue.

See to it that all of your children have meaningful roles within the family. They need a strong sense of self in order to have a positive outlook on life.

Ask your children to experiment with the feelings an optimistic outlook creates by going through the next couple of hours trying to see the good in people and in situations around them. This strategy might be just what they need to get them out of their pessimistic slump, and over time they may very well internalize this attitude.

Never nag your children to be more positive. It doesn't work. Sometimes you just need to leave them alone. Try choices: "When you feel like talking about what's bothering you, then I'll be here to listen."

Use questioning: "You're feeling pretty negative about things. What do you think made you bring this attitude on?" (See how this question makes creating this attitude *her* responsibility?) "How do you feel when you think this way?" "How do you feel when you're more positive?"

NIGHTMARES

WHY THEY DO IT

Since children are learning new things, making new realizations about life, and undertaking new skills, they tend to have anxieties that will be vented in their dreams.

LOGICAL CONSEQUENCES

They shouldn't suffer any consequences, because this isn't considered a punishable "offense."

SOLUTIONS TOWARD SELF-DIRECTION

Teach your children strategies for breaking a recurrent nightmare. For instance, if your children have one about a great white shark, have them close their eyes in bed and make happy changes in their dream before they fall asleep. Maybe they can pretend that the shark turns into a ballerina and starts to dance with them. It's important to have some component of the change include your children interacting with the source of fear so that they can feel they have control over it.

Acknowledge the fears that arise from their bad dreams. And when they're lucid enough, discuss these dreams and any related issues that might be plaguing them in the present. This discussion will help them develop the internal dialogue necessary to tackle their fears in life.

Noisiness

Why they do it

Children are expressive and uninhibited beings by nature, including how they express themselves vocally.

Logical consequences

If your children are too noisy indoors, toss them outside. Tell them they can come back in when they're willing to use their "indoor voices."

If they turn up their stereo too high, make them turn it off. Tell them you're afraid they'll damage their ears, and, since your job is to ensure their safety and health, the stereo's taboo until they've decided to listen at an acceptable decibel range. If this approach doesn't work, take their stereos away from them for a while.

If your children are noisy in a public place, take them home.

Solutions toward self-direction

Allow for an acceptable amount of "happy noise" in your house. If you have kids, don't expect things to be so quiet that you can hear a pin drop, 'cause it ain't gonna happen in this lifetime, folks. Don't yell or scream when they're noisy. Smells like a fishy double standard to them.

Don't nag or punish your children for their noisiness, because this approach only motivates them to turn it into a big (and usually noisy) externally directed power struggle.

Use observations when they're being nice and quiet: "You guys are playing so quietly together. That makes our whole house so calm and happy!"

Give information and impartial descriptions: "We allow only indoor voices in the house." "Your noisiness is starting to hurt my ears. You will have to go outside."

Use questioning: "How do *you* feel when someone's being noisy while you're concentrating on something?" "What do you need to do now to make things quieter?"

PESTERING, POKING, AND SHOVING
WHY THEY DO IT

When children can't be aggressive with their siblings and friends overtly, they'll do so on the sly. The ultimate goal is to get the other kid to cry or whine so much that *they* wind up getting into trouble instead. Children pester because they have low self-esteem, don't receive enough attention, or don't feel a sense of belonging.

LOGICAL CONSEQUENCES

Be aware of the interactions your children have with others. If possible, let them suffer the natural consequences that are sure to occur, like being alienated or hollered at by that friend, having their behavior reciprocated, getting the other child's parents on their backs, and so on.

If they pick on children who are too young to deliver these kinds of consequences, separate them from those kids. If they can't behave nicely with others, they'll have to be stuck with themselves as playmates.

SOLUTIONS TOWARD SELF-DIRECTION

Use observations when they refrain from pestering under circumstances when they ordinarily would have: "Henry, you kept your cool when your brother opened his birthday presents. I know how hard it is to do sometimes. Now he's willing to play with you, and you're both having a great time!"

Give information: "Pestering people makes them not want to have anything to do with you." "We treat others like we want to be treated in our family."

Use questioning: "What are our rules about shoving and poking other people?" "How do you think that makes your sister feel? Do you think she'll want to play with you now?" "How does it make *you* feel when you're treated like that? What do you need to do to make her feel better?"

Give choices: "Do you want to play nicely with Bradley or go up to your room and play by yourself?"

PORNOGRAPHY AND SEXUAL IRRESPONSIBILITY

WHY THEY DO IT

All children are eventually curious about sexuality and will end up satisfying this curiosity if their parents don't beat them to the punch.

LOGICAL CONSEQUENCES

Define and enforce clear rules about what you consider appropriate ways for them to learn about sexuality. If you find pornographic magazines, take them away and withhold their allowance until you feel comfortable that they won't spend it on things of this nature.

If your children call those infamous 900 numbers that are for "mature audiences only," make them cough up the dough to pay the bill and remove their phones from their rooms.

If you find out that your children are visiting pornographic Web sites, take away their computer privileges for a month. The same goes for those times when you catch them communicating with strangers on the Internet. "Buddies online" services that allow them to chat with their friends directly are much safer options.

SOLUTIONS TOWARD SELF-DIRECTION

Address your children's questions about sexuality openly. If you're too embarrassed, trust me, someone else will do the job for you.

Don't wait until your children ask you about sex. When you think they're ready to understand such concepts, explain them in an age-appropriate way. You can buy them books to help cover some of the subject, but this reading shouldn't completely replace your role as their teacher in such matters. I like the book for adolescents by Dr. Ruth Westheimer entitled *Dr. Ruth Talks to Kids*. It covers each subject candidly and appropriately without making sex out to be some kinky or shameful act.

Never make your children feel they should be ashamed of their own sexual curiosity by scolding, shaming, ridiculing, or punishing them for sexual exploration (in both their actions and their questions) that is normal and healthy for their age.

Use the correct words for body parts. Using words like "weenie," "boobs," or "balls" shows your children that you think sexual aspects of the body are shameful, disgusting, or embarrassing.

Use questioning: "I notice that, nowadays, sex is more about image and power than love. Do you think that's right? Do you sometimes feel social pressure in anything relating to sex?" "Do you think you have all the answers you need concerning sex? Are there any questions you have about this subject?" "What are the consequences of having sex before you're ready?" "Do you know anyone at school who has made mistakes where sex is concerned? What consequences have they had to experience because of it?"

Use impartial descriptions: "You seem very interested in boys now. Let's share what you and I know about sex. Maybe I can fill in some of the gaps."

PROMISE BREAKING

WHY THEY DO IT

Children make promises they don't intend to keep in order to bribe and manipulate others into doing whatever they want. Some simply change their minds. Others . . . well, maybe they're budding politicians.

LOGICAL CONSEQUENCES

It's your job to help your children uphold their integrity, and this character development means making sure they keep their promises. Many deals will be broken without you ever knowing it, but not to worry, those whom your children disappoint will take their revenge. The outside world is brutal that way. Their friends will alienate them, they'll have trouble gaining the trust of others, and those they betray won't have nearly as much regret when they compromise their own integrity in the relationship. Reality bites.

SOLUTIONS TOWARD SELF-DIRECTION

If extenuating circumstances cause you to break a promise or commitment with your children, apologize and explain the situation in detail. Let them know that keeping promises is important to you and that you, also, are disappointed at having to go against your word.

Teach your children how to get what they want (or at least *try*) without resorting to manipulative tactics like breaking promises.

Make keeping promises part of your family's identity with statements like, "We keep our word in this family."

Use questioning: "Why did you find it necessary to go against your word?" "How do you think that makes Taylor feel about you? Do you think she'll trust you in the future?"

Use impartial descriptions: "I thought you gave your sister that yo-yo. She seemed very disappointed when you took it away from her."

Notice when they *do* keep their promises: "I see you stuck to your promise to help Jimmy with his math after school. I know that's tough since you have football practice later. Jimmy must think it's pretty cool to have a friend like you to rely on."

PUBLIC HASSLES
WHY THEY DO IT

I truly believe that children aren't taught to respect public places. Practically from the day they're born, without teaching them the proper way to behave in public, we start taking them to all sorts of joints. So they grow to think the public is some faceless and over-tolerant being they can have their way with as they please. I'm amazed at some of the behavior I see parents allow in restaurants and grocery stores today. They plead and bribe their children to act nicely, so that the kids' antisocial actions are almost rewarded, in a way.

LOGICAL CONSEQUENCES

If your children act badly in a public place, hightail it home. If this public misbehavior is a recurrent problem, set them up for a bigger fall. For instance, tell them you're all going to go to see that movie that they've been drooling over for the last two weeks. The rules are, if they're nice, they stay; if they're not, they go. And at the least hint of commotion, take them home. NO SECOND CHANCES.

If your children are responsible for any acts of vandalism, have them make or pay for any repairs of the damage. If your children litter, have them pick it up along with all of the litter nearby. If a fine is imposed, make them pay it.

SOLUTIONS TOWARD SELF-DIRECTION

Define and explain clear rules and boundaries for public behavior for them to incorporate into their internal dialogue.

Never give in to your children when they're making a scene in public. They'll just mark that in the "this trick works great" column.

Never bribe your children. You want them to behave because it's *right*, not because it'll get them something they want. This bribery only encourages them to grow up feeling they're entitled to everything.

Don't threaten your children with shame: "Those people are looking at you. How embarrassing! I bet they think you're a spoiled brat!" This shaming makes children think that the opinions that others have of them are crucial to their self-worth.

Don't use the ever-popular threat, "Do you want *the* man to come over here and make you behave?" I bet my children grew up having horrible nightmares about evil waiters and grocery store security guards. But this threat just sends the message that you can't handle their bad behavior and need to call upon a higher authority. The faceless "man" becomes an external influence to which they react blindly.

Use questioning: "What's the rule about behaving in public (or littering, loitering, etc.)?" "How do you think others feel about your actions?" "What do you intend to do to make things right again?"

When they do behave well in public, let them know you noticed. "Billy, you're acting so grown up here in the store. I really enjoy your company when you make such good choices."

Use impartial descriptions and give information: "People can't hear the movies when there's lots of noise in the theater." "This noise level seems to be bothering that couple at the next table." "We don't allow this kind of behavior in the store."

Offer choices: "When you find ways to settle yourself down, then we can go back into the theater." "You must sit at the table properly or leave the restaurant."

Try the minimalist parent approach: "Christopher . . ." (Then place your index finger to your lips to signal him to be quiet.)

RUNNING AWAY FROM HOME
WHY THEY DO IT

There are several reasons children run away from home. Some do so because of an unstable family situation (divorce, a death in the family, sexual or physical abuse, or drug or alcohol problems in the parents). Some run away as a response to over-control, neglect, or conditional love. Some seek to wield power over, get undue attention from, manipulate, or punish their parents. Some suffer acute personal crises like pregnancy, substance abuse, or trouble with the law. Some are depressed, and some just seek adventure or are influenced to run away by their peers.

LOGICAL CONSEQUENCES

There are certainly no acceptable natural consequences for running away, but there are logical ones. You can tighten the reins by becoming their little shadow. Tell them that until you feel certain they won't fly the coop, you're on them like white on rice.

Solutions toward self-direction

If they're little and are obviously bluffing at the door with their empty suitcases in hand, say your good-byes without looking up from your paper. "I'm sorry to see you leave, Billy. I'm really going to miss you, but it's your choice. Write if you get work." That way, they can't use the threat as a manipulative ploy. Their problem remains theirs alone.

Take a long, hard look at the family dynamics. Are your children being over-controlled? Do they have plenty of choices? Help them define their role or niche in the family. They must understand how important they are to the entire family.

Using the walk-through, pros and cons list, and other techniques mentioned earlier in the book, help your children deal with any problems they may be running away from.

Communicate, communicate, and communicate. Take the time to listen and understand your children without refuting their word, trying to have the last say, or letting it go in one ear and out the other. Most kids who run away complain that their parents don't understand or listen to them.

Use questioning: "What troubles are you having that made this seem like the only solution for you?" "What other options can you think of?"

Try providing information: "Your Uncle Phil ran away when he was sixteen and here's what consequences he had to endure." (List as many as you can, and make it as graphic as the law will allow!)

Safety-Rule Breaking
Why they do it

Some rules are nonnegotiable regardless of the circumstances. This includes most safety rules. Wandering away from us in public, running out into the street or parking lot, playing with matches, and, yes, that timeless classic, "sticking a knife in the toaster," are just a handful. Some kids break these rules because they forget, they don't understand the reasoning behind them, or they just want to get a rise out of us!

LOGICAL CONSEQUENCES

If your children break a safety rule outside the home, take them home immediately. Say something like, "I'm afraid you're going to get hurt because of the bad choices you're making. We'll try this again when I think you'll choose to be safe."

If your children play with matches, take them away. If they are overly curious, put them in a bathtub full of water, and let them light matches under your watchful eye until they're sick and tired of it.

SOLUTIONS TOWARD SELF-DIRECTION

Come up with a list of safety rules you want your children to follow. Explain each one along with the logic involved. Use questioning: "What's our rule about playing with firecrackers?" "What do you need to do now to be safer?"

Offer choices: "When you make better choices with your Boy Scout knife, then I will return it to you." "When you have your seat belt on, then I can start the car."

Try the minimalist parenting technique: "Erik ... bike helmet."

Don't use scare tactics. Reading the gruesome front-page news about child abductions will just make your children overly fearful of their surroundings. This kind of fear will make them react blindly to external threats, perceived or real. For instance, say things like, "Leaving Mommy in the grocery store is not safe," instead of terrorizing them with the details of what could happen. For the same reasons, don't make them fear others by telling them not to speak to strangers. Anyway, sometimes it's people they already know that can put them in harm's way. I tell my children not to go anywhere with anyone unless they have my personal OK, even if they're just going to the park with Uncle Larry.

SCHOOL MISBEHAVIOR
WHY THEY DO IT

So much of that energy that's tolerated at home can't possibly be tolerated in a school setting, where children must pay attention and learn something other than the sounds that come out of Mary's mouth when her pigtails are tugged. Occasionally, children will misbehave in school because they don't get enough attention at home, have low self-esteem, or don't feel they have a niche or role in the class. Poor conduct is their misguided way of meeting these needs.

LOGICAL CONSEQUENCES

Give teachers your complete permission to levy appropriate consequences for misbehavior. If your children are still disruptive, have the school call you to pick them up. Believe it or not, children seldom see leaving school early as a bonus. At least not under these circumstances. But just in case, don't let them have any fun when they get home. Keep them in their room to do schoolwork, whether they have any assignments or not.

Have them make amends for the disruption they caused. If necessary, have them apologize to the entire class. If they don't want to be embarrassed, they need to make better choices.

SOLUTIONS TOWARD SELF-DIRECTION

Ask the teacher if you can help out in the classroom one afternoon a week for awhile. You can observe a lot while you're cutting out little brown teddy bears from paper sacks, and this presence might give you some insight into what motivates your children to behave the way that they do. With this insight, you can better help your children solve their school behavioral problems.

Use questioning: "What are our rules about behaving at school?" "How easy do you think it is for your friends to learn and finish their work when you disrupt the class like that?"

Use impartial descriptions and give information: "Your teacher tells me you've been distracting the other classmates. Behavior like this makes it more difficult for you and your friends to learn. When learning becomes hard, your relationships with your teacher and the rest of the class might become more challenging."

Talk to the teacher about helping your children find their roles in the class. When children feel as if they have something to contribute, their behavior improves. I particularly like finding a role that somehow ties in to their behavioral problem. For instance, if Suzy has a problem talking in class, put her in charge of giving everyone a secret signal to settle down when they're getting noisy. If Jimmy tends to run all over the place when the class walks in line to the cafeteria at lunchtime, make him the line leader for a few days.

SCHOOL PHOBIA
WHY THEY DO IT

Some children are over-protected and too dependent on a parent. Some are agoraphobic (they have a fear of public places and crowds), some suffer from depression, and some have a heightened fear of criticism, evaluation, and failure.

Logical Consequences

Hey, going to school is not negotiable. They're going no matter what. If they want to go in their pajamas, that's their choice.

Solutions toward Self-Direction

Acknowledge your children's fear: "I know you don't want to go to school, and you'll be a little nervous at first, but I have faith in you to work out those fears."

Don't cling to your children because of any separation anxiety *you* have! They can pick up on the subtlest of signals that you don't have faith in them to work out their problem on their own.

Give your children age-appropriate responsibilities early on. Don't do everything for them or rescue them from difficult experiences and mistakes. You need to send a constant message that you have faith in them to be self-reliant.

Teach your children the skills to recover from defeat, as addressed earlier in the book, so that they aren't afraid of taking risks and making mistakes.

Use impartial descriptions and give information: "It's common to be nervous about going to school." "When people face whatever they're afraid of, they usually get less and less afraid over time."

SEX BEFORE THEY'RE READY

See under "Pornography and Sexual Irresponsibility" and "Growing Up Too Soon." Basic message: polish that shotgun. (Not really. What I really mean to say is—don't allow it!)

SHARING AND POSSESSIVENESS

Why they do it

Children have trouble sharing because they're afraid of losing things to someone else's control. Some feel as if their private property is the only thing in their lives over which they have any power.

LOGICAL CONSEQUENCES

Don't force, but strongly encourage your children to share. Any disciplining should be targeted at the conflicts they create when they choose not to share, like bickering, yelling, and hitting.

If your children don't share with their siblings or friends, they'll suffer natural consequences like losing a friendship or having no one to play with.

SOLUTIONS TOWARD SELF-DIRECTION

Don't even expect your children under three to share at all. They have no concept of other people's feelings at this age. After that age, teach your children how to respectfully ask another child to share a toy and to take good care of that toy while it's in their possession.

Teach your children about the benefits of sharing. I tell mine that if they don't share a toy, they just have the toy, but if they share the toy, they have both a toy and a friend.

If your children fight with someone else over a possession, don't take sides. Either don't interfere at all, or, if the noise level bothers you, take it away from both of them until they work things out.

Give choices: "Johnny wants to play with one of your trucks. Do you want to let him play with the dump truck or the backhoe?"

Use impartial descriptions: "I see you shared your favorite toy with Timmy. I know how hard that must have been. Look how happy Jimmy is now."

Shyness

Why they do it

Some children are shy because that's their temperament. Some are shy because they're over-controlled or over-protected by their parents. Some aren't taught the necessary skills to handle stress or failure. Some aren't raised to be independent and self-reliant.

Logical consequences

There aren't any effective logical consequences that won't backfire and make your shrinking violets wilt even more.

Solutions toward self-direction

Never force your children to socialize. Never coax them to come out from hiding behind you and speak, for instance. This makes them learn to react mindlessly to others in fear. But don't let them use their shyness as an excuse to avoid things.

Allow for differences in personality, and let your children know that you accept these differences as part of their uniqueness. Don't speak for your children.

Give your children plenty of age-appropriate responsibilities to increase their sense of competence. Teach your children skills to recover from defeat. They must experience and learn how to handle failure to feel competent.

Encourage friendships that provide the right chemistry. Try not to encourage them to befriend aggressive, manipulative, or bossy kids. Role-play various peer interactions they might find uncomfortable.

Encourage, but don't force, your children to have new experiences. Expose them to their world as much as you possibly can.

Help your children find their roles within the family. Offer them ways to contribute.

SIBLING RIVALRY

WHY THEY DO IT

Children fight with their siblings because they're struggling to find their special niche within the family. Sometimes, it's to suck you into the fray and get attention. And once you get close, it's like a black hole. Even light can't escape its clutches.

LOGICAL CONSEQUENCES

Let them work it out for themselves. Never take sides, come to the youngest one's rescue, or assume the eldest is to blame. Your attention might be just the thing they seek.

If your children fight over seating arrangements, nobody sits anywhere until they work out a system. If they fight over television channel choices or time at the computer, nobody gets to use either until they come up with a plan everyone can agree upon.

SOLUTIONS TOWARD SELF-DIRECTION

Acknowledge your children's feelings. If your daughter says, "Mommy, I hate Erik! He's always so mean to me," say something like, "I know how upset you must be when he teases you. I used to get mad at my older brother, too." Don't dismiss her feelings with remarks like, "You can't possibly feel that way. He's your brother, for goodness' sakes!" This response only creates confusion in their minds about their conflicting feelings of love and annoyance.

Talk about the sibling wars you experienced as a child, and then let your children know how rewarding your relationships with your siblings are now. If those relationships aren't as close as you had hoped, discuss where and why things went sour, what regrets you have, and what you could have done differently growing up together. Our children can learn from our mistakes.

When a new sibling is born, give the older sibling age-appropriate ways to help care for him or her. This involvement makes them feel needed, rather than threatened, by the new arrival.

Use questioning: "I see you and your sister aren't getting along well. You did great yesterday. What's different now?" "How does not getting along make you feel, compared to when you're friends?" "How do you think your sister is feeling now? What are you going to do about it?"

Use impartial descriptions: "I see you're getting along so well together. And it looks like you're having a lot more fun playing than fighting. Look how happy you both are." "When you fight with your brother, I find that you complain about not having anyone to play with."

SPITTING
WHY THEY DO IT

Children spit to create an effect, to look tough, or to show aggression when they don't know how to resolve their conflicts with words.

LOGICAL CONSEQUENCES

If your children spit on someone else, they should be required to help clean the spittle off and make amends. If they spit on anything other than a person, they should clean up after themselves and apologize to any onlookers. If spitting is a big problem, separate them from their grossed-out "victims." After all, if they can't behave properly with others, they'll have to be removed from them.

Use humor: Make an official announcement that the Fox family lives in a no-spitting zone. Pretend you're reading news in the newspaper about the Spit River cresting past the floodplain at the Johnsons'.

Teach your children verbal ways to settle their conflicts.

Offer choices: "When you decide to use words instead of spitting to solve your disagreements, then you can play with your friends again."

Use impartial descriptions and give information: "I saw you spit on the sidewalk. Most people find spitting disgusting." "TB and other diseases can be spread by spitting."

Use questioning: "What's our rule about spitting?" "How do you suppose Nadine feels right now?" "How do you feel when someone spits on you?" "What do you need to do to make it up to her?"

SPORTSMANSHIP (POOR)

WHY THEY DO IT

Some children just don't take to competition well. Whenever they lose, they perceive it as a personal attack against their self-worth and retaliate with sour comments, insults, flying board game pieces, and gnashing teeth. The fact that society (including some parents) encourages a winner/loser attitude and is so focused on competition adds fuel to the fire.

LOGICAL CONSEQUENCES

If your children show poor sportsmanship, they shouldn't be allowed to continue with the competition. If their bad conduct occurs at the end of the game, they can't play in the next one. Say something like, "I can't let you play until I'm sure you're going to be a better sport." Have your children make amends with whomever they subjected to their poor sportsmanship.

Solutions Toward Self-Direction

Encourage cooperative games over competitive ones, especially in younger children who don't yet have the social and cognitive maturity to deal with defeat. Don't let your children win all the time when you play games with them. They need to understand that they can't possibly expect to win at everything.

Make good sportsmanship part of your family's identity: "We're good sports in our family."

Give your children the unconditional love they need. When they win or lose some form of competition, focus your comments on how hard they tried, whether they were good sports, whether they had fun, and how well they played as part of a team.

If your children are involved in a competitive sport or game that has one of those coaches with that "Let's crush the competition! Win! Win! Win!" attitude, pull them out. The same goes for those sports where the parents of the team members are thirsty for blood.

Use questioning: "I see you're pretty upset about losing your soccer match. What are our rules about good sportsmanship?" "How does behaving like a poor sport make you feel—better or worse?"

Role-play situations that prompt poor sportsmanship from your child.

Use impartial descriptions and give information: "I see you're being such a good sport. I know how hard that is when you've lost an important match. You must feel pretty proud of yourself. And it looks like you've earned the respect of your friends with your conduct, too."

Whenever you watch sports or games of any sort with your children, point out and discuss good and bad sportsmanship in the competitors.

STEALING AND SHOPLIFTING

See "Committing Crimes."

SULKING AND POUTING

WHY THEY DO IT

Sulking and pouting are really just silent forms of tantrums. And frankly, they're not restricted to children! People use this form of behavior to get their way, to get attention, or to seek revenge. Children who are over-controlled sulk or pout because they've never been given a chance to learn how to get what they want verbally. Children who have permissive parents sulk because it works.

LOGICAL CONSEQUENCES

Make it a rule that if your children try to get something by sulking or pouting, they definitely won't get it under *any* circumstances.

No sulkers or pouters allowed in your personal space. They'll have to take it elsewhere. So, make them leave until they're finished with their "poor little me" act.

SOLUTIONS TOWARD SELF-DIRECTION

Never make their problem seem more important to you than to them. Don't reprimand, threaten, punish, or tease your sulker or pouter. Just let children work their problem out on their own. If you feel compelled to interfere, leave the room. Remember, "ho hum."

Role-play situations that tend to incite the child to sulk or pout.

Use questioning: "What are you trying to tell me? I need words to understand you." "Do you think your behavior will accomplish what you want it to?" "Do you like it when other people sulk or pout with you?" "How do you feel about them when they do?"

Give choices: "Do you want to pout in your room or stay here and think of a solution to your problem?"

Use the minimalist parenting technique: Get your child's attention by calling out his name. Then lift your pouting lip off the bottom of your chin and use your fingers to transform your mouth into a smile.

TANTRUMS (PHYSICAL AND VERBAL)
WHY THEY DO IT

Tantrums. Every parent's nightmare. When our children are in the throes of one, we feel helpless, as if we're watching an eruption from Mount Krakatoa. And they smell our fear, people. They smell our fear.

There are tons of reasons children throw fits. Some don't have the necessary skills to express their frustration, disappointment, anger, and desires verbally, some want attention, some want revenge, some want to get their way, or some just don't know what else to do.

LOGICAL CONSEQUENCES

Never give in to your children when they have tantrums. Keep that "ho hum, take care of your problem on your own, buddy" attitude.

Wait quietly until he gives up, or pick him up (or lead him by the hand) and take him to another room without uttering a peep. The fewer words, the better. If your child has a tantrum in public, take him home.

Solutions toward self-direction

Never nag, plead, bribe, coax, wheedle, or threaten your children when they have tantrums, or it'll become more entrenched as an externally directed reaction. Just leave them alone.

It's perfectly acceptable to acknowledge their feelings: "I know how angry you feel, and it's OK to be angry. I'll just hold you until you're finished."

Give choices: "It's OK to be upset. You can either express it in a quiet and acceptable way, or you can have your tantrum in your own space."

Use questioning *after* the tantrum is over, preferably *long* after: "You were upset in the grocery store today. Did you accomplish what you wanted with that behavior?"

Role-play whatever event prompted the tantrum. Have your child play one side, then the other.

Tattling

Why they do it

Children tattle because they don't know how to solve their own problems, they want attention, or they feel they must undermine someone else to improve our opinion of them. Bottom line: If we try to fix it, it'll stay broken. It's like trying to fix a Swiss watch. You're going to be picking up little pieces all day long if you do.

Logical consequences

When your children tattle, they'll incur the wrath of whoever it is they're betraying.

Solutions toward self-direction

Establish tattling rules. Basically, children shouldn't be allowed to tell on someone unless life, limb, or property are at stake. Teach your children how to resolve their own conflicts verbally.

Have a "tattle box" somewhere handy. Once they're old enough, require your children to write out their concerns and place them in the box to be addressed later. This delay will help eliminate those times they tattle just to get your attention on the fly. It also motivates them to reflect inwardly on whether they should handle the situation themselves.

Try one of these approaches:

"You aren't tattling, are you?" (Message: I ain't gettin' sucked into this one, buddy!)

"I know how angry you feel with Billy. What are you going to do about it?" (Message: I understand how you feel and expect you to handle it.)

"I know you and Billy can work things out." (Message: I have faith in you.)

Use questioning: "You're tattling. What are the rules about tattling?" "What can you do to work out your problem without my help?"

Make observations when they take care of their own conflicts: "Jonathan, I noticed you handled things on your own when Tommy called you names. Wow, that's pretty grown up!"

TEASING AND NAME-CALLING

WHY THEY DO IT

Children verbally torture when they're jealous, when they want revenge, when they want to seem tough and powerful, or when they're angry and don't know how to work out their conflicts in acceptable ways.

LOGICAL CONSEQUENCES

If your children tease or call someone else names, they'll usually get all of the natural consequences they need from others. As they grow up and get an earful of teasing themselves, they'll stop. But if things seem out of hand, remove them from the other child after requiring them to make amends in some way. Tell them they can join their friends when you think they can be kinder.

Solutions toward self-direction

Teach your children skills to resolve conflicts. Role-play situations where your children are being teased and vice versa.

Use questioning: "I saw you teasing Danielle. What are our rules about teasing? What made you feel you had to do it? How do you think she felt when you teased her? How do *you* feel when you get teased? What are other ways you could have handled your feelings?"

Give choices: "Do you want to go inside, or stay and be kind to your friends?"

Use impartial descriptions and give information: "I overheard you teasing Jane. We use kind words in our family." "Name-calling is hurtful and causes problems rather than solves them. If you have a disagreement with someone, handling it with kind words is very effective."

Telephone, TV, Electronic Game, and Computer Addiction

Why they do it

Children have so many opportunities to commune with electricity, it'd make Benjamin Franklin, Thomas Edison, and those other electricity wizards proud. Kids love handing their brains over to some piece of equipment as though it were a hatcheck lady at the restaurant. After all, passive entertainment is mindless, hypnotic, and relaxing. They don't have to meet anyone's demands or expectations, and they're transported from the relentless criticisms and evaluations of the outside world.

As far as telephones are concerned, I truly believe there's a need for a new type of medical specialist, the "telephonilogical surgeon," because most adolescents need emergency surgery to remove the telephone receiver that has fused to their ear. At a certain age, friends are the center of their little universe, and telephone wires are the umbilical cords that connect them.

LOGICAL CONSEQUENCES

If your children break the rules you've established for using any of these gadgets, take those privileges away.

If your children are cranky after their little one-on-one relationships with electronics, take away that privilege for a week. The same goes when they don't comply with your requests while they're using the telephone, computer, and so on.

SOLUTIONS TOWARD SELF-DIRECTION

Establish clear and reasonable rules on when and for how long your children can watch television, use the telephone, play electronic games, and use the computer.

Teach your children how to entertain themselves without machinery. Help them make up a list of choices, and post it on the refrigerator.

Use questioning: "What are the rules about using the phone? Why do you think those rules are so important? What do you need to do now?"

Offer choices: "You can either try to abide by the Nintendo limits on your own, or I can keep the machine in my room and have you sign in and out for it."

Use impartial descriptions and give information: "You've been playing video games past your limit, and your homework isn't finished yet. Bedtime is 9:30 no matter what." "Playing outside is good for your mind and body."

When your children *do* create forms of play that don't involve electronics, make observations: "I see you're making something out of papier-mâché! That looks like fun. How creative you are!"

THUMB AND FINGER SUCKING

WHY THEY DO IT

Children suck their thumbs and fingers because it feels good, because it's a habit, or because they're experiencing stress.

LOGICAL CONSEQUENCES

It isn't necessary to render consequences for this behavior, because it's perfectly normal. After all, what's the worst thing that can happen? Pick your battles! It's a lot easier to let them suck away than it is to hassle with their unrequited urges and anxieties.

SOLUTIONS TOWARD SELF-DIRECTION

Never tease, shame, nag, or punish your children for thumb or finger sucking. Never try maneuvers like bedtime mittens or hot sauce. Not only is this ineffective, but it fosters external direction.

Allow your children to communicate their fears openly. Encourage them to discuss with you those things that might be sources of stress for them.

Intervene only if this habit bothers your children and they ask for your help. Then consult with their dentist about thumb guards.

TOILET TRAINING TROUBLES

WHY THEY DO IT

Trust me, your children aren't going to come home from football practice wanting their Pull-ups changed. Children potty-train at different rates because they don't all mature at the same time rates, emotionally or physically.

LOGICAL CONSEQUENCES

The only consequence your children should experience is the fact that they have something warm, wet, or stinky in their diapers. Some kids can't bear it, and others couldn't give a hang.

SOLUTIONS TOWARD SELF-DIRECTION

Never tease, shame, threaten, nag, or punish your children for their toilet-training accidents. Berating them only creates a relentless externally directed power struggle that makes the Korean War look like a lovers' spat. And never reward or bribe your children for their toilet-training successes.

Give your children your unconditional love regardless of their toilet-training status.

If they're old enough, ask them how they feel about their toilet-training progress. One hopes they won't be so old you can ask them to prepare a dissertation on the subject.

Don't compare siblings in the trials and tribulations of their toilet training.

If your children are stinking up the area with their smelly little diapers and they refuse to have them changed, give them a choice: "You can either let me change you, or you can go outside until you're ready for a clean diaper."

Use observations when they're successful: "Well, you made it to the potty on time! I bet you're glad to be wearing dry pants instead of wet ones."

TOUCHING EVERYTHING

WHY THEY DO IT

Children love exploring their world with all of their senses, and their grubby little paws are certainly no exception!

LOGICAL CONSEQUENCES

Provided your children understand the rules about what they can and can't touch, take them out of the store, for instance, if they choose to disregard those rules. Tell them you can't take them with you again until you feel certain they're going to make wiser choices.

SOLUTIONS TOWARD SELF-DIRECTION

Establish clear rules on what your children can and can't touch, but don't be overly restrictive.

Never nag, threaten, or punish your children for touching things all the time, unless you like those little parent-child externally directed power struggles.

Use questioning: "What are our rules about touching breakables? What would you be required to do if you accidentally broke something you touched?"

Use observations when they're being good about keeping their hands to themselves: "I notice you're not fingering everything, even though there are so many tempting things in this store. I love taking you with me when I'm not nervous about things being broken."

Give choices: "If you can keep your hands to yourself, we can stay and look around longer."

TRUANCY

WHY THEY DO IT

Children skip school when they're struggling academically, when they want to test the limits of their power, when they're experiencing peer pressure to do so, when they're depressed, or when they're trying to avoid any other sources of stress at school, including challenging social situations.

LOGICAL CONSEQUENCES

If your children are truant, tell them you have to escort them to their class and set them in their seats personally until you feel certain they won't skip school again. If this procedure embarrasses them, tough bananas. Have them apologize to their teachers for missing class.

SOLUTIONS TOWARD SELF-DIRECTION

Teach your children the value of an education. Keep the lines of communication open between you and your children. Encourage them to air their troubles at school by freely lending them an empathic ear.

Use impartial descriptions and give information: "Your teacher told me you played hooky twice last week. Kids who miss a lot of school are required to repeat that grade. I bet you'd feel pretty bad seeing your friends leave for the next grade while you stay behind."

Use questioning: "What are our rules about not skipping school? Why do we have those rules?" "What do you need to do to keep yourself from being tempted in this way?"

Offer choices: "When you decide to stop skipping school, then I won't have to walk you there myself."

Examine the friendship circles your children are in. If the friends, too, are recurrent truants, forbid the association until your children can make better choices in their company. Talk to the other parents to come up with a united plan.

UNRELIABILITY AND IRRESPONSIBILITY

WHY THEY DO IT

Children who have everything done for them and are consistently rescued from the consequences of their bad decisions grow to be unreliable and irresponsible adults.

Logical Consequences

If your children don't fulfill their responsibilities, they should bear the consequences. If they forget to turn in their library book, they should have to pay the fine themselves. If they aren't reliable in those things you ask them to do, take away some of their privileges. Tell them that the level of privileges must match the level of reliability and responsibility, both of which tie in to their level of maturity.

Solutions Toward Self-Direction

Don't rescue your children from their mistakes. Don't shelter them from experiences.

Give your children age-appropriate responsibilities from the beginning rather than doing everything for them all the time. Teach your children skills to recover from defeat as discussed earlier in this book.

Never nag, threaten, label, or punish your children when they don't come through on their responsibilities.

Use questioning: "You didn't do your paper route this morning. Why do you suppose it's so important to be reliable in your responsibilities? Do you think you might lose your job because of your bad decisions?"

Use impartial descriptions and give information: "Mrs. Jones says you didn't get her mail while she went on vacation, as you promised. We believe in fulfilling our commitments in our family."

Remark on those times when they *are* reliable: "I notice you gathered up the video rentals for me to take back to the store. That sure makes my job easier. And I like feeling that I can depend on you."

VANITY

WHY THEY DO IT

Children become obsessed with their outward appearance when they believe it's pivotal to their acceptance by others and by themselves. Unfortunately, society sends them messages that how they look is more important than what kind of human beings they are.

LOGICAL CONSEQUENCES

Children who are vain are often alienated by their peers. One hopes they'll get the message.

SOLUTIONS TOWARD SELF-DIRECTION

De-emphasize the importance of their external appearance. Instead of telling them how pretty they look, point out one of their character strengths instead. Don't buy them designer fashions, fancy makeup, and other things that encourage vanity.

Try not to make comments, negative or positive, about other people's looks on TV, in movies, in public, etc.

Use questioning: "Why is there so much pressure to look perfect, nowadays? Do you think this is good or bad?" "How do you feel about those who are overly concerned with their looks?"

Use impartial descriptions and give information: "You seem to be so concerned with the way your hair looks now. Most of your friends care more about their appearance than yours. What they do care about in others are things like compassion, integrity, loyalty, and so on."

WASTEFULNESS

WHY THEY DO IT

Children are wasteful when they haven't had to experience or don't understand the consequences of this behavior.

LOGICAL CONSEQUENCES

If your children are wasteful, they should do without or replace what they waste. For instance, if they serve themselves huge portions of food and eat only a small fraction, they'll have to finish it for the next meal. If they waste all the toner in the copier by photocopying their butts 300 times, take them to the office supply store to buy a refill with their own money. If they purposely break their last pencil in half, they should do without and have to use crayons to finish their homework.

SOLUTIONS TOWARD SELF-DIRECTION

Teach your children the importance of conserving resources of any kind.

Use questioning: "What are our rules about wasting things? Why do we have those rules? How do you intend to make up for your waste?" "What would happen if everyone were wasteful?"

Use impartial descriptions and give information: "You left your bedroom light on when you left for school. Our electricity bill is already high enough in the summer." "We don't believe in wasting food in our family." "Water is a precious resource. It's a good idea to turn the faucet off while brushing your teeth."

Offer choices: "If you're still hungry, you can finish that second serving you gave yourself, or you can have it for lunch tomorrow." "When I can be certain you won't be so heavy-handed with the glue, then I'll let you use it without supervision."

Use observations when they're not being wasteful: "I notice you were careful about not keeping the lights in your room on when you left this morning. Over time, that really lowers our electric bill. I really appreciate that."

Whining

Why they do it

Children whine because they want undue attention, because they seek revenge, because they want to test the limits of their power, or because it works.

Logical consequences

If your children whine, their request should be immediately denied. Refuse to listen until they can talk in a "big girl" or "big boy" voice. If they don't stop right away, leave the room or make *them* leave the room.

Solutions toward self-direction

Sometimes children whine because they don't feel a sense of belonging. Help them find appropriate roles within the family.

Try humor: Tape-record your children while they're whining and play it back when they're in a good mood. Ask them what they think about the sounds they were making. But never use this tactic as a form of mockery.

Never nag, threaten, mock, ridicule, or punish your children when they whine. It just encourages them to engage you in an externally directed power struggle. To them, negative attention is better than no attention at all.

Use questioning: "What is our rule about whining? Why do we have that rule?" "How do you think it makes me feel when you talk to me in that tone of voice?" "How do you feel when you hear other people whining?"

Use observations when they aren't whining: "I notice you asked for dessert without whining today. I really enjoy listening to you when you speak in a respectful tone of voice."

Use impartial descriptions and give information: "I see you're whining. That strategy has no effect on me."

Give choices: "You can either talk to me in a more pleasant voice or leave the room." "When you stop whining, then I can listen to you."

WITHDRAWAL TO THEIR ROOM

WHY THEY DO IT

Sure, some parents with teenagers think this withdrawal is a bonus rather than a problem, but it's fairly natural and predictable. Why? Most adolescents have many uncertainties about how their bodies are changing and the increasing responsibilities in their lives. This uncertainty gives them the illusion that they have less control, so they seek refuge in familiar surroundings that are wholly their own. Some children feel over-controlled, under-appreciated, and neglected by us. Many children this age have (gulp) done things they know we'd disapprove of and hide themselves in their rooms because they're afraid their facial expressions, body language, or loose lips will give them away. On rare occasions, our children become hermits because they're depressed or have an antisocial disorder.

LOGICAL CONSEQUENCES

Hey, sometimes they're going to miss out on some cool stuff.

SOLUTIONS TOWARD SELF-DIRECTION

Let them communicate openly without fear of ridicule or evaluation. Never refute, criticize, or reject their opinions. In fact, encourage them to find their own beliefs.

One of the best times to talk with your adolescents is at bedtime. I love to sit on the edge of their beds, stroke their hair, and listen to their concerns and joys. This companionship lets them know you enjoy their company.

Spend plenty of one-on-one time with them. Try to do things *they* like to do. For instance, take the boys to the hardware store to check out the newest tractors. You're not going to drag them off to help you shop for lingerie. Not if you want to live, that is.

Acknowledge and accept their imperfections, and model how you accept your own. If you're perfect, take this book back for a refund and go talk to Martha Stewart.

Let your children know that you expect them to make mistakes and will love them no matter what. Discuss some of the mistakes you made when you were their age.

Respect their privacy. Don't barge into their rooms without permission, and don't force them to discuss their day. Just let them mumble. (Are there any foreign language classes in Mumble-ese?)

Try humor. Sprinkle M&M's from their door to the dinner table.

When you're lucky enough to spend time with your teenagers, let them know how you feel with remarks like, "I really enjoy your company."

Use impartial descriptions and give information: "You've been in your room all day. That's fine, but we do expect to see you at the dinner table at 6:00." "I know you value your time alone, and that's OK, as long as your responsibilities here at home are met." "It's rare to find someone who enjoys their own company."

A Note from the Author

I want so much to hear from all of my readers so that I may learn as much from you as you learn from me. Much of what I hear will help shape the nature and content of future books. You can contact me at *medhus@earthlink.net*. My Web site: *http://www.drmedhus.com*.

Level System
for Teenagers

DEFINITION OF LEVELS

LEVEL 3:

You have full privileges such as going out with friends, having full access to your possessions, and having the phone back in your room. Your bedtime and phone time will be extended by thirty minutes. You might expect occasional surprise perks from happy parents.

LEVEL 2:

You lose phone (including cell phone) and social privileges like having friends over. You may listen to CDs, watch TV, use the computer, play video games, play outside, nap, bathe, draw, etc. These must be within the agreed upon time limits, wherever applicable.

LEVEL 1:

All privileges are suspended. You can do little more than homework, reading schoolbooks or newspapers, and hanging around the house. This means nothing pleasurable can be done, like biking, napping, eating desserts or snacks, bathing, drawing, playing with any material possessions, going on errands, having more than brief conversations with other members of the household, etc.

RULES

- YOU WILL START EACH DAY AT LEVEL 3.
  There is one exception to this rule: If the infraction occurs after 8:00 P.M., the demotion begins the next morning.
- Any of the infractions listed below will cause you to be demoted to the next level (level 3 to level 2 to level 1).
- *We* decide if that demotion should occur. That decision is not yours.

INFRACTIONS

- Disrespect, talking back (depending on intensity and frequency)
- Yelling, screaming (verbal tantrums)
- Cursing (depending on intensity and frequency)
- Fighting with siblings (depending on intensity and frequency)
- Hitting or other forms of physical retaliation
- Cruelty
- Dishonesty
- Abusing privileges (phone, curfew, etc.)
- Not fulfilling responsibilities at school or home

Resources

BOOKS

DEFEAT RECOVERY SKILLS/FAILURE

How Children Fail, by John Holt, Dell Publishing, 1964.

See Jane Win, by Dr. Sylvia Rimm, Crown Publishing, 1999.

What Kids Need to Succeed, by Peter Benson, Ph.D., Free Spirit Publishing, 1998.

What Teens Need to Succeed, by Peter Benson, Ph.D, Judy Galbraith, M.A., and Pamela Espeland, Free Spirit Publishing, 1998.

EMPATHY

Creating Harmonious Relationships, by Andrew LeCompte, Atlantic Books, 2000.

INDEPENDENT THINKING

Raising a Thinking Child, by Myrna Shure, Ph.D., Henry Holt Publishing, 1994.

INTUITION

Awareness, by John Stevens, Bantam, 1973.

Centering Book, by Gay Hendricks and Russell Wills, Prentice Hall, 1975.

The Wise Child, by Sonia Choquette, Ph.D., Three Rivers Press, 1999.

Your Sixth Sense, by Belleruth Naparstek, Harper, 1997.

PARENTING

1-2-3 Magic, by Thomas Phelan, Ph.D., CMI, 1995.

200 Ways to Raise a Boy's Emotional Intelligence, by Will Glennon, Jeanne Elium, and Don Elium, Conari Press, 2000.

Bringing Up Kids Without Tearing Them Down, by Dr. Kevin Leman, Nelson Publishers, 1995.

Children: The Challenge, by Rudolf Dreikurs, M.D., Plume, 1990.

How to Raise a Child with a High EQ, by Lawrence E. Shapiro, Ph.D., Harper Perennial, 1997.

How to Talk So Kids Can Learn, by Adele Faber and Elaine Mazlish, Simon and Schuster/Fireside, 1995.

How to Talk So Kids Will Listen and Listen So Kids Will Talk, by Adele Faber and Elaine Mazlish, Avon, 1980.

Liberated Parents, Liberated Children, by Adele Faber and Elaine Mazlish, Avon, 1994.

The Moral Intelligence of Children, by Robert Coles, Plume Publishing, 1998.

Parenting Isn't for Cowards, by Dr. James C. Dobson, Word Books, 1987.

Parents as Mentors, by Sandra Burt and Linda Perlis, Prima Publishing, 1999.

Positive Discipline A–Z, by Jane Nelsen, Prima Publishing, 1999.

Raising a Daughter, by Jeanne Elium and Don Elium, Celestial Arts, 1995.

Raising a Family, by Jeanne Elium and Don Elium, Celestial Arts, 1997.

Raising a Son, by Jeanne Elium and Don Elium, Celestial Arts, 1996.

Raising a Teenager, by Jeanne Elium and Don Elium, Celestial Arts, 1999.

Raising Good Children, by Dr. Thomas Lickona, Bantam Publishing, 1994.

Raising Good Kids in Tough Times, by Dr. Roger McIntire, Summit Crossroads Press, 1999.

Raising Positive Kids in a Negative World, by Zig Ziglar, Ballantine, 1985.

Raising Self-Reliant Children in a Self-Indulgent World, by H. Stephen Glenn and Jane Nelsen, Ed.D., Prima Publishing, 1989.

The 7 Habits of Highly Effective Families, by Stephen R. Covey, Golden Books, 1998.

The 7 Secrets of Successful Parents, by Randy Rolfe, Contemporary Books, 1997.

The Seven Spiritual Laws for Parents, by Deepak Chopra, M.D., Harmony Books, 1997.

The 7 Worst Things Parents Do, by John and Linda Friel, HCI Publishing, 1999.

Siblings Without Rivalry, by Adele Faber and Elaine Mazlish, Avon, 1998.

Spoiled Rotten, by Fred Gosman, Warner Books, 1993.

What Do You Really Want for Your Children?, by Dr. Wayne W. Dyer, Avon, 1985.

SELF-ESTEEM/SELF-CONCEPT

100 Ways to Enhance Self-Concept in the Classroom, by Jack Canfield and Harold Clove Wells, Allyn and Bacon, 1994.

101 Ways to Develop Student Self-Esteem and Responsibility, by Jack Canfield and Frank Siccone, Allyn and Bacon, 1995.

150 Ways to Increase Intrinsic Motivation in the Classroom, by James P. Raffin, Allyn and Bacon, 1996.

365 Ways to Build Your Child's Self-Esteem, by Cheri Fuller, Pinon Press, 1994.

Choices: A Teen Woman's Journal for Self-Awareness and Personal Planning, by Mindy Bingham, Judy Edmondson, and Sandy Styker, Advocacy Press, 1983.

The Four Conditions of Self-Esteem, by Reynold Bean, ETR Associates, 1992.

Inner Work, by Robert Johnson, Harper and Row, 1986.

Passionate Purpose, by Reed Daugherity, Book Partners, 1998.

Self-Esteem Revolutions in Children, by Thomas Phelan, M.D., Child Management, Inc., 1996.

The Self-Esteem Workbook, by Lynda Field, Element Publishing, 1995.

Something More, by Sarah Ban Breathnach, Warner Books, 1998.

Through My Eyes: A Journal for Teens, by Linda Kranz, Rising Moon, 1998.

BENEVOLENT SELFISHNESS

The Art of Selfishness, by David Seabury, Cornerstone, 1972.
The Virtue of Selfishness, by Ayn Rand, Signet, 1964.

SEXUALITY

Raising a Child Conservatively in a Sexually Permissive World, by Sol Gordon, Ph.D., and Judith Gordon, M.S.W., Simon and Schuster, 1983.
A Return to Modesty, by Wendy Shalit, Free Press, 1999.

SIMPLICITY

Simplifiy Your Life with Kids, by Elaine St. James, Andrews McMeel Publishing, 1997.

SOCIAL ISSUES

A Kid's Guide to Service Projects, by Barbara Lewis, Free Spirit Publishing, 1995.
The Kid's Guide to Social Action, by Barbara Lewis, Econo-Clad Books, 1996.
Kids with Courage: True Stories About Young People Who Make a Difference, by Barbara Lewis, Free Spirit Publishing, 1992.
The Youth Charter, by William Damon, The Free Press, 1997.

WIN-WIN MENTALITY

All the Best Contests for Kids, by Joan and Craig Bergstrom, Tricycle Press, 1996.
Everybody's a Winner: A Kid's Guide to New Sports and Fitness, by Tom Schneider, Little, Brown and Co., 1976.
Everybody Wins!, by Cynthia MacGregor, Adams Media, 1998.
Learning the Skills of Peacemaking, by Yogesh Ghandi, Jalmar Press, 1995.

Web Sites

www.dushkin.com/connectext/psy/ch11/survey11/mhtml for a locus of control test.

www.paragongeneration.co.za/tips/tips3.html for tips on how to be intrinsically motivated.

www.plato.acadiau.ca/courses/educ/piper/motivate.html on the importance of internal motivation.

www.queendom.com for the test that determines whether you have an internal or external locus of contol.

www.unsoundart.com/inner.htm for a poem on inner locus of control.

Catalogs

Back to Basic Toys—toys that stimulate creativity and imagination. 800.356.5360.

Chinaberry Books—focuses on high quality books. 888.793.9481.

Family Pastimes—cooperative games. 613.267.4819.

Hearthsong—high quality books and toys for personal growth. 800.422.0755.

Just Pretend—toys for newborn to twelve years. 800.286.7166.

Other Resources

Directory of American Youth Organizations, by Judith Erickson, Ph.D., Free Spirit Publishing, 1996.

International Network for Children and Families—Committed to creating new generations of responsible children who have higher self-esteem and better cooperation skills. 904.377.2176.

Kidsrights—Prevention and education materials. 1.800.892.KIDS.

Children's Books

The Bad Beginning, by Lemony Snicket, HarperCollins, 1999.

The Cay, by Theodore Taylor, Avon/Camelot, 1969.

Daniel's Duck, by Clyde Robert Bulla, HarperTrophy, 1979.

The Fire Cat, by Esther Averill, HarperTrophy, 1988.

Frindle, by Andrew Clements, Aladdin, 1998.

Hatchet, by Gary Paulsen, Aladdin Publishing, 1996.

Hey, New Kid!, by Betsy Duffey, Puffin Books, 1996.

Kids' Random Acts of Kindness, by Rosalyn Carter, Conari Press, 1994.

My Father's Dragon, by Ruth Stiles Gannett, Random House, 1979.

Skinny Bones, by Barbara Parks, Random House, 1997.

Toestomper and the Caterpillars, by Sharleen Collicott, Houghton Mifflin, 1999.

The Voyage of the Frog, by Gary Paulsen, Bantam, 1995.

Young Wolf's First Hunt, by Janice Shefelman, Random House, 1995.

Index

A

accidents, 160–161
accountability, 138, 174–176
addiction, telephone, TV, electronics, 262–264
aggressive physical acts, 161–163, 240–241.
    See also violence
alcohol consumption, 134–137, 163–164.
    See also substance abuse
allowances (spending money), 204
anger
    accidents and, 160
    cursing/inappropriate language, 196–197
    discipline and, 96–98
    property destruction, 205
    punishment and, 90
    questioning in, 52, 109
    reprimands and, 34
    violence among children, 137–139
animal cruelty, 164–165. *See also* violence
anorexia/bulimia, 208–210
anticipatory parenting, 101
apologies. *See also* consequences, logical
    crimes committed, 190
    school misbehavior, 249
    spitting, 255
    truancy, 267
approval, conditional, 13, 25–27, 30–34,
    42–43. *See also* love, unconditional
arguing disrespectfully, 166–167. *See also*
    disrespectful behavior
asset within a group, 9–11, 44. *See also*
    belonging desire
attention seeking
    clinging behavior, 186–188
    crime in, 189–190
    crying inappropriately, 192–193
    demanding behavior as, 200–201
    helplessness behavior, 219–221
    homework hassles, 221–222
    illness faking, 222–223
    interrupting behavior, 223–224
    laziness, 226–227
    pestering, poking, shoving, 240–241
    procrastination/dawdling, 197–198
    school misbehavior, 249–250
    sulking and pouting, 258–259
    tantrums, 259–260
    tattling, 260–261

violence among children, 138
whining, 271–272
avoidance behavior
    illness faking, 222–223
    laziness, 226–227
    shyness, 252
    truancy, 266–267

B

bathing hassles, 168–169. *See also* hygiene
beauty perception/body image, 151–154,
    176–177, 209, 269
bedtime hassles, 169–170
bed-wetting, 171–172
begging, 172–173. *See also* manipulative
    behavior; whining
belonging desire
    asset within a group, 9–11
    body image/beauty perception, 151–154
    bullying, 182–183
    cliques, 188–189
    competition and, 154
    consumerism in, 145
    cult involvement, 193–195
    friend hassles, 212–214
    gang involvement, 215–216
    jealousy and, 225
    laziness and, 225
    negativity, 237
    pestering, poking, shoving, 240–241
    school misbehavior, 249–250
    violence and, 137–139
birthday hassles, 173–174
blaming (accountability lack), 174–176, 191
body image/beauty perception, 151–154,
    176–177, 209, 269
body piercing/embellishments, 176–177
boredom, 178–179, 208–210
borrowing without returning, 179–180
bragging, 180–181
bribes. *See also* reward
    as discipline, 104–105
    messiness, 234
    public hassles, 245
    tantrums, 260
    toilet training troubles, 265
bulimia/anorexia, 208–210
bullying, 182–184

C

car hassles, 184–185
character development
cheating in school, 185–186
    intuition in, 72
    morality in, 8–9
    promise breaking, 243–244
    selfishness in development of, 77–79
    values in, 49, 139
cheating in school, 185–186
choices limited technique (discipline). See also
        specific situations, e.g. tantrums
    examples of, 111–112
    internal dialogue, 56
chores. See responsibilities
clinging behavior, 186–188
cliques, 188–189
clothing hassles, 206–208
compassion. See empathy
competence, 7–8
competition, 154–156. See also failure;
        sportsmanship
complaining, 191–192. See also whining
computer/games addiction, 178–179, 262–264
conditional behavior, 13, 25–27, 30–34,
        42–43. See also love, unconditional
conflict resolution
    aggressive physical acts, 162
    bullying, 183
    friend hassles, 214
    teasing and name calling, 262
    violence and, 37–38, 139
    win-win mentality, 156
conformance pressure (over-controlling
        behavior), 40–42
consequence list, 59–60
consequences, logical. See also discipline;
        punishment; specific situations,
        e.g. tantrums
    discipline and, 118–120
    opportunities denied as, 123–124
    substance abuse, 136–137
    technological irresponsibility, 141
    time-outs, 114–117
    violence and, 139
consumerism, 145–147. See also demanding
        behavior
control and domination (parental). See
        domination and control
counseling. See professional help
courtesy (lack of), 231–232. See also
        disrespectful behavior
crime
    parenting challenge, 189–190
    physical punishment and, 37–38
    property destruction, 205, 215–216, 245

criticism. See also lecturing; nagging;
        reprimands
    body image/beauty perception, 154
    as control strategy, 32–33
    discipline and, 110, 119
    in questioning technique, 109
    self-development and, 13
criticism (situational examples)
    bed-wetting, 171
    friend hassles, 214
    habits, annoying, 165
    helplessness behavior, 220
    hygiene, 181
    lying and, 228–229
    school phobia, 250–251
    withdrawal (to their room), 272
crying inappropriately, 192–193
cult involvement, 193–195
curfew breaking, 195–196
cursing/inappropriate language, 196–197

D

dating, 217–219
dawdling/procrastination, 197–198, 221–222
decision-making skills, 6, 39, 51, 56, 208
defiance, 198–200
demanding behavior, 200–204. See also
        consumerism
depression, 250–251, 266–267, 272–273
dialogue, internal (introspection)
    conflict resolution, 69
    consequence list, 59–60
    decision-making, 51, 56
    discipline and, 89–91
    empathy development, 82–84, 86–87
    modeling, 56–57
    praise in, 60–65
    pros and cons list, 58–59
    questioning technique, 52–54
    role-playing, 57–58
    self-talk in, 14, 21
    statement prompts, 54–56
    truth facing, 68–69
    unhealthy, 66–68
directing (over-controlling behavior), 36–37
direction. See also self-direction
    external, 6, 11–14, 20–24
    internal, 6, 11–14, 89–91
disappointment, parental, 34
discipline. See also consequences; punishment;
        specific situations, e.g. tantrums
    alternative approaches, 34
    anger and, 96–98
    of behavior (not child), 98–99
    bribes in, 104–105
    children as problem owners, 99–100

choices limited technique, 111–112
consistency in, 94–95, 139, 144
criticism and, 110, 119
dialogue, internal, 89–91
fairness in, 118–120
goal of, 89–90
humor in, 113–114
ignoring as, 104
impartiality/specificity technique, 109–111
impulse control and, 139
lecturing in, 119
level system for teenagers, 117–118,
    275–276
minimalist approach, 100–101, 112–113
mirroring technique, 110
misbehavior rescued, 105–107
modeling behavioral choices, 95–96
negative, 101–103
non-degrading, 34
over-controlling behavior in, 37–38
positive, 101–103
problem-solving skills and, 102–104
punishment vs., 90–91
questioning technique in, 108–109
reprimands in, 119
rescue and, 99–100, 105–107
respect for children, 93–94
rewards as, 65
rules in, 91–93
scare tactics in, 248
self-control in, 96–98, 139
self-worth and, 90
shame as, 30–31
substance abuse, 137
this or that technique, 111–112
threats in, 38, 104–105
time-outs, 114–117
violence among children, 139
disrespectful behavior, 166–167, 205–206,
    231–232
domination and control (parental), 25–27
    comparisons used in, 42–43
    criticism as, 32–33
    father knows best, 32–40
    food as, 209
    guilt, 30–31
    judgments and evaluations, 33–34
    labels and generalizations, 43–44
    manipulative behavior, 230
    martyrdom, 30–31
    over-controlling, 36–38
    pressure to conform, 40–42
    punishment and, 34–35, 90, 91
    reasons for, 29
    reprimands in, 34–35
    rescuing, 38–40

shame, 30–31
thought indoctrination, 35–36
dressing hassles, 206–208
Dr. Ruth Talks to Kids (Westheimer), 242
drug use, 134–137, 163–164, 189–190. *See also*
    substance abuse

E

eating hassles, 208–210, 232–233
electronic game addiction, 262–264
emotions (expression of), 23–24
    aggressive physical acts and, 161–163
    birthday hassles, 173–174
    crying inappropriately, 192
    cursing/inappropriate language, 197–198
    eating and, 208–210
    negativity, 236–237
    tantrums, 259–260
    teasing and name calling, 261–262
empathy. *See also* selfishness, benevolent
    aggressive physical acts, 162
    benevolent selfishness and, 78
    defined, 77
    development of, 47, 81–85
    forgetfulness, 211
    I messages in, 85–86
    modeling, 83, 86–87
    reading recommendations, 277
    showing, 178, 213, 227
    sincerity importance, 82
    suffering's role in, 130–131
    teaching, 87
empathy triad, 79–81
entitlement expectations, 22–23
enuresis, 171–172
evaluation. *See* criticism; judgment

F

failure. *See also* competition; mistakes
    accountability and, 176
    attempting, value of, 124–125
    fear of, 121–122
    grades (bad), 168
    independence and, 128–129
    parental admission of, 123, 124
    past downplayed, 126–127
    perfection and, 125–126
    praise and, 62
    procrastination and, 197–198
    reading recommendations, 277
    rebounding from, 121–131
    school phobia, 250–251
    self-worth and, 129–130
    suffering's role in, 130–131
    tolerance of, 127–128
false-self, 36–38, 134

family identity
    bragging, 181
    importance of, 48–50
    manners (good), 231
    promise keeping, 243
    rules and, 91
    sportsmanship, 257
    truth telling, 229
fidgeting, 210–211. *See also* habits
fighting. *See* violence
finger sucking, 264
food hassles. *See* eating hassles; mealtime
    hassles
forgetfulness, 211–212
friend hassles, 212–214

G

gang involvement, 215–216
giving vs. getting, 146, 174. *See also*
    demanding behavior
going somewhere other than where they said.
    See lying
grades (bad), 167–168
gratification, immediate, 147, 201. *See also*
    demanding behavior
growing up too soon
    (makeup/dress/dating/sex), 217–219
guilt technique, 30–31

H

habits
    annoying, 165–166
    fidgeting, 210–211
    thumb and finger sucking, 264
happiness (stories), 3–5
helplessness behavior, 219–221
homework hassles, 221–222
honesty (inner) modeling, 69
humor in discipline
    accidents, 161
    arguing disrespectfully, 167
    bedtime hassles, 170
    begging, 173
    complaining, 192
    curfew breaking, 196
    demanding behavior and, 202, 203, 204
    dressing/clothing hassles, 208
    forgetfulness, 212
    grades (bad), 168
    habits, annoying, 166
    helplessness behavior, 220–221
    homework hassles, 222
    hygiene (poor), 169, 182
    manners (lack of), 232
    mealtime hassles, 233
    messiness, 234

property destruction, 216
spitting, 256
value of, 113–114
whining, 271
withdrawal (to their room), 273
hurried lifestyle, 142–144. *See also* simple
    lifestyle
hygiene hassles, 168–169, 181–182

I

if-then technique (discipline), 111–112
ignoring as discipline, 104
illness faking, 222–223
I messages, 85–86, 229
impartiality/specificity technique (discipline),
    109–111. *See also* specific situations, e.g.
    tantrums
impulse control, 14, 138–139, 161–163
independence encouragement
    clinging behavior, 186
    crying inappropriately, 192–193
    demanding behavior and, 202
    helplessness behavior, 220
    importance of, 8, 128–129
indulgence demands. *See* demanding behavior
Internet resources, 274, 281
interrupting, 223–224
introspection techniques
    about, 51–52
    choices, 56
    consequence list, 59–60
    modeling, 56–57
    praise and reward, 60–66
    pros and cons list, 58–59
    questioning, 52–54
    statement prompts, 54–56
    walk-throughs/role-playing, 57–58
intuition, 71–75, 277
irresponsible behavior, 267–268

J

jealousy, 224–226, 261–262
judgment (evaluation), 12–13, 33–34, 160

L

labels and generalizations (over-controlling
    behavior), 43–44, 47
laziness, 226–227
lecturing. *See also* criticism; nagging
    in discipline, 119
    dressing/clothing hassles, 208
    minimizing, 100–101, 112–113
level system of discipline, 117–118, 275–276
limited choice technique (discipline). *See*
    choices limited technique (discipline)
losing things, 227–228

love, unconditional. *See also* approval, conditional. *See also* conditional behavior
demonstration examples, 25–27
grades (bad), 168
self-development and, 12, 13
self-esteem and, 7
sportsmanship (poor), 257
substance abuse, 137
lying, 174, 216–217, 228–229

M

make-up wearing, 217–219
manipulative behavior, 172–173, 229–231, 232–233
manners (lack of), 231–232. *See also* disrespectful behavior
martyrdom technique, 30–31
materialism, 145–147. *See also* demanding behavior
mealtime hassles, 232–233. *See also* eating hassles
media. *See also* real-world influences
body image/beauty perception, 152
electronic entertainment/Internet, 140
sexuality development, 151
substance abuse, 135–136
violence among children, 138
meditation, 74, 162. *See also* visualization techniques
messiness, 233–235
minimalist approach to discipline
about, 100–101, 112–113
accidents, 161
bathing hassles, 169
grades (bad), 168
habits, annoying, 166
public hassles, 246
safety-rule breaking, 248
sulking and pouting, 259
mirroring technique in discipline, 110
misbehavior
and discipline, 104, 105–107
opportunities denied for, 123–124
in public, 244–246
rescued, 105–107
in school, 249–250
mistakes. *See also* failure
blaming (accountability lack), 175
contests of, 126
encouraging, 128
over-reacting to, 127–128
parental admission of, 69, 123, 124, 175, 219
withdrawing due to, 273
mocking. *See* ridicule
modesty, 148. *See also* sexuality

morning hassles, 235–236. *See also* dressing hassles
movies. *See* media

N

nagging. *See also* criticism; lecturing
as control strategy, 32
in discipline, 119
dressing hassles, 208
habits, annoying, 165–166
irresponsible behavior, 268
messiness, 234
morning hassles, 236
noisiness, 239
thumb and finger sucking, 264
toilet training troubles, 265
touching everything, 266
unreliability, 268
whining, 271
nail biting, 165–166
name calling , 261–262
Naparstek, Belleruth, 71
negativity, 236–238
nightmares, 238
noisiness, 239–240
nose-picking, 165–166

O

over-controlling parental behavior. *See also* domination and control; rescuing; threats
about, 36–38
arguing disrespectfully and, 166–167
conformance pressure, 40–42
cult involvement, 194
curfew breaking, 195–196
defiant behavior and, 198–200
demanding behavior and, 200–204
directing as, 36–37
discipline and, 37–38
disrespectful behavior and, 205–206
false-self creation and, 36–38
gang involvement, 215–216
labels and generalizations, 43–44, 47
messiness, 233–235
ultimatums, 38, 69
withdrawal (to their room) and, 272–273
over-eating, 208–210
over-protective behavior, 199, 250–251. *See also* rescuing

P

pack animal instinct, 9–11. *See also* belonging desire
parenting
anticipatory, 101
consistency and follow-through in, 94–95

disagreement handling, 231
permissive, 200–204
reactive, 101
reading recommendations, 277–279
peer pressure
  crime, 189–190
  friend hassles, 212–214
  substance abuse, 134
  truancy, 266–267
perfection expectations
  body image/beauty perception, 151–154
  conditional approval and, 25–27
  excellence striving vs., 125–126
  failure and, 122–123
permissive parenting, 200–204
pestering, poking, shoving, 240–241. *See also*
  aggressive physical acts
pornography, 241–243. *See also* sexuality
positive discipline. *See* praise
possessiveness, 251–252
pouting, 258–259. *See also* tantrums
powerlessness
  bullying, 182
  crying inappropriately, 192–193
  gang involvement, 215–216
  property destruction and, 205
  sharing and possessiveness, 251–252
  substance abuse, 134
  violence among children, 138
power struggles. *See* manipulative behavior
praise (positive discipline). *See also* reward
  accidents, 160, 161
  accountability, 176
  achieving, 101–103
  computer/games addiction, 264
  dialogue, internal, 60–65
  fidgeting, 211
  independent behavior, 188
  irresponsible behavior, 268
  laziness, 227
  messiness, 235
  morning hassles, 236
  pestering, poking, shoving, 240
  promise keeping, 244
  public hassles, 246
  for quietness, 239
  school misbehavior, 249–250
  self-development and, 13
  tattling, 261
  telephone/television addiction, 264
  toilet training troubles, 265
  touching everything, 266
  truth telling, 229
  unreliability, 268
  wastefulness, 271
  whining, 272

precocious behavior, 217–219
problem-solving skills
  dialogue, internal, 69
  discipline and, 102–104
  intuition in, 73
  rescuing and, 39
  tattling, 260–261
procrastination/dawdling, 197–198, 221–222
profanity. *See* cursing
professional help
  aggressive physical acts, 163
  animal cruelty, 164
  bullying, 184
  eating disorders, 209
  substance abuse, 163
promise breaking, 243–244
property destruction, 205, 215–216, 245.
  See also crime; violence
pros and cons list, 58–59, 247
public hassles, 244–246
punishment. *See also* consequences; discipline
  bed-wetting and, 171
  discipline vs., 90–91
  fear and, 35
  food as, 209
  helplessness behavior, 220
  homework hassles, 221
  illogical, 34–35, 69, 90, 123–124
  irresponsible behavior, 268
  noisiness, 239
  physical, 37–38
  self-worth and, 90
  sexuality, 242
  sulking and pouting, 258–259
  thumb and finger sucking, 264
  toilet training troubles, 265
  touching everything, 266
  truth facing and, 69
  truth telling and, 217
  unreliability, 268
  whining, 271

Q

questioning technique (discipline). *See also*
  specific situations, e.g. tantrums
  body image/beauty perception, 153
  dialogue, internal, 52–54
  discipline and, 108–109
  sexuality, 149–150
  substance abuse, 136
  technological irresponsibility, 141
  violence among children, 139

R

reactive parenting, 101
real-world influences. *See also* media

beauty perception/body image, 151–154
competition, 154–156
consumerism, 145–147
hurried lifestyle, 142–144
sexuality, 147–151
substance abuse, 134–137
technology, 139–142
violence and, 137–139
reasoning skills, 6, 7, 11–14, 36
reciprocity/entitlement expectations, 22–23
relaxation techniques. *See* meditation
repression (of self-expressiveness), 27–29
reprimands. *See also* criticism
in discipline, 119
fear and, 35
judgmental, 34–35
lying and, 228–229
truth facing and, 69
rescuing (over-controlling behavior)
as control strategy, 38–40
crying inappropriately, 192–193
discipline and, 99–100, 105–107
in failure, 130–131
forgetfulness, 211–212
homework hassles, 221
irresponsible behavior, 267–268
negativity, 237
unreliability, 267–268
respect for children
choices as, 112
clothing choices, 208
defiant behavior and, 199
discipline and, 93–94
personal property, 216
withdrawal (to their room), 273
responsibilities (chores), age-appropriate
accountability, 176
irresponsible behavior, 268
jealousy and, 225
laziness and, 226
school phobia, 251
shyness, 252
unreliability, 268
revenge
crime and, 189–190
crying inappropriately, 192–193
cult involvement, 193–195
gang involvement, 215–216
helplessness behavior, 219–221
manipulative behavior, 229–231
property destruction and, 205
substance abuse, 135
tantrums, 259–260
teasing and name calling, 261–262
whining, 271–272
reward, 65–66, 209, 222, 265. *See also* praise

ridicule. *See also* criticism
bed-wetting and, 171
clothing choices, 207
whining, 271
withdrawal (to their room), 272
role play
bragging, 181
bullying, 183
cliques, 188
complaining, 192
crying inappropriately, 192
cursing/inappropriate language, 197
drug and alcohol peer pressure, 135
in empathy development, 84–85
friend hassles, 213
of internal dialogue, 57–58
interrupting behavior, 224
jealous behavior, 225
running away from home, 247
sexuality development, 149
sportsmanship (poor), 257
sulking and pouting, 258
tantrums, 260
violence among children, 139
rudeness, 231–232
rules
borrowing without returning, 179
computer/games addiction, 263
demanding behavior and, 204
discipline and, 91–93
growing up too soon, 218
precocious behavior, 218
public hassles, 245
safety-rule breaking, 247–249
self-direction and, 159–160
tattling, 260
telephone/television addiction, 263
touching everything, 266
running away from home, 246–247

S

safety-rule breaking, 247–249
scare tactics, 248
school-related problems
cheating, 185–186
misbehavior, 249–250
phobia, 250–251
truancy, 266–267
self-confidence, 27, 28, 128–129
self-deceit, 66–68, 95–96, 212, 233
self-definition
comparisons in, 42–43
criticism and, 32
development of, 11–14
judgments and evaluations in, 33–34
labels and generalizations in, 43–44

self-direction
    family identity and, 49
    intuition development and, 71–75
    judgments/evaluations and, 33
    motivation in, 38
    qualities/characteristics, 6–10, 43, 44, 51,
        77–87, 125
    reason as foundation for self-direction, 6
    self-esteem and, 7
self-esteem/self-confidence
    bragging, 180
    developmental critical point, 13
    pestering, poking, shoving, 240–241
    praise and, 64
    reading recommendations, 279–280
    school misbehavior, 249–250
    self-direction and, 7
self-evaluation, 43, 44, 60–66
self-expressiveness, 28, 176–177
self, false, 36–38, 134
selfishness. See also empathy
    benevolent, 78–79
    defined, 28
    reading recommendations, 280
    self-confidence vs., 77
self-sacrifice, 78–79
self-talk/self-monitoring skills. See dialogue,
    internal
self-worth
    entitlement expectations and, 23
    excellence striving not perfection, 125–126
    failure vs., 129–130
    punishment and discipline, 90
    sportsmanship (poor), 256–258
sexuality
    growing up too soon, 217–219
    irresponsibile behavior, 241–242
    irresponsible behavior, 150
    pornography and, 241–243
    precocious behavior, 217–219
    reading recommendations, 242, 280
    real-world influences, 147–151
shame as discipline. See also criticism
    bed-wetting, 171
    lying and, 228–229
    public hassles, 245
    in questioning technique, 109
    sexuality, 242
    thumb and finger sucking, 264
    toilet training troubles, 265
    value of, 30–31
sharing, 251–252
Shelly, Mary Wollstonecraft, 83
shoplifting. See crime
shyness, 252–254
siblings

borrowing without returning, 180
car hassles, 184
influences, 44–48
jealous behavior, 225
rivalry among, 254–255
toilet training and, 265
simple lifestyle, 145–147, 280. See also hurried
    lifestyle
smoking, 163–164. See also substance abuse
societal problems/social issues
    causes of, 6
    physical punishment and crime, 37–38
    reading recommendations, 280
    reciprocity/entitlement expectations, 23
    technology (real-world influences), 139–142
spanking. See punishment, physical
spitting , 255–256
sportsmanship, 154–156, 256–258. See also
    failure
statement prompts (internal dialogue), 54–56
stealing. See crime
substance abuse
    alcohol use, 134–137, 163–164
    drug use, 134–137, 163–164, 189–190
    smoking, 163–164
success focus, 102–103, 128–129
suffering's role in failure, 130–131
sulking, 258–259. See also tantrums
swearing. See cursing
sweets eating, 208–210

T
tantrums, 258–259, 259–260
tattling, 260–261
tattoos, 176–177
teasing, 261–262, 264, 265
technology (modern), 139–142
teeth brushing, 181–182. See also hygiene
telephone addiction, 262–264
television addiction, 262–264
television watching, 178–179. See also media
thinking, independent, 277
this or that technique (discipline), 111–112
thought indoctrination, 35–36
threats (over-controlling behavior)
    discipline and, 38, 104–105
    idle, 107
    irresponsible behavior, 268
    messiness, 234
    public hassles, 245
    sulking and pouting, 258–259
    tantrums, 260
    toilet training troubles, 265
    touching everything, 266
    truth facing and, 69
    unreliability, 268

whining, 271
three-level system of discipline, 117–118,
   275–276
thumb sucking, 264
time-outs, 114–117, 161, 184
toilet training troubles, 264–265
touching everything, 265–266
truancy, 266–267
trust development, 180
truth facing, 68–69
truth telling, 217, 229

U

ultimatums (over-controlling behavior), 38, 69
unreliability, 267–268

V

values, instilling, 49, 139. *See also* character
   development
vandalism, 245. *See also* crime
vanity, 269. *See also* beauty perception
verbal torture. *See* teasing
violence
   aggressive physical acts, 161–163, 240–241
   among children, 137–139, 212–214
   animal cruelty, 164–165
   conflict resolution and, 37–38, 139
   physical punishment and, 37–38
   property destruction, 205, 215–216, 245
visualization techniques, 73, 225. *See also*
   meditation

W

walk-throughs. *See* role play
wastefulness , 270–271
web site (author's), 274
Westheimer, Ruth, 242
when-then technique (discipline), 111–112, 165
whining , 104, 178, 220, 271–272. *See also*
   begging; complaining; manipulative
   behavior
winner-loser mentality , 154–156. *See also*
   failure; sportsmanship
win-win mentality, 156, 280
withdrawal (to their room) , 272–273

BEYOND WORDS PUBLISHING, INC.

OUR CORPORATE MISSION

Inspire to Integrity

OUR DECLARED VALUES

We give to all of life as life has given us.
We honor all relationships.
Trust and stewardship are integral to fulfilling dreams.
Collaboration is essential to create miracles.
Creativity and aesthetics nourish the soul.
Unlimited thinking is fundamental.
Living your passion is vital.
Joy and humor open our hearts to growth.
It is important to remind ourselves of love.

To order or request a catalog, contact
Beyond Words Publishing, Inc.
20827 N.W. Cornell Road, Suite 500
Hillsboro, OR 97124-9808
503-531-8700 or 1-800-284-9673

You can also visit our Web site at *www.beyondword.com*
or e-mail us at *info@beyondword.com*.